ROMANTIC
ESCAPES

in the

CARIBBEAN

Lovetripper Guide

ROMANTIC
ESCAPES

in the

CARIBBEAN

Lovetripper Guide

Paris Permenter & John Bigley

HUNTER

Hunter Publishing, Inc.
130 Campus Drive, Edison, NJ 08818
732-225-1900 / 800-255-0343 / fax 732-417-1744
e-mail: hunterp@bellsouth.net
www.hunterpublishing.com

In Canada
Ulysses Travel Publications
4176 Saint-Denis, Montréal, Québec
Canada H2W 2M5
514-843-9882, ext. 2232 / fax 514-843-9448

In the UK
Windsor Books International
The Boundary, Wheatley Road
Garsington
Oxford, OX44 9EJ England
01865-361122 / fax 01865-361133

ISBN 1-55650-914-6
© 2001 Paris Permenter & John Bigley

Cover: Sint Maarten © 2001 Paris Permenter & John Bigley
Back cover: © Douglas G. Ashley
Interior images © 2001 Paris Permenter & John Bigley
unless otherwise noted

Maps by Kim André & Kim Foley MacKinnon
© 2001 Hunter Publishing, Inc.
Indexing by Jan Mucciarone

About the Authors

*A*uthors John Bigley and Paris Permenter fell in love with the Caribbean over a dozen years ago and have turned their extensive knowledge of the region into an occupation. As professional travel writers and photographers, the pair contribute travel articles and photographs about the US and the Caribbean to many national consumer and trade publications.

The husband-wife travel writing team are the authors of numerous Hunter guides: *Adventure Guide to Jamaica*; *Adventure Guide to the Cayman Islands*; *Antigua, Barbuda, St. Kitts & Nevis Alive!*; *Jamaica: A Taste of the Island*; *Jamaica Alive!*; *Nassau & the Best of the Bahamas Alive!*; *Adventure Guide to Anguilla, Antigua, St. Barts, St. Kitts & St. Martin*; and *Bahamas: A Taste of the Islands*.

Paris and John are also frequent television and radio talk show guests on the subject of travel. Both are members of the prestigious Society of American Travel Writers (SATW) and the American Society of Journalists and Authors (ASJA).

Readers can follow the couple's travels on their websites: Travels with Paris and John (www.parisandjohn.com) or Lovetripper Romantic Travel Magazine (www.lovetripper. com).

☙✻❧

Contents

Appendix

Index

Maps

Introduction

$\mathcal{B}$efore we start examining the individual islands, let's look at the region as a whole. The Caribbean spans an area that stretches over 2,000 miles east to west and 1,000 miles north to south, starting just off the coast of Florida and reaching down to the coast of South America.

This part of the world is blessed with year-round sunshine, with water warmed by Caribbean currents and shores cooled by gentle trade winds. Winter and summer temperatures differ by only a few degrees.

Geography

The islands arch out like a cracking whip, with the largest islands to the west and the small islands to the east, curving on down to South America and ending with a "snap" back to the west at the ABC islands: Aruba, Bonaire and Curaçao.

The whole formation of islands is referred to as the **Antilles**, usually divided into the **Greater Antilles** and the **Lesser Antilles.** The Greater Antilles, as the name suggests, are the Caribbean's largest islands: Cuba, Hispaniola (an island shared by the Dominican Republic and Haiti), Jamaica, and Puerto Rico. The term Lesser Antilles encompasses the other islands.

Often, the area is just divided up into the Eastern and Western Caribbean. The Eastern islands are the same as the Lesser Antilles; the Western Caribbean is the Greater Antilles and the Cayman Islands.

The multiple names given to this region is your first hint at the diversity the Caribbean boasts. In researching and writing this book, we traveled to the Caribbean every few weeks and many friends asked us, "Are you getting bored visiting the same area again and again?" Besides the fact that it would be pretty tough to tire of perfect weather, postcard-pretty scenes, and a sea as clear as glass, the Caribbean holds an endless fascination for us, and hopefully for you, because it offers so many different types of experiences.

Although every one of these countries is an island surrounded by the Caribbean Sea, they differ in many ways. The political structures range from crown colonies to independent nations. Some islands span hundreds of square miles; others can be covered by bicycle in a single afternoon. Languages vary as well; English, Spanish, French, Dutch, and even a beautiful mélange of languages called **Papiamento** greet visitors, though you'll find that English is spoken in just about every resort area.

Although technically not part of the Caribbean, the Bahamas share its azure waters and perpetual summer. Bermuda is also beyond the Caribbean's reaches, though it, too, offers a romantic island atmosphere.

How Do You Say....

The Caribbean contains a few tongue twisters. So you can sound like a local, here's how to say some of the toughest:

Anguilla................... an-GWIL-a
Antigua .... an-TEE-ga
Barbuda .... bar-BOO-da
Nevis....................... NEE-vis
Saba........................ SAH-buh
Statia .... STAY-sha
St. Barths .... St. Barts
St. Croix .... St. Kroy
St. Lucia .... St. LOU-sha

Getting Started

Okay, it's time to make some decisions. Which island will you choose? It's a question that only the two of you can answer, based on your own personal tastes. Do you want high-rise lux-

Caribbean Islands

Florida

CUBA

Cayman
Islands

JAMAICA

Bahama Islands

Turks &
Caicos

HAITI

DOMINICAN
REPUBLIC

PUERTO
RICO

Virgin
Islands

Anguilla

St. Martin/Sint Maarten

St. Barts

St. Kitts
& Nevis

Barbuda
Antigua

Guadeloupe
Dominica

Martinique

St. Lucia
St. Vincent
Mustique
Grenada
Margarita

Barbados

Trinidad &
Tobago

Atlantic Ocean

Bermuda

Caribbean Sea

Aruba   Curaçao

YUCATAN

HONDURAS

NICARAGUA

COSTA
RICA

PANAMA

COLOMBIA

VENEZUELA

NOT TO SCALE

© 2001 HUNTER PUBLISHING, INC

ury or Robinson Crusoe-type seclusion? Glitzy dinner shows or evening serenades from tiny tree frogs? Days spent shopping, snorkeling, scuba diving, or just sunning on a sandy beach?

When friends ask us for help in selecting a destination, we advise them to first identify their preferences. We sometimes like the bustling atmosphere of busy islands like Jamaica, St. Thomas, or Puerto Rico; other times we long for the serenity of St. Kitts, Nevis, or Virgin Gorda.

To help you make this major decision, begin by asking yourself these questions:

- ♥ Is our budget a major factor in our choice?

- ♥ Will this be a quick three- or four-day getaway or a leisurely vacation of a week or more?

- ♥ Do we enjoy casino gambling and shows?

- ♥ Are we looking for luxurious accommodations?

- ♥ Would we prefer the convenience of an all-inclusive resort?

- ♥ Do we want to rent a car and explore on our own?

- ♥ What activities are most important to us? Snorkeling? Scuba? Tennis? Windsurfing? Sailing? Hiking? Shopping?

- ♥ Do we want a lush, tropical environment?

- ♥ Do we want white sand beaches? Nude beaches?

- ♥ Do we want the simplicity of remaining on US turf or would we rather experience a different culture?

Sit down together and consider your answers. Then take a look at your choices. Thoughout this book, we have indicated with a heart (♥) in the margin any restaurant or accommodation we think is especially romantic.

Vacation Options

Budget Getaways

There's no good way to put this, but you'll find out soon enough that a trip to the Caribbean isn't cheap. Even if you select a budget hotel, transportation to the islands is a big expense that you just can't avoid.

However, some islands are less expensive than others. These destinations are high volume, bringing in commercial and charter flights on a daily basis. This may mean more crowds, but your airfare will probably be cheaper than flights to more secluded islands.

> *Some destinations offer packages that include air, hotel, and ground transportation for one affordable price. Jamaica, Puerto Rico, the US Virgin Islands, the Bahamas, and the Dominican Republic offer these kinds of deals.*

A tropical setting on Nevis.
Courtesy of Nisbet Plantation Beach Club.

Charter airline companies serve most of these islands as well. For more information on low-cost carriers, see *Travel Information*, page 33.

Quick Getaways

If you're planning a three- or four-day retreat, make the most of your visit by minimizing travel time. These islands are the easiest jumps from the US: the Bahamas, Turks and Caicos, Cayman Islands, Puerto Rico, and Jamaica (if you stay in the Montego Bay area; Negril and Ocho Rios are nearly two hours from the airport, Port Antonio is even farther). From the UK, you'll find the best connections to Barbados, Antigua, and Bermuda.

Mega Resorts

Twenty-four-hour room service, full-treatment spas, and satellite TV aren't commonplace throughout the Caribbean. However, the two of you can be pampered at full-service properties in Puerto Rico, Aruba, the Bahamas, Jamaica, Barbados and St. Lucia in hotels that offer more than the comforts of home.

Where to Stay

Whatever you're looking for in the way of accommodations – high-rise hotel, seaside bungalow, bed-and-breakfast inn, small traditional hotel, or private villa – you'll find it in the Caribbean.

Just as varied as the type of accommodations available is the range of prices at these properties. Everything from budget motels with spartan furnishings to private islands that attract royalty and Hollywood types is available.

This guidebook covers things in-between, places where the everyday vacationing couple can enjoy safety and comfort in surroundings where romance can flourish. The resorts, hotels, and villas featured on these pages offer all levels of activity. Some have round-the-clock fun and evening theme parties; others point the way for guests to find their own entertainment. Some are located on the beach; others up the mountains with spectacular views. Some are full-service properties with every-thing from beauty salons to jewelry shops to a half-dozen bars and restaurants located right on property; others are simple ac-commodations where the guests enjoy dinner in former greathouses built over 200 years ago.

Choosing a Caribbean accommodation is more important than selecting a hotel at other destinations. A Caribbean hotel, un-like a property in a downtown US city, for example, becomes your home away from home. This is not just where you spend your nights, but also a good portion of your days, languishing on the beach, lying beneath towering palms, and luxuriating in a warm sea.

What form will your paradise take? White sandy beaches? Rug-ged limestone cliffs perched above baby blue water? Mountain-side vistas? A resort with daily activities and a pulsating nightlife? A historic inn furnished with Caribbean antiques? Or a quiet getaway where the only footprints are your own?

The choice is yours.

Prices

Hotel prices vary drastically between high and low season and also by view. Garden view rooms are generally the least expen-sive, followed by ocean view, then oceanfront. Suites are the priciest accommodations, with rates that can be more than dou-ble that of a standard room.

Rather than provide specific prices, which come and go as quickly as a hibiscus blossom, we've given price ranges for ac-commodations. These rates reflect high winter season for a standard room for two adults for one night (expect prices to be as much as 40% lower during the off season); prices are in US dollars. You'll find a price scale at the beginning of each *Sweet Dreams* section for each island.

All-Inclusive Resorts

As the name suggests, all-inclusive means that all activities, meals, drinks, airport transfers, and tips are included in the price.

This policy means that you're free to try anything you like without worrying about spending your vacation budget for the next five years. Ever been curious about windsurfing? Take a lesson. Want to know how to reggae dance? Throw off your shoes and jump in line. Wonder how those brightly colored drinks with the funny umbrellas taste? Belly up to the bar. You're free to try it all.

Some folks don't like all-inclusives because of the concern (not unfounded) that once you've paid for the whole package you'll be unlikely to leave the property to sample local restaurants and explore the island. The all-inclusive confinement is, however, up to the individual couple. Perhaps your goal for this trip is to languish away the mornings in bed (this is, after all, a guide for lovers), roll out to the beach, grab a rum punch in one hand and your partner's hand in the other, and sit there until the sun slowly sinks into the sea. An all-inclusive is just right for you. You won't have to worry about taxis or rental cars or dinner reservations.

Or maybe the two of you want to try it all: scuba diving, sailing, windsurfing, golf, or tennis. An all-inclusive is just the ticket for you as well. The one-price-pays-all policy will be a better deal than paying for individual lessons.

Who else should check out an all-inclusive? Those who are:

- ♥ On a tight budget. You'll know how much to put aside for the entire vacation before you ever buy your ticket. Once you arrive, live like a king and you never have to count how much money's left or how high the tally's going on your credit card. All-inclusives, like other hotels, come in a varied price range.

- ♥ Traveling with the kids. You can still have a romantic trip thanks to all-inclusive resorts with children's programs. The kids will have fun doing age-appropriate activities, making new friends, and learning about a new culture, while the two of you enjoy a romantic respite.

- ♥ Receiving the trip as a gift. All-inclusive resort vacations are increasingly popular as wedding gifts. They permit the gift-giver to pay for the trip up front and for honeymooners to enjoy themselves without feeling like they're running up a huge tab for parents or in-laws.

♥ Getting married on your honeymoon. Several all-inclusives offer free weddings; all offer various wedding packages. You'll find experienced wedding planners at these resorts who can simplify paperwork and make your wedding a special, hassle-free day.

We love all-inclusive resorts, but we are careful to balance a stay there with island tours or visits to off-property restaurants so as not to miss island culture. Even with these extra expenditures, we've found most of these resorts to be economical choices.

In selecting an all-inclusive, read through the offerings carefully. Are all drinks included or just wine with dinner? Are tips included? Airport transfers? Watersports but not motorized sports? Scuba diving? Know what features are important to the two of you and see if those are included in the package price.

Jamaica is the king of the all-inclusive, but you'll find them on several other islands, especially Aruba, Barbados, St. Lucia, Antigua, the Bahamas, and the Turks and Caicos.

Bed & Breakfasts and Small Inns

If you're looking for peace and quiet, B&Bs and small inns offer good getaways and a chance to immerse yourself in more of the local atmosphere.

These small inns, many built around historic greathouses on former plantations, are intimate properties that host only a handful of guests at a time. Here, the two of you will be part of just a small group and you'll get to know each other as you would aboard a small cruise. Often, the owners of the inn reside right on property, so you'll receive personal attention.

Our favorite inns make us feel like we're guests of the family returning for another stay. We enjoy chatting with other guests, usually experienced travelers, and with the owners, who give us an insight into island life. Over the years, we've shared dinner conversations with hoteliers about hurricanes, gardening, local dining specialties, sports, and island life in general. It has given us a perspective on these destinations that we would never have received at a larger property.

Ask plenty of questions before booking a stay in a B&B or small inn. These properties may offer limited services and be more restrictive than a traditional hotel. If applicable, be sure to ask:

- ♥ Is smoking permitted indoors?

- ♥ Are children allowed as guests?

- ♥ Is breakfast served at one time or as guests wander in?

- ♥ Are intimate tables available or are meals served family style? Are special dietary considerations met?

- ♥ Is there a minimum stay?

- ♥ Does a remote location necessitate a rental car?

Villas

For some couples, the idea of real romance is a private villa, without other guests. Just the two of you – alone, except for the occasional visit by a cook or maid who is there to meet your special requests, introduce you to island cuisine, and make you feel pampered in what really is your home away from home. St. John, St. Thomas, Jamaica, and Barbados are especially popular islands for villa rentals.

Villas vary in price, services, and level of luxury. Before you make a commitment, check:

- ♥ *Cleaning service.* Many villas offer cleaning service before your arrival and after your departure; additional cleaning can be arranged for a surcharge. At other properties, you may have daily maid service.

- ♥ *Groceries.* Ask if you might send a deposit for groceries and have a cook stock up before your arrival. Finding a refrigerator and cabinets ready with your favorites can be comforting after a long flight.

♥ *Cook service.* Many villas can arrange for cook service as you choose: three meals a day, dinner only, or just one special meal. In Jamaica, villas typically include cook service.

♥ *Check your options.* Don't assume your villa is air conditioned; ever-present trade winds make this an optional feature. If it's more of a necessity than an option to you, inquire.

♥ *Car rental.* Many villas are located away from the resort areas. See if you should rent a car to avoid pricey taxi rides for long hauls.

♥ *Minimum stay.* Unlike hotel minimums of three nights, villas often require a minimum seven-night rental.

Many resorts also offer villa rentals. These homes are located on the resort property and guests enjoy the security and services of the resort while at the same time having the space and facilities of a villa home. Some resorts that include villa homes are Peter Island, Four Seasons Nevis, Jumby Bay, and Bitter End Yacht Club in the British Virgin Islands.

How Long to Stay?

Package vacations usually come in three- , four- , and seven-night lengths, with the option to add extra nights if you like. If you're setting up your own vacation, then the sky (okay, your budget) is the limit. All but the smallest islands have daily air service, so you can usually schedule arrival and departure whenever you like.

We've found that three-night trips are just a little too short, even for a quick getaway. Three nights sounds like it should also include four days, but you have to be realistic. Usually your arrival day will be lost; departing from Texas we arrive in the Caribbean no earlier than mid-afternoon and sometimes much later than that. If you're arriving from the West Coast, expect a full travel day. You'll probably miss both dinner and the evening show and just be ready to roll into bed after you check in. The departure day is also lost. With a two-hour international flight

Introduction

check-in, you often need to leave for the airport just after breakfast.

So, on a three-night, four-day package, expect two full days of vacation: the days between your arrival and your departure. We've done it, but it's not relaxing and can, especially if you've never been to the island before, be very frustrating. If you do consider a three-night package, re-read the *Quick Getaways* section, page 6, just prior for the list of the easiest destinations to reach from the US.

If budget is a major factor or if you need to hurry back to the kids, we suggest a four-night trip. You'll have a little time to relax and, although it's not as glorious as a week-long stay, you'll start to get into the island groove and state of mind.

On a week-long trip you'll have a chance to really relax and take some day-trips around the island.

Two-week trips are the epitome of luxury. They're usually enjoyed by Europeans rather than Americans, who generally have shorter vacations than their trans-Atlantic neighbors. If you're lucky enough to afford, both in time and money, a long getaway, you might think about island-hopping. See page 33 for tips on inter-island flights.

> *T IP: If you will be arriving very late, consider staying the first night at an inexpensive hotel close to the airport. A business hotel, without the amenities of a resort, will look just fine if you're coming in just in time to hit the sack. The next morning, get up and take a taxi to your resort hotel. You'll arrive early and have all day to enjoy the resort and feel like you're really getting your money's worth. You may have to store your luggage until your room is ready, but most resorts have changing facilities so you can go ahead and hit the beach.*

When to Go

Seasonal Pricing

Room rates are at their highest from mid-December through mid-April (and at all-time highs during the holiday weeks), and generally fall about 40-50% during low season. Resorts that seem out of reach in the winter months may be right in your price range during the summer.

Of course, into any scene a little rain must fall, and in the Caribbean that means low season. Low season covers the summer and early fall months, for two reasons. First, these are the warmest months in the Northeast US, the area of the country that often flees to the sunny Caribbean during the chilly winter months, so demand is down. Second, this is hurricane season.

Climate

Mention the Caribbean and weather in the same sentence, and one concern quickly arises: **hurricanes.** These deadly storms are a threat officially from June through November, although the greatest danger is during the later months, basically August through October. (September is the worst.)

Keep in mind, however, that the Caribbean is a large region. We've been in the Western Caribbean when storms were picking up force in the eastern reaches and never felt a gust of wind or saw a wave over ankle high.

To minimize the chances of a hurricane ruining or postponing your trip, plan a vacation outside the hurricane season or outside the hurricane zone. In the far southern reaches, the islands of Aruba, Bonaire, and Curaçao (also known as the ABC islands) and Trinidad and Tobago are below the hurricane zone and are safer bets during the summer and fall months.

Except for the hurricane season, weather in the Caribbean is a wonderfully monotonous topic. (In Papiamento, the language of the Dutch islands, there is no word for weather. It's almost always perfect, so why waste a word?)

In the summer, days peak in the low 90s, with lows in the 70s. In the winter, temperatures run about 5 to 10 degrees cooler. The sea remains warm enough for comfortable swimming year-round. (Note: The Bahamas are technically not part of the Caribbean, and you'll find the temperatures here are slightly cooler.)

If budget is not your prime consideration, then when's the best time to go to the Caribbean? Any time!

Festivals

Whatever time you visit the Caribbean, chances are good that an island festival of some sort will be in progress, offering you the chance to take part in local celebrations of life. **Carnival** is the biggest bash in the islands and is held in January in Trinidad, April in St. Thomas, and February in St. Martin.

When it comes to Carnival, no island's festivities can beat Trinidad's pulsating party, perhaps second only to Rio de Janeiro's celebration. Held the Monday and Tuesday prior to Ash Wednesday, this pre-Lenten party is preceded by weeks of parties, balls, competitions, and calypso shows. J'Ouvert, Carnival Monday, starts at two in the morning as Trinidadians take to the streets in costume. Grab your mate and practice Carnival dances: chipping (a slow shuffle down the street), jumping up (you can picture that one), and wining (a pelvic dance that would put Elvis to shame). Soca music pulsates from giant trucks while people playing steel pans deliver traditional calypso sounds. The two of you can jump in and shuffle along as the whole parade gyrates down the street.

Carnival dancer on Sint Maarten.

Caribbean Cuisine

For most couples, dining is an important part of their trip. It's a chance to further delve into a culture, to learn more about the bounty of the land and the sea.

A richly diverse region, the Caribbean is filled with a full menu of offerings that reflect the many cultures that settled this area. From East Indian rotis served throughout Trinidad and Tobago, to Dutch keshi yena served on Aruba, Curaçao, and St. Maarten, the islands are a cornucopia of cultures and cuisines.

One thing island cuisines have in common is attention to flavor. Dishes are rich with tastes and are often spicy. Some dishes trace their origin back to when the Arawak Indians first barbecued meats. Later, distinctive seasonings were developed by Africans, who came to the islands as slaves.

A century later, Chinese and East Indian influences made their way to the Caribbean, when indentured laborers who replaced slaves after emancipation also brought their own culinary talents. Today curried dishes grace nearly every menu, using local meats such as goat, chicken, and seafood.

Unique Island Dishes

Breakfast

Ackee and saltfish, the national dish of Jamaica. Ackee is a small fruit that is harvested only when it bursts and reveals its black seeds; before that time the fruit is poisonous. Once cooked, it resembles and tastes much like scrambled eggs.

Johnnycakes and **boiled fish** are morning dishes in the Bahamas.

Soups

Pepperpot, a spicy stew in Jamaica.

Asopao, a chicken and rice soup in Puerto Rico.

Stoba di cabrito (goat stew) in Curaçao.

Entrées

Fried fish.

Stewed lamb with *pan bati* (pancake) on Dutch islands.

Keshi yena, a hollowed wheel of Edam cheese filled with meat and baked to combine flavors served on Dutch islands.

Conch (pronounced Konk), a shellfish served chopped, battered and fried in conch fritters.

Grouper, a large fish caught in the waters just offshore; appears on every menu.

Flying fish. This fish, often fried, is a favorite in Barbados.

Pattie, a turnover filled with spicy meat that's a favorite lunch snack with locals in Jamaica.

Jerk is a style of cooking, made with pork, chicken, or fish. The dish is marinated with a fiery mixture of spices, including Scotch bonnet peppers, pimento or allspice, nutmeg, scallion, and thyme. This is a favorite in Jamaica.

Empanadillas, little meat turnovers, in Puerto Rico.

Roti, a burrito-like fast food that traces its roots to India; served in Trinidad and Tobago. Look for "buss up shot" at most diners; this is a roti that's torn up like a "busted up shirt" and is eaten with a fork rather than by hand.

Escovitch, a style of cooking using vinegar, onions and spices brought to Jamaica by the Spanish Jews. Often used when cooking fish.

Ital food (eye-tal), is the food of the Rastafarians, a vegetarian cuisine that does not use any salt. Look for the red, green and gold Rasta colors on dining establishments as a clue to locating Ital eateries, often small restaurants in Jamaica.

Stamp and Go. You could call them fast food or appetizers, but stamp and go is much more descriptive. Stamp out these little fish fritters in the kitchen, grab some for the road, and go.

Side Dishes

Fried plantains, similar to bananas.

Breadfruit. Similar in taste to a potato, and served in as many ways on most Caribbean islands.

Peas (usually red beans or pigeon peas) and rice: the number one side dish in the Caribbean.

Cou-cou (a cornmeal and okra dish) in Barbados.

Jug-jug (made of Guinea corn and green peas) in Barbados.

Christophine, a type of squash, served on most Caribbean islands.

Dasheen, a root vegetable similar to a potato and served on most Caribbean islands.

Mofongo, fried plantains mixed with fried pork rinds and seasoned with garlic, in Puerto Rico.

Afungi, a pudding of cornmeal and okra, served on several islands, including Antigua & Barbuda.

Fungi (pronounced foon-GEE), a tasty accompaniment that's somewhat like cornbread dressing, in the Virgin Islands.

Dessert

Ducana, a pudding made from grated sweet potato and coconut, sugar, and spices, and boiled in a banana leaf, in Antigua.

Flan, a wonderful custard, served primarily in Dominican Republic and Puerto Rico.

Tembleque, a custard made with coconut milk and sprinkled with cinnamon in Puerto Rico.

Duckanoo. This delicious dessert, originally from Africa, is concocted with cornmeal, coconut, spices and brown sugar. The ingredients are tied up in a banana leaf (hence its other name, Tie-A-Leaf), and slowly cooked in boiling water.

Spectacular Sunsets

Most Caribbean days draw to a close with a thrilling blaze of tropical colors. Enjoying the sunset is an island obsession, so pick your spot with care (and try to arrive early). In St. Thomas, **Paradise Point** and a bar named, appropriately enough, **The Bar,** offer romantic sunset viewing. Below in the city where shoppers hustle to pick up a few last bargains before the boutiques close their doors, the lights trickle on one by one, competing with a deepening sunset the color of a blooming hibiscus.

On the western reaches of Jamaica, lovers end their day in Negril at **Rick's**, one of the most famous sunset bars and restaurants in the Caribbean. Nearby, divers plunge off the cliffs to hearty cheers from onlookers. When the sun dips low, however, the crowd turns its attention to the west and to a blaze of color that marks the end of another day in paradise.

Activities

You want activity. Spirited watersports. Pulsating nightlife. Hedonistic delights. Your mate wants leisure time. Days spent under a coconut tree. Nights lulled by trade winds and the rhythm of lapping waves, as the moon rises over a silver sea.

In the Caribbean, you both will be happy. Whether your idea of a romantic getaway brings to mind a fiesta or a siesta, this sprawling region delivers. Year-round warm weather makes possible the sensual delights for which the islands are known. Slip out of bed for a midnight dip in a private plunge pool or jog side by side on a sandy beach as the first rays of light illuminate the sky. Even during the winter months, the only goosebumps you'll experience are ones your lover delightfully produces.

Activities on each island vary with its size and atmosphere. Pick one of the bigger destinations like Jamaica, St. Thomas, Grand Cayman, Puerto Rico, St. Martin-Sint Maarten, or Nassau for your choice of nonstop fun. For plenty of peace and quiet, head to one of the smaller isles such as Anguilla, known for its fine dining; St. Barts, recognized for its unique European atmosphere; Tobago, rich with natural delights; or Nevis, a tropical paradise that's been discovered by few.

We've rated activities on each island from 0 to 5. A score of 0 means the activity isn't available; 5 means it's world-class.

ISLAND ACTIVITY RATINGS	Snorkeling	Scuba	Boating	Hiking	Fishing	Shopping	Casinos	Dining
Anguilla	4	4	3	2	3	1	0	4
Antigua	3	3	5	3	3	4	2	3
Aruba	2	2	3	3	3	4	4	3
Bahamas	3	4	3	2	3	4	4	4
Barbados	2	2	3	3	3	3	0	3
Bermuda	2	3	3	2	2	4	0	4
BVI	4	3	4	4	3	1	0	3
Cayman Islands	4	5	3	2	4	4	0	3
Curaçao	3	3	3	2	3	2	0	2
Dominican Republic	3	3	2	4	3	3	1	3
Jamaica	3	3	2	4	3	2	1	3
Puerto Rico	3	3	3	4	3	4	4	3
St. Barts	3	3	3	3	3	2	0	4
St. Kitts & Nevis	3	4	3	5	3	2	1	4
St. Lucia	4	3	3	5	3	3	0	3
St.Martin-Sint Maarten	3	3	5	3	3	5	3	4
Trinidad & Tobago	3	4	3	5	3	2	0	3
Turks & Caicos	4	4	3	1	3	1	1	3
St. Croix (USVI)	4	3	4	4	3	4	1	3
St. John (USVI)	4	3	4	4	2	1	0	2
St. Thomas (USVI)	4	4	4	4	3	5	0	3

Sports

Scuba & Snorkeling

The clearest water for these activities is generally found around those islands without rivers or steep hills to create runoff. Add underwater features, such as coral reefs and walls or submerged shipwrecks, and you have a diver's paradise. Among the best dive destinations in the Caribbean are the Turks and Caicos, the Cayman Islands, and Bonaire.

Golf

Golf courses are popping up like hibiscus blossoms throughout the region. The top choices are Puerto Rico and Jamaica, each offering championship courses designed to keep even the most dedicated golfer happy. You'll also find courses on St. Croix, St. Thomas, Nevis, St. Kitts, Aruba, and Barbados.

Golfing in the Bahamas.
Courtesy of Radisson Cable Beach Resort.

Tennis

Top tennis facilities are available in resorts on Puerto Rico, Jamaica, Antigua, and St. Croix.

Windsurfing

Windsurfers will find excellents spots in these warm waters. Aruba is the top windsurfing destination in the Caribbean due to ever-present trade winds. Puerto Rico also offers windsurfing (taught by a former member of the US Olympic Team) as well as the BVI, home of an annual international tournament.

Sailing

The Caribbean Sea around the British Virgin Islands is a sailor's paradise. Opportunities abound for voyages of all durations and beginners are reassured by the fact that one is seldom far from land. The Moorings (☎ 800-521-1126 or 284-494-2332) and other services catering to the sailor are numerous here as well. Other top sailing destinations are Antigua and St. Martin-Sint Maarten.

Shopping

Those who are ready to shop-'til-they-drop should head to the US Virgin Islands for the Caribbean's highest duty-free allowance. Shoppers in St. Thomas, St. Croix, and St. John can bring back more goodies (twice as much as some Caribbean islands) without paying duty. Other shopper's delights are Nassau (Bahamas), St. Martin-Sint Maarten, and Grand Cayman.

Beaches

White Sand Beaches

Caribbean sand comes in all shades (ranging, literally, from black to white – and even pink in some areas). If your vision of paradise includes chalk-white beaches, head to the Turks & Caicos, Bahamas, St. Thomas, St. John, Antigua or Anguilla.

Nude Beaches

The clothing-optional beaches are of two types. There are the resort beaches where nudity is encouraged (and, in a couple of cases, even dictated) on a separate, specified area of the shore. These locations tend to be safe and somewhat crowded but close to amenities like food, drink, tables, and restrooms. Look to the French islands, such as St. Martin, and Jamaica (especially Negril) for resorts featuring nude beaches. The other type of nude beach can be found on many islands where access to undeveloped, isolated beaches means that nudity is more-or-less tolerated. While this may seem to be the more romantic of the two types, that on some islands, such as St. Lucia, public nudity is actually illegal.

Lovers taking a beach stroll.
Courtesy of Casa de Campo, DR.

Tropical Delights

Within the Caribbean, landscapes can range from desert to jungle, with everything in between. Even more surprising is the fact that some islands include both desert and rain forest climates. However, if your Caribbean adventure must be backdropped by tropical splendor, head to Jamaica or St. Lucia for lush scenery punctuated by brilliant hibiscus and bougainvillea and every imaginable tropical fruit and vegetable. Every island has wonderful beaches to walk on hand in hand.

Culture

Although all islands boast a rollicking Caribbean spirit, their cultures also borrow heavily from their founding fathers. Visitors who would rather remain in the US and skip the hassles of passports, immigration cards, and currency exchange can choose Puerto Rico or the US Virgin Islands: St. Thomas, St. John, and St. Croix.

Dutch architecture creates picturesque waterfront communities in Aruba, Bonaire, Curaçao, and Sint Maarten. A rich Spanish heritage pervades the Dominican Republic and Puerto Rico. The British Virgin Islands, Montserrat, the Cayman Islands, and the Turks and Caicos still operate as British dependencies. In the former British colonies – the Bahamas, Antigua and Barbuda, Barbados, St. Kitts and Nevis, Trinidad and Tobago, and Jamaica – the British influence is still strong.

Driving is on the left side of the road and the Royal Family is seen smiling back from postage stamps.

Adventures

Get Set to Get Wet

Every Caribbean island is surrounded by miles of liquid paradise. Whether you prefer a leisurely afternoon paddle aboard a sea kayak to a pristine beach or a night dive to look at fluorescent marine creatures in a sea as warm as a bath, the Caribbean has the spot for you.

Fun on the water in Nassau.
Courtesy of Radisson Cable Beach Resort.

Scuba diving is a top activity throughout many of these islands. Here, the two of you can swim hand in hand through waters as clear as white rum and enjoy visibility that often tops 150 feet. Travelers are drawn by reef dives, with coral heads dotted with sea flora and fauna as colorful as gumdrops, and wreck dives to explore the remnants of old pirate ships preserved in these warm waters.

And if the two of you don't yet scuba but would like to learn a new sport together, now's the chance. Many hotels offer resort courses and, after a lesson and some practice in the pool, you and your mate can share your virgin dive offshore the same afternoon.

Or, you can act out your Jacques Cousteau fantasies with a snorkel trip. With just a few minutes of quick instruction, you're ready to take a peek at the marine world just offshore. One of the Caribbean's most popular snorkel sites is **Stingray City** in Grand Cayman. Here you can stand in about four feet of water and hand-feed southern Atlantic stingrays that nuzzle against you as gently as kittens. Another popular snorkeling spot is at **Buck Island Reef National Monument** in St. Thomas. Here, in about 12 feet of water, swim hand in hand as you follow a marked trail for a self-guided tour of this undersea world.

On Land

Often portrayed as a destination for water-lovers, the Caribbean presents myriad outdoor challenges on land as well: cycling, hiking, golfing, tennis, parasailing – just about any type of warm-weather sport imaginable. The pace goes from mild to wild – whatever the two of you choose.

One of the most challenging activities in the islands is an all-day hike up St. Kitts' **Mount Liamuiga**. Climb this dormant volcano all the way to the mile-wide crater rim to view a spectacular cloud forest and steaming sulphur vents in the volcanic region. The hike is a tough one, so come prepared with very good walking shoes and a can-do spirit.

Is biking more your speed? Grab your partner and a mountain bike and head for the challenges of Jamaica (where you can tour the lofty **Blue Mountains** on guided rides) or the ease of flatter islands like Little Cayman.

How about something a little easier? The US Virgin Islands offer a whole range of milder pursuits. Save some energy for shopping on St. Thomas, where poinciana-covered hills overlook streets filled with some of the Caribbean's finest duty-free shopping stores. Eco-tourists especially enjoy St. John, where nature lovers can camp and hike in the national park that covers two-thirds of this unspoiled island.

*Don't miss St. John's **love bush**, an indigenous species with slightly frayed leaves. Follow the local legend to test your love: pick a leaf and carve your and your mate's initials into it. Plant the leaf. If it takes root and grows, so will your love.*

Sightseeing

Part of the fun of visiting the islands is soaking up their unique cultures. The best way to do that is to explore. Sign up for a guided tour or rent a car for the day and take a look at the local sights.

Don't forget – driving is on the left in many islands!

The islands blossom with romantic sites, places where the two of you can feel like Adam and Eve in a tropical paradise. St. Lucia, a fertile utopia, is home of the **Diamond Waterfalls and Gardens**. Garden trails lead to a cascade that leaves a spray of "diamond" twinkles in the air. If you stop by on a Sunday, you can also enjoy a soak in the mineral baths originally built by French King Louis XVI for use by his troops. See page 283 for more details.

The island of Jamaica is also known for its waterfalls and tropical splendor. Although the north coast's Dunn's River Falls is far more visited, on the island's southern reaches **Y.S. Falls** offers couples a much quieter paradise. Cascading in steps through tropical forest, the falls can be climbed with the help of a guide, then swimmers can enjoy clear waters under a canopy of fern. For more on the falls, see page 235.

Not every island is known for tropical lushness. Some are rugged reminders of the power of the elements and the raw energy of the sea. On the friendly Dutch island of Curaçao visit **Boca Tabla,** a sea cave carved by pounding Atlantic waves. Kneeling in the darkness of the grotto you can sneak a kiss while crystal blue waves surge within feet of you, roaring into the cave and back out to sea.

Nightlife

Casinos

The click of the roulette wheel and the ring of slot machines are being heard on more and more Caribbean islands. The top gaming destinations are Puerto Rico, Aruba, Bahamas (Grand Bahama, but especially Nassau), and Dutch Sint Maarten. More limited gaming is also found in the Turks & Caicos, the Dominican Republic, St. Croix, Curaçao, St. Kitts, and Antigua.

Most casinos open at noon and remain open until early morning. Many have dress codes which require semi-formal attire; leave the shorts, tank tops, and flip-flops in the room for your night at the tables. This is your chance to dress up and party. Note: In Puerto Rico you may be surprised to learn that alcohol cannot, by law, be served in casinos. You will find bars in each hotel, but no drinks are served on the casino floor.

Music

Music lovers will recognize the name of **Bankie Banx,** Anguilla's best known musician. The reggae singer is also the owner and operator of **The Dunes Preserve,** a charming bar and restaurant set up high above the seashore. Constructed entirely of recycled ship parts and driftwood, this open-air roost gives visitors the feeling they're visiting Robinson Crusoe. Every Friday night Bankie performs his lively tunes; at other times you'll find him behind the bar serving drinks. (See page 69.)

There's nothing like the pulsating energy found in local bands to make your heart beat a little faster. Nightlife is usually pretty quiet on the island of Tobago, but once a week calypso and soca rhythms bring residents and vacationers out into the streets to dance. **"Sunday School,"** held every Sunday in the community of Buccoo Village, is an open-air street party that doesn't get cranked up until near midnight. The two of you can move to a Caribbean beat and soak up the atmosphere at this unique island party.

Just Doing Nothing

"The number one activity is to do nothing," says Tom Lewis, general manager at **Ocean Club** in the Turks and Caicos. Located on the tranquil island of Providenciales, this resort recognizes that many travelers and especially honeymooners come to make their own fun. Here, island visitors enjoy all that lovers could want from a Caribbean getaway: peace, privacy, and mile after mile of pristine beach.

And those elements – enjoyed by you and your lover – ensure that any island getaway can turn into a romantic seaside tryst. No matter how the two of you define fun, your island in the sun is a surefire guarantee of romance.

Romantic dining in Jamaica.
Courtesy of the Half Moon Golf, Tennis & Beach Club.

Travel Information

What to Pack

When we first began to travel in the Caribbean, we envisioned an elegant destination where visitors wore the most stylish sportswear and fine evening wear. It was an image created by stories of Caribbean travel earlier this century, when wealthy travelers made the long journey with steamer trunks and remained in the islands for weeks at a time. Today's jet travel has shortened the length of stay – and diminished the necessary amount of luggage – for a Caribbean journey.

We carry all the necessary accessories (which, on some islands, can be expensive or difficult to buy):

- ❑ camera and film, extra camera batteries
- ❑ sunscreen (two bottles of different strengths)
- ❑ snorkel gear (certified divers must bring a "C" card)
- ❑ insect repellent
- ❑ all prescriptions (in original prescription bottles)
- ❑ 2 pairs of sunglasses each
- ❑ 1 or 2 paperback books
- ❑ antiseptic for bug bites
- ❑ aloe vera lotion for sunburn

❑ first aid kit with aspirin, stomach medicine, bandages, etc.

❑ mini-address book for postcard writing

We quickly learned that in the Caribbean, the key wardrobe words are comfort and cool, not necessarily chic. Even if you'll be staying at the poshest resort and dining in the toniest restaurants, comfort comes first. A few restaurants require jackets for men (especially during high season), and we've identified those throughout this guidebook. Neckties are rarely seen.

We keep a permanent packing list for our Caribbean trips. For a four-night trip, we bring:

His	*Hers*
2 pairs casual slacks	1 pair nice slacks or khakis
2 T-shirts	1 T-shirt
2 polo or short sleeve shirts	2 short sleeve/sleeveless blouses
2 swimsuits	2 swimsuits, 1 cover-up
1 pair walking shoes	1 pair walking sandals
1 pair sandals or tennis shoes	1 pair evening sandals
1 pair water shoes	1 pair water shoes
	1 casual skirt
	2 pairs shorts
	1 dress or sundress

This may seem sparse, but we always carry on our luggage if possible (although sometimes we've had to surrender bags on small propeller planes). Toting bags may seem like a hassle, but it does minimize the chance of lost luggage. When we deplane, we're first in line for customs and immigration, so we breeze through and add a little precious time to our island vacation.

Getting to the Islands

Once the two of you have decided where you'd like to go, here's your second hurdle: getting there. Fortunately, you have several options because most islands are served by multiple air carriers; many are also served by cruise ships.

Caribbean Air Carriers

Just as you would with accommodations, shop around for an airline. Start early, be patient, and do some research. Check with several carriers, even those that aren't the primary airlines in your region. The chances are, unless you are starting from an East Coast hub, that you'll be making connections along the way, so sometimes it's cheaper to do some creative routing – although you will pay for it in travel time.

Travel to Caribbean destinations is easier than ever with ample airlifts to even the smallest islands. Most connections from major mainland US cities are made through either Miami or San Juan, Puerto Rico's Luis Muñoz Marin Airport, the American Airlines hub for many Caribbean flights. From San Juan, American Eagle serves many neighboring islands.

Frequent Flyer Programs

When you purchase your airline ticket, sign up for the frequent flyer program. Also, check to see if the resort you are visiting is part of the program.

Today you can earn mileage in many ways other than flying. Long distance companies, credit card companies, dining programs, and others offer miles, sometimes as many as five for every dollar spent.

Some Internet sites where you can buy tickets include: www.priceline.com; www.cheaptickets.com; www.travelocity.com; and www.etravelplans.com.

The following carriers offer flights to at least one Caribbean destination. You'll find that the flight schedule varies by season (the most flights, and for some airlines, the only flights, are offered during peak season from mid-December to mid-April).

Air Carriers		
Air Aruba	☎ 800-88-ARUBA	www.airaruba.com
Air Canada	☎ 888-247-2262	www.aircanada.ca
Air Jamaica	☎ 800-523-5585	www.airjamaica.com
ALM	☎ 800-327-7230	www.airalm.com
American Airlines	☎ 800-433-7300	www.im.aa.com
Bahamasair	☎ 800-222-4262	www.bahamasair.com
BWIA	☎ 800-JET-BWIA	www.bwee.com
Cayman Airways	☎ 800-422-9626	www.caymanairways.com
Continental	☎ 800-525-0280	www.continental.com
Delta Air Lines	☎ 800-221-1212	www.delta.com
Northwest	☎ 800-447-4747	www.nwa.com
TWA	☎ 800-221-2000	www.twa.com
United Airlines	☎ 800-538-2929	www.ual.com
US Airways	☎ 800-622-1015	www.usair.com

Air-Land Packages

Several airlines offer package deals that provide a complete vacation: room, transfers, air, and, for all-inclusives, meals, drinks, and tips. Is this cheaper than putting a package together on your own? Usually. Check it out for yourself by calling the hotel reservation numbers, asking for their room rate and adding it to the cost of an airline ticket. You'll usually see a substantial savings since the airlines buy rooms in bulk and therefore have much more purchasing power than an ordinary consumer.

Some travelers worry about the term "package," imagining a trip where they'll be herded on a bus full of tourists and have no choices of what to do. Have no fear. Some packages include the services of a greeter at the airport who will welcome you and show you the way to the transfer bus to your hotel, but beyond that you're on your own. If you want to rent a car and explore, go to it.

Packages are also offered by charter airlines, carriers that offer service at lower cost, usually with few frills. (Often, only one class of service is available, seat assignments are given only at check-in, and carry-on allowances may be only one bag per passenger due to an increased number of seats onboard.) Some charter companies offering Caribbean service include **Adventure Tours, FunJet, Apple Vacations, GoGo**, among others. Talk to a travel agent for details on these tours.

If you don't want the package vacation, some of these charters also sell "air-only," just the airline tickets themselves.

Island-Hopping

Want to island-hop? It's fun and, if you're visiting small islands, a necessary part of a Caribbean vacation.

Two carriers offer special passes designed for island-hopping. **LIAT,** ☎ 800-468-0482, and **BWIA,** ☎ 800-JET-BWIA, each offer a special pass that permits you to hop from island to island – with certain restrictions. Check with the airlines for special rules and more information on these passes.

Island-hopping passes must be purchased and ticketed (a very important detail) within the continental US. They cannot be purchased in the Caribbean. Check with other carriers about other multi-island passes.

When traveling on small carriers, be prepared to carry on only one small bag. You'll be able to check other luggage at the ticket counter or right at the airplane door as you board (our choice so we can make sure the bags board the same plane as we do).

Service may be limited on some flights. A few times we have flown on prop planes when the only staff members were the pilot and co-pilot, seated just a couple of rows ahead of us. The flights are generally short, though, and really give you a bird's-eye view of the islands that can't be beat.

Check-in requirements are not flexible with the small carriers. Requirements vary from carrier to carrier, but make sure you arrive at the airport by the requested check-in time. Some flights have been known to leave early, so make sure that you check in ahead of schedule. Call the night before and reconfirm your seats, then arrive at the airport at the stated check-in time.

Cruises

For many couples, the idea of cruising the Caribbean is romantic bliss. Waking up to a new port each day can be a great way to get a real feel for several islands as you vacation.

Numerous cruise ships ply these waters; some travel the Caribbean only during winter months. Here's a list of several cruise lines that offer Caribbean cruises:

Cruise Lines	
Carnival Cruise Line	☎ 888-CARNIVAL www.carnival.com
Celebrity Cruises	☎ 888-313-8883 www.celebritycruises.com
Clipper Cruise Line	☎ 800-325-0010 www.clippercruise.com
Cunard Lines	☎ 800-7-CUNARD www.cunard.com
Fred Olsen Cruises	☎ 01473-292222 (in the UK) www.fredolsen.co.uk
Holland America	☎ 800-426-0327 www.hollandamerica.com
Norwegian Cruise Line	☎ 800-327-7030 www.ncl.com
Princess Cruises	☎ 800-PRINCESS www.princesscruises.com
Royal Caribbean Cruises	☎ 888-313-8883 www.royalcaribbean.com

Travel Agents

Travel agents offer a free service, making hotel and air reservations and issuing airline tickets. They can shop around for the lowest rate for you and often hear about sales that aren't known to the general public.

They can't however, read your mind. We've seen couples go to a travel agent and say "We'd like to go somewhere warm." That – as you can see in this book – covers a lot of territory!

Every vacation is a once-in-a-lifetime opportunity. The two of you may return to the islands, but no other trip will be exactly like this one. Each is unique and offers wonderful opportunities for you to explore the world together. Part of the fun of travel is the anticipation of the trip. Read through this book together and talk about your options.

Entry Requirements

S pecifics vary from country to country (we'll discuss those in individual chapters), but plan to bring along either a current passport or a certified copy of your birth certificate (some islands accept voter registration card), and a photo ID. Passports are the easiest form of entry (plus you'll get the neat immigration stamps as a free souvenir).

> *T IP: If you're headed to the Caribbean on your honeymoon (or if you'll be getting married while in the tropics), don't have your airline tickets issued under your new name. Your tickets must match the name on your passport that you'll be using for entry. If you are presenting your certified birth certificate and you have changed your name since birth, bring along a copy of your marriage license as well.*

Obtaining a Passport

To obtain a passport, you may apply in person at the nearest passport office (see *Appendix*, page 382 for offices) or at one of the several thousand federal or state courts or US post offices authorized to accept passport applications. Not every post office offers this service; usually just the largest offices in the city. For your first passport application, you must apply in person.

We can't stress enough the importance of applying for a passport early. The heaviest demand period is January through August. September through December is the speediest period, but you should still allow at least eight weeks for your passport application to be processed.

To obtain a passport, first get an unsigned passport application (DSP-11) from your local passport office or post office that handles passport applications. Do not sign the application. You'll also find passport applications online at the US Department of State's website, travel.state.gov/passport_obtain.html.

You'll need to provide proof of US citizenship. This can be an expired passport, a certified birth certificate (that means one with a raised, impressed, embossed, or multicolored seal). If you do not have a certified copy of your birth certificate, call the Bureau of Vital Statistics in the city where you were born. It's a handy document to have, so request it.

You also must provide identification, which can be an expired passport, a valid driver's license, a government ID card or certificate of naturalization or citizenship. (Here's what won't work: Social Security card, learner's permit, or temporary driver's license, credit card, expired ID card.)

Passport Photos

Next, you must provide two recent identical photographs of yourself no larger than 2x2 inches (the image of your head from the bottom of your chin to the top of your head must not be less than one inch or more than 1⅜ inch). Passport photos can be either color or black and white but they may not be Polaroids or vending machine photos. The easiest way to get passport photos is to go to a quick copy store and ask for passport shots.

$\mathcal{P}$rice

Passports for adults 16 and over are $60 and are valid for 10 years. You may pay in person by check, bank draft, or money order. At passport agencies you may also pay in cash; some (but not all) post offices and clerks of court accept payment in cash.

When you receive your passport, sign it. The next step is to fill in the emergency contact information (use a pencil in case you need to make changes).

$\mathcal{G}$etting Information

Need to talk with someone? The only public phone number for passport information is for the **National Passport Information Center** (NPIC). You can call here for information on passport emergencies, applying for a US passport, or to obtain the status of a passport application. Automated information is available 24 hours a day and live operators can be reached on weekdays from 8 am to 8 pm, Eastern Standard Time. (Services are available in English, Spanish, and by TDD.) This is a toll call: the charge is 35¢ per minute for the automated system or $1.05 per minute for live operators. Call ☎ 900-225-5674 for either automated or live service; ☎ 900-225-7778 for TDD service. Calling from a number blocked from 900 service? Call ☎ 888-362-8668 (TDD ☎ 888-498-3648); you will be required to pay by credit card at a flat rate of $4.95 per call. For passport offices, see the *Appendix,* page 382.

$\mathcal{L}$ost $\mathcal{P}$assports

If you lose your passport or have it stolen, immediately report the loss to the local police. Get a police declaration, then report to the local consulate or embassy for a replacement passport. We've had this happen and relied on the State Department to help us replace a lost passport (caused by the sinking of a boat we were traveling in) with an emergency passport.

> $\mathcal{W}$e can't emphasize enough how important it is to carry a copy of the identification page of your passport tucked somewhere in your belongings.

Caribbean Embassies & Consulates

Run into problems on your trip? You will find consulates and embassies on some of the larger islands. These offices can assist you with lost or stolen passports, emergencies, etc.

If you are involved in an emergency situation, go to the nearest US embassy or consular office and register as an American citizen in the region. Bring along your passport and a location where you can be reached. Offices are listed in the *Appendix,* page 385.

The consular office can also be contacted for a list of local doctors, dentists, and medical specialists. If you are injured or become seriously ill, a consul will help you find medical assistance and, at your request, inform your family or friends. The State Department cannot assist you in funding an emergency trip back to the States – that's what travel insurance is all about.

Travel insurance can cover the cost of a trip that you have to cancel, trip delay expenses. and medical expenses that your regular insurance policy might not handle. You can purchase travel insurance through your travel agent or call an insurance agency directly. (Don't buy insurance through a tour operator; if the business should close, your insurance policy will probably be terminated along with it.)

Customs

When you leave the US and when you return home, you will pass through US Customs at your point of US entry. (A few islands have Customs Pre-Clearance so you can go through the declaration before returning home, usually a faster process.)

You'll complete a customs declaration form, one per household, identifying the total amount of your expenditures while out of the country. Each person has an exemption of either $400, $600 or $1,200 (depending on the island you visited). Families can pool their exemptions, so a family of four can bring back $1,600, $2,400, or $4,800 worth of merchandise without paying duty.

Some items cannot be brought back to the US (even if you're just coming through for a return flight to the UK). These include:

- ♥ books or cassettes made without authorized copyright ("pirated" copies)

- ♥ any type of drug paraphernalia

- ♥ firearms

- ♥ fruits and vegetables

- ♥ meats and their by-products (such as pâté)

- ♥ plants, cuttings

- ♥ tortoise-shell jewelry or other turtle products (which you will see sold in the Cayman Islands, among others)

TIP: Keep your sales slips handy and pack so your purchases can be reached easily. Get a copy of the "Know Before You Go" brochure (Publication 512) from the US Customs Service, at your airport or by writing the US Customs Service, PO Box 7407, Washington, DC 20044. Check out the US Customs website: www. customs.ustreas.gov.

Island Life

*T*he Caribbean is the land of "no problem" and, for the most part, it's just that. Travel here is easy and carefree, and residents are generally as warm as the weather.

You are, however, entering a different culture, one that has its own traditions and customs. And, as with travel to any part of the world these days, there are a few precautions to take to ensure that yours is a safe and healthy vacation.

Dress

The citizens of the West Indies are modest, conservative people who generally frown upon displays of skin. Although nudity or topless bathing is permitted on some beaches, it is typically not practiced by locals. Most islanders follow a more conservative style of dress than seen in US beach communities.

Bathing suits are appropriate only for swimming; when off the beach grab a cover-up. Bare chests are also frowned upon outside the beach. However, leisure wear – T-shirts, shorts, sundresses and sandals – will be readily accepted in any Caribbean community.

> *TIP: Throughout the West Indies, it is customary to greet folks before blurting out a question or request. A polite "good morning" or "good afternoon" will help you fit in and get your interaction off to a good start.*

Patois

English is the primary language of most Caribbean islands, but you'll quickly find that you may not understand everything, especially if locals are talking to one another. English is spoken with a distinct Caribbean lilt, a delightful sing-song rhythm. Each island has its own patois as well, local words which are often a mixture of African languages dating back to the island's slave days. Jamaica's patois is perhaps the most distinctive and also most difficult to understand.

Taxis

Modes of transportation vary from island to island, but for the most part taxis are the best means of travel. Even the smallest islands like tiny Salt Cay in the Turks & Caicos have taxi service, and you'll find that they're generally operated by professionals who are happy to talk about their island. We've had some of our most interesting conversations about island life with taxi drivers, who are well informed about history and tourist attractions. Often drivers will present their business card at the end of the journey in case you have further need for transportation.

Potential Problems

Crime

Crime in the Caribbean, like anywhere else in the world, can be a potential problem, albeit an infrequent one. Along with their everyday cares, some vacationers unfortunately also leave behind their everyday precautions. On vacation, use the same common sense you would exhibit at home, especially at night. Don't bring expensive jewelry; locally-produced shell necklaces can give you an island look without tempting thieves. Use safes and safety deposit boxes provided by hotels. Also, don't leave valuables on the beach while you are in the water – one of the most common scenarios for theft.

Drugs

Depending on the island you visit (Jamaica is the most notable example), you may be offered illegal drugs from a smooth-talking local salesman. These ingenious entrepreneurs offer their goods both on and off land. We've had more than one swim interrupted by salesmen in canoes, boats, and, once, even on horseback in the shallow water. A polite "no, thank you" usually ends the contact without further problems.

Marijuana, or "ganja" as it's known locally, is illegal throughout the Caribbean. Drug penalties are becoming stiffer, and drug prevention measures more stringent in many countries.

We also caution vacationers not to carry any packages that they have not personally packed. We have been approached by locals asking us to mail packages for them once we arrived in the US. The requests may have been legitimate, but the risk is too great.

Food & Drink

Stomach problems from food and water are rare in the Caribbean. Most stomach distress is caused not by the food itself, but by larger-than-usual amounts of food (combined, for many vacationers, with large amounts of rum).

Water is potable on nearly every island, although some resorts offer bottled water because the tap water produced by desalinization is slightly unusual to the taste. In the Dominican Republic, we would recommend drinking only bottled water, due to possible contamination. However, most islands offer excellent water supplies (and some, like St. Kitts, are so above average that cooks swear it accounts in part for their delicious cuisine).

Sunburn

Nothing will destroy romance on a vacation any faster than a sunburn, your biggest danger in the Caribbean. You'll be surprised, even if you don't burn easily or if you already have a good base tan, how easily the sun will sneak up on you. At this southern latitude, good sunscreen, applied liberally and often, is a must. (And for those of you frequenting those nude beaches, let's just say you need to be extra generous with the sunscreen or even sunblock for the sake of your romance.)

Insects

Oh, those pesky bugs! While the number of mosquitoes are generally fewer than in the American South (the omnipresent sea breeze keeps them at bay), the worst insects in the Caribbean are sand fleas. Popularly known as "no-see-'ums," these pesky critters raise itchy welts where they bite, usually along the ankles. Use an insect repellent if you'll be on the beach near sunset, the worst time of the day for these unwelcome beach bums.

Manchineel Trees

Manchineel (*Hippomane mancinella*) trees, found on most Caribbean islands, present an unusual danger. These plants, members of the spurge plant family, have highly acidic leaves and fruit. During a rain, water dropping off the leaves can leave painful burns on your skin, and the tree's tiny apples will also burn you if stepped on. In most resorts, manchineel trees have been removed or are clearly marked, often with signs and with trunks painted red.

Marine Dangers

For the two of us, a trip to the Caribbean isn't complete without snorkeling in the warm waters which circle every island.

While some inhabitants of these waters look scary, most pose little danger. Exceptions are scorpionfish (a mottled pinkish fish that hangs out on coral and is so ugly it actually looks dangerous), sea urchins (painful if you step on their brittle spines), jellyfish (which cause painful stings with their tentacles), and stingrays (which are dangerous if stepped on; they can be avoided by dragging your feet when wading). Fire coral, of which there are many varieties, but all edged in white, will burn you to defend itself if you brush against it.

The best precaution is to follow your mother's advice: look, but don't touch.

Heat Dangers

In the Caribbean you'll find the mercury regularly rising to high levels on many days and high humidity levels can make the temperature feel much higher. In these conditions, you'll need to take extra precautions to make sure you don't overdo your sun exposure.

The first concern is heat cramps, muscle cramps caused because of lost water and salt in the body. From there, it's not far to heat exhaustion, when the body tries to cool itself off and the victim feels, well, exhausted and even nauseous. Finally, heat stroke can set in, a life-threatening condition.

What can you do to avoid these conditions?

♥ First, drink water – lots of water. Don't wait until you're thirsty to reach for the water jug. Thirst is an early sign of heat stress, so start drinking before it reaches that point.

♥ Slow down. Curtail your activities whenever possible and do like the animals do in the high heat – move slowly.

♥ Take lots of breaks.

Travel Information

- ♥ Stay out of the direct sun.

- ♥ Make sure you are both protected from the sun. Wear wide brimmed hats and caps as well as sunglasses.

- ♥ Wear sunscreen. Sunburned skin is a definite no-no.

- ♥ Avoid the sun between the hours of 10 am and 2 pm; that's when the sun's rays are the strongest. Enjoy an early morning hike then kick back and take a swim break that afternoon.

Time Zones

The Caribbean straddles two time zones. The western islands – Jamaica and Cayman – fall in the Eastern time zone, the same as the East Coast of the US. The eastern islands fall in the Atlantic time zone, one hour ahead of Eastern time.

The Caribbean islands do not observe Daylight Saving Time. During the summer months, the western islands are the same as the Central time zone; the eastern islands the same as the Eastern time zone.

But why worry about the time? Forget the time zones and enjoy island time. When the sun is up, roll out of bed. When it sets, head off the beach and get cleaned up for dinner. When you're hungry, eat, and when you get tired, go to bed.

Currency

You'll find that US currency is accepted on many Caribbean islands, although you'll often receive change back in the local currency.

We recommend using a credit card for everything but tips and street purchases. Besides avoiding the hassle of currency conversion (and back again when you leave), you'll usually receive the best possible exchange rate with a credit card. Credit card companies shop for the best exchange rate for you – saving you some extra pennies and time along the way. Also, many companies limit your liability if your card is stolen.

Island Romance
Weddings

Would you like to get married on your honeymoon? Destination weddings are becoming more and more popular with couples eager to skip the fuss of a traditional wedding and jump right into the fun. Many hotels and resorts offer on-site help to plan your wedding, everything from details like obtaining the license, to extras such as music and photos. Whether the special day involves just the two of you or whether you'll be inviting friends and relatives to join in the occasion, a destination wedding can be a way to create wonderful memories.

But first, the downside. These weddings aren't for everyone. If you're in love with the idea of a large wedding with all your friends and family, skip this. Even with a year of planning, it's just about impossible to get everyone's schedules coordinated for this kind of event. You have to decide what is most important to you.

Tying the knot in St. Thomas.
Courtesy of The Ritz-Carlton.

Destination Weddings

Destination weddings have caught on for several reasons. According to hotels and resorts around the Caribbean, they're especially popular with couples who:

- ♥ are on a budget and don't want the expense of an elaborate wedding.

- ♥ don't want the fuss of a wedding and all that goes with it at home.

- ♥ are on their second marriage looking for something a little different or need to bring along children on the honeymoon. The children's programs at many resorts offer privacy for the couple and a chance to enjoy a vacation with their new family.

- ♥ are bringing a small wedding party. Sometimes the bride and groom stay at one resort and the wedding party at a neighboring resort, giving everyone privacy.

- ♥ are bringing a sizable wedding party and would like to take over a resort.

Many couples say "I do" to island weddings not only as a way to make the occasion more special, but also as a means of simplifying the whole process. "Just say the word, and we'll take care of everything," explains Ava Burke-Thompson, Director of Guest Services at the Sheraton Grand Resort, Paradise Island, Bahamas. "We can arrange for the marriage license; minister, priest or rabbi; florist and photographer; wedding cake and champagne; and the rehearsal dinner and wedding reception."

At resorts like the Sheraton Grand, on-site wedding coordinators take care of every last detail, some with just a one-day notice. "We do it all the time," says Burke-Thompson. "It's now legally possible to get married in the Bahamas with 24 hours' notice."

Island ceremonies also give way to another joyous celebration: island anniversaries. Couples who wed in the Caribbean find it romantic to revisit the very spot where they married.

Easy to Arrange

Recognizing the Caribbean wedding trend, islands are relaxing their marriage requirements. "We are pleased to see that many of the islands are meeting the current trend of destination weddings by enacting legislation making it easier for tourists to get married in the Caribbean," said Michael Youngman, director of marketing for the Caribbean Tourism Organization. "In addition, many hotels and resorts offer wedding and honeymoon packages, making getting married in the Caribbean a memorable and affordable experience."

You'll find that island weddings are becoming increasingly easier to arrange, with shorter (or no) residency periods, simplified paperwork, and usually no required blood tests. Many resorts have full-time staff members to simplify paperwork.

Details, Details

Before you say "I do," plan to do a little research into the "do's" – and "don'ts" – of the local marriage laws. Many islands have loosened their marriage regulations, making it easier for foreigners to tie the knot. Even so, you'll need to do some research. "The reason some couples have problems with their overseas wedding is that they are unfamiliar with the marriage laws, rules and regulations of where they want to be wed," explains Ruth Keusch, co-owner of Ottley's Plantation Inn in the Caribbean federation of St. Kitts & Nevis. In researching your destination wedding, Keusch recommends that couples make sure they find out in advance:

- ♥ if their home country will recognize a wedding in the designated country as valid.

- ♥ the minimum residency period required before the marriage can be performed.

- ♥ what paperwork you'll need to bring from your hometown house of worship if you're planning a religious ceremony.

- ♥ what proof is required if you're divorced or widowed.

Weddings

♥ if blood tests are required and, if so, if you can bring them from your home doctor or whether they must be performed locally.

♥ if there will be English-speaking staff members available to assist you.

♥ costs and fees.

♥ typical weather during the month of your wedding.

♥ special hotel rates for members of the wedding party.

♥ what previous experience the hotel or resort has in planning foreign weddings.

Planning

The simplest way to plan an island wedding is to work through your resort's wedding coordinator. This staff member counsels guests before their stay so you know what necessary papers to bring. After arrival, the coordinator helps couples complete necessary paperwork, explains where to go if the country requires an in-person visit to obtain a marriage license, arranges for a minister or other officiating party, and helps with wedding extras such as photography and music.

Once you decide on a resort, call the local number and ask to speak with the wedding coordinator. Also, inquire about wedding packages to make your special day that much more extraordinary.

> *Typically, most countries require you to send documents and complete paperwork before your stay. If this is the case, do not send documents by surface mail. Mail service throughout most of the Caribbean is extremely slow. Rely on fax transmissions and courier services such as Federal Express for delivery of papers. Also, bring copies of all paperwork to the island with you, just in case.*

The resort staff will work with you down to the last detail. We recently spoke with Angus Sexius, Guest and Public Relations Manager for the Royal St. Lucian, who handles weddings at the popular property. "I try to meet with the clients the morning after they arrive so they can relax before the ceremony. We then make an appointment and go to the lawyer's office," Sexius says. The paperwork then goes to the attorney general's office, where the marriage license is issued.

Sexius notes several points for travelers planning to wed. St. Lucia has public beaches. "When we have beach weddings we cannot tell people to get off the beach." The Royal St. Lucian moves ceremonies as close as possible to the hotel property. "Most guests are mindful of the ceremony and are discreet." Also, the marriage officer in Castries has the final say over the exact time of the wedding. Finally, says Sexius, "The thing I need to be mindful of is that I have no control over the weather. We must put in a contingency plan in case of bad weather."

Two Top Wedding Packages

In the Caribbean, two all-inclusive resort chains really stand out in the destination wedding and honeymoon market: **SuperClubs** and **Sandals**. These resorts offer extensive wedding packages and on-site coordinators to make the day memorable as well as extra special.

Sandals

With resorts in Antigua, Jamaica, Bahamas, and St. Lucia, Sandals has also performed thousands of weddings. Call or contact the Sandals wedding division for a wedding form and details; www.sandals.com; 888-SANDALS.

The "Wedding Moon" package includes document preparation; legal fees; minister or other officiating party; witnesses; wedding announcement cards; champagne and hors d'oeuvres; bouquet and boutonniere; Caribbean wedding cake; video of your ceremony; 5x7 photo; candlelight dinner for two; "Just Married" T-shirts; continental breakfast in bed the morning after the wedding; decorated wedding area; and taped musical accompaniment. Check with Sandals for the present fee. Lately they've been offering the package free with a minimum stay.

Additional services can be purchased and include manicure/pedicure; full body massage; hairstyling make-up session in your room; additional photos; "Sunset Hour" Moët and Chandon with hors d'oeuvres; floral decorations, and more.

Wedding times at Sandals properties are 10 am, noon, 2:30 pm, and 4:30 pm.

If you'll be getting married at one of the Sandals locations in Jamaica, you'll need to send notarized copies, that include both the notary stamp and notary's signature of your birth certificates, (as well as final divorce decrees or death certificates, if one of you was previously married) to **Unique Vacations** at 4950 SW 72nd Avenue, Miami, FL 33155. ☎ 305-284-1300.

> *I*mportant: You have to supply documents at least a month before the wedding. Be sure to send notarized copies, not originals!

If you select one of the Sandals properties in St. Lucia, the Bahamas, or Antigua, you'll need to send photocopies of your documents to Unique Vacations at least 30 days before the date, then hand carry your original documents with you to the hotel. (We've suggested this before, but it's worth another mention: be sure to hand-carry those documents with you; never put them into checked luggage!)

SuperClubs

This resort has locations in Jamaica and the Bahamas, and offers guests free weddings and vow renewals with ceremonies that include marriage license, minister, witnesses, tropical flower bouquet and boutonniere, champagne, music, and a wedding cake, as well as best man, maid of honor and witnesses, if needed. A mininum stay is required. Additional packages are available for a fee including video and still photography.

SuperClubs has a variety of properties for all types of guests, so you can select one that meets your personal interests and the profile of your wedding guests, if you're bringing some along. Elegance is the name of the game at the Lido properties: **Grand Lido Negril, Grand Lido Braco,** and **Grand Lido Sans Souci.** Sports and fun is the theme at the Breezes properties: **Breezes Bahamas, Breezes Montego Bay,** and **Breezes Runaway Bay.** And it's pure party, anything goes at **Hedo-**

nism II in Negril and **Hedonism III** in Runaway Bay (where you can even get married in the nude if you choose!). Visit www. superclubs.com; ☎ 877-GO-SUPER in the US; 0208-390-7652 in the UK.

Before you go, you'll work with a wedding coordinator to supply papers including certified copies of both your birth certificates, which must include your fathers' names. You'll also need to supply your professions. If either of you was previously married, you'll need either a certified copy of the final divorce papers or death certificates.

T IP: Start the paperwork process as least three weeks before your trip.

Horse and carriage rides are popular with honeymooners.
© Len Kaufman

Weddings

When you arrive at SuperClubs, the wedding coordinator will take you on a personal tour of the property so you can select the perfect spot for exchanging your vows. If you're staying at one of the Jamaica properties, you'll need to be on the island at least two days before exchanging vows, and all the paperwork is handled by the wedding coordinator. If you're staying at Breezes Bahamas, you'll need to be on island two days before the ceremony and will need to appear at the Registrar General's office in person between 9:30 am and 4:30 pm, Monday through Friday, to complete your paperwork.

Other Wedding Packages

Just about every hotel in the Caribbean offers a special wedding package. Some of these packages include accommodations; some cover the wedding only. Check with your property for a wedding package and ask about the features you're interested in, whether it's a steel pan band or a videographer. Also ask about guests. One property may have restrictions on the number and age of guests. Another may have discount packages available for guests staying on property. Some hotels do weddings for guests only; others allow people staying at other properties to exchange vows at their hotel.

Wedding Requirements

Here's a quick look at individual island marriage requirements. Fees are given in US dollars.

Anguilla: Two-day waiting period; $284 fee. No blood test.

Antigua & Barbuda: One-day waiting period; $240 for wedding license. No blood test.

Aruba: Civil ceremonies are not legal unless one member of the couple is either a Dutch citizen or was born on Aruba.

Bahamas: 24-hour residency requirement; $40 for marriage license. No blood test.

Barbados: No residency requirement; fee of $62.50. No blood test.

Bermuda: No residency requirement; fee of $205. No blood test.

British Virgin Islands: Three-day waiting period; $110 for marriage license, plus fee of $35 to be married in Registrar's Office; $100 to be married outside the office. No blood test.

Cayman Islands: No waiting period; $200 for marriage license. No blood test.

Curaçao: Three-day residency; $167 for marriage license. No blood test.

Dominican Republic: No residency period; $20 for marriage license. Couples must write the American Consulate in Santo Domingo in advance of intended wedding date asking permission to marry in a civil ceremony. All documents must be translated into Spanish. No blood test.

Jamaica: 24-hour residency; $54 for marriage license. No blood test.

Puerto Rico: No residency; $2 stamp fee for copy of license. A VDRL blood test no older than 10 days prior to the wedding is required.

St. Barts: One person in couple must be resident for 30 days; no fee. Blood test required.

St. Kitts & Nevis: Two-day residency; $80 for marriage license. No blood test.

St. Lucia: Two-day residency and two days for license; $198 for marriage license. No blood test.

St. Martin: One person in couple must be resident for 30 days; no fee. Blood test required.

Sint Maarten: 10 days before the ceremony couples must register at the Office of Civil Registry. Fee $152. No blood test.

Trinidad & Tobago: Three-day residency; $55 fee. No blood test.

Turks & Caicos: 24-hour residency requirement; approval by a marriage officer may take two days. $50 fee. No blood test.

USVI: Must wait eight days from receipt of notarized application, but the couple does not need to be on island during this time. $50 for marriage license; $200 fee to be married in the court by a judge. No blood test.

Weddings

Honeymoons & Anniversaries

Let your hotel know when making reservations that you will be celebrating a special
occasion. Although most have honeymoon-
anniversary packages that you can purchase for extra amenities, such as breakfast
in bed or champagne on arrival, many hotels
like to recognize honeymooners and those
celebrating an anniversary. Some hotels offer a special gift or even a room upgrade if
available. Remember, as much as you want
to have a good time, the hotel also wants to
make this an extra-special trip for the two of
you. What better way to bring back return
guests than to help create a wonderful occasion?

Romantic Sites in the Caribbean

This region boasts enough idyllic sights to ignite a spark in any
romance. Lovers will find these sites especially inspiring:

1. DIAMOND WATERFALLS AND GARDENS, ST. LUCIA
Blooming with tropical splendor, garden trails lead to the Diamond Waterfalls, a cascade that leaves a spray of "diamond"
twinkles in the air. If you stop by on a Sunday, you can also enjoy a soak in the mineral baths originally built by French King
Louis XVI for use by his troops. See page 283.

2. THE BATHS, VIRGIN GORDA, BVI
This beach is littered with massive granite boulders as smooth
as riverbed stones. They form shadowy caves where you can
swim in water as warm as a bath. See page 157.

3. Y.S. FALLS, JAMAICA
Although the north coast's Dunn's River Falls is far more
heavily visited, these secluded falls offer couples a much quieter paradise. Cascading in steps through tropical forest, the
falls can be climbed with the help of a guide, then swimmers
can enjoy clear waters under a canopy of ferns. See page 235.

4. OLD SAN JUAN, PUERTO RICO

Dotted with historic sites and rich with the atmosphere of Spanish conquistadors, here couples can stroll hand in hand where lovers have walked for centuries. The most recognized site in Old San Juan is **Fuerte San Felipe del Morro**, better known as El Morro. See page 248.

5. BOCA TABLA, CURAÇAO

Pounding Atlantic waves carved this sea cave. Kneeling in the darkness, you'll watch the surge of crystal blue waves as they come within feet of you, roaring into the cave and back out to sea. See page 188.

6. WEST END, NEGRIL, JAMAICA

Negril's famous Seven Mile Beach gives way to rugged cliffs on its west side and visitors find one of the best sunset lookouts in the Caribbean. Every day crowds arrive at Rick's, one of the region's best known sunset bars, for the chance to watch another island day draw to a close. See page 238.

7. SOUTH PENINSULA, ST. KITTS

Until a few years ago, this stretch of land was accessible only by boat. Today a modern highway makes the island's most beautiful, pristine beaches accessible. Keep an eye out for the vervet monkeys that live in this remote region. See page 264.

8. NATURAL BRIDGE, ARUBA

This symbol of Aruba marks the line where tumultuous sea waves crash against the windward coast. Walk out on the bridge for a cool sea spray and breathtaking view. See page 96.

9. PARADISE POINT, ST. THOMAS

Aboard ski-lift gondolas, you'll rise to one point that never sees snow: the top of Flag Hill, for a view of the Charlotte Amalie harbor dotted with cruise ships. Gondolas ascend to the point from 9 am to 4:30 pm every day. See page 374.

10. MARACAS BAY, TRINIDAD

About an hour from Port of Spain, the drive to this area is a treat in itself, winding through the Northern Range with views of forests where species such as howler and capuchin monkeys, ocelot, Amazon parrots, and wild pigs can be found. The beach at Maracas Bay offers a full day of fun and is the place to see and be seen in Trinidad. See page 324.

Weddings

The Islands

Anguilla

$\mathcal{T}$his island is well known among the well-to-do and is a favorite getaway for those couples who are really looking to escape. Don't expect mega-resorts here; it is definitely for couples looking to discover their own fun. It's an easy order to fill.

This tiny island is the king of the Caribbean beach world, a mecca for beach buffs in search of that perfect stretch of sand. Although only 16 miles from end to end, and little more than 35 square miles in all, the island packs in over 30 beaches and numerous nearby cays to tempt sunlovers, snorkelers, sailors, scuba divers, and those just looking for a good beach walk or hike. A few beaches bustle with activity, but most are quiet, pristine boundaries between land and sea.

Festivals

Although Anguilla enjoys a festive atmosphere year-round, definitely the biggest blowout of the year for romantic travelers is Carnival. Starting on the first Monday in August and continuing to mid-August, Carnival brings colorful parades, pageants, and lots of music to the island. Swimsuit competitions, a bands festival, street dancing, arts and crafts exhibitions, and Caribbean Night with calypso, soca and reggae artists are scheduled. Carnival also brings boat racing – the island's number one sport.

Boat racing is considered the national sport of Anguilla. Races are conducted using sleek vessels, 15 to 28 feet in length. The boats are made on the island and recall the history of Anguilla. Boat racing dates back to the early 1800s to the days when Anguillians, realizing that the low rainfall made sugar cane and other agricultural crops unsuccessful, turned to the sea. Sailors and fishermen worked the waters around the island in boats about 17 to 20 feet in length. Like today's racing boats, these vessels did not have a deck and were powered by a jib and mainsail held by a single 25-foot mast. At the end of a workday, fishermen often raced each other back to shore.

By the early 1900s, boating wasn't just a way to quicken the commute back to Anguilla, it became a competition. Fishermen and sailors raced back to Anguilla to take part in competitions such as August Monday, the start of the island's largest festival. Today the boats are primarily constructed in Island Harbour on the northwest side of the island. On competition days, Anguillians and visitors line the shores to cheer on the competitors.

You'll see the boats, their sleek, shiny hulls reflecting the Caribbean rays, as you drive around the island. Most are kept dry docked in their captain's front yard, proud reminders of the racing sport that binds together Anguillians many times a year. Races are scheduled on festival days, including:

- ♥ New Year's Day
- ♥ Easter Monday
- ♥ Anguilla Day, late May
- ♥ Whit Monday, late May
- ♥ Queen's Birthday, mid-June
- ♥ Heineken Regatta, August
- ♥ August Monday, early August
- ♥ August Tuesday, early August
- ♥ August Wednesday, early August
- ♥ August Thursday, early August
- ♥ Champion of Champions Race, mid-August

The viewing grounds are typically at Island Harbour or Sandy Ground, and occasionally at Blowing Point or Meads Bay.

Sweet Dreams

Price Chart

Rates reflect high winter season (expect prices to be as much as 40% lower during the off season) for a standard room for two adults for one night; prices are in US dollars.

$ . . . . under $150
$$ . . . . between $150 and $300
$$$ . . . . between $300 and $450
$$$$ . . . . over $450

Altamer Villa
Shoal Bay, West End
Reservations: ☎ *888-652-6888*
www.altamer.com
$$$$

This new villa is one of several that will soon offer luxury accommodations to a few lucky couples. Rates include meals prepared by Altamer's gourmet chef and spirits/beverages (except fine wine, cognac and cordials). This four-story, 12,000-square-foot beachfront villa was designed by modern architect Myron Goldfinger. Three more villas are scheduled to be completed by 2004.

Altamer features a game room with custom-built pool table and flat screen plasma television with DVD player, computer with Internet connections, plus bars on multiple levels. A full-time staff of five operates from a separate concierge building, ensuring privacy and quality service. The main villa is one of the few handicapped-accessible in the islands, with an elevator in one of the towers.

Special Features/Activities: beachfront, marble baths with whirlpools, gourmet professional kitchen, pool, fitness center, tennis.

The Islands

Cap Juluca

Maundays Bay
☎ *264-497-6666; fax 264-497-6617*
Reservations: ☎ *888-858-5822*
www.capjuluca.com
$$$$

Cap Juluca, named for the native Arawak Indian Rainbow God, is an exclusive getaway that offers privacy and pampering. The 58 guest rooms and junior suites, seven suites, and six pool villas all offer complimentary mini-bar, marble baths, and hair dryer. Some units include kitchen with refrigerator and dining room.

Special Features/Activities: beachfront, tennis courts, croquet, beach, pool, Sunfish, kayaks, windsurfing, fitness center, snorkel trips, sunset cruises.

Cove Castles Villa Resort

Shoal Bay West
Reservations: ☎ *800-223-1108, 264-497-6801; fax 264-497-6051*
www.covecastles.com
$$$

This luxury villa resort includes two four-bedroom grand villas with over 5,000 square feet; four three-bedroom villas; and eight two-bedroom beach houses. The resort caters to the guest looking for privacy, peace, and quiet. The stark white structures have a contemporary exterior and a tropical décor inside. Complimentary amenities include snorkeling gear, Sunfish sailboats, sea kayaks, bicycles, tennis facilities, video players and library, concierge service, cable TV, and a personal housekeeper. Also available at additional charge are deep-sea fishing and sailing excursions, tennis instruction, massage, and more.

Special Features/Activities: All villas include the services of a personal housekeeper, video player and library, CD player and library.

CuisinArt Resort and Spa

PO Box 2000, Rendezvous Bay
Reservations: ☎ *800-937-9356; 264-498-2000; fax 264-498-2010*
www.cuisinartresort.com
$$$$

This new 93-room resort is filled with whitewashed villas with blue Mykonos-inspired domes. Beyond, the sea provides a beautiful backdrop. Couples have a variety of room types from which to choose. All are decorated with Italian fabrics and international furniture; baths have Italian marble. Some suites also include a private solarium for sunning. Couples can start their day with a complimentary continental breakfast served in their room or on their patio.

Special Features/Activities: beachfront, three restaurants, cooking classes, health and beauty spa, fitness center, two bars, pool, tennis, snorkeling, watersports.

♥ Malliouhana

Meads Bay
Reservations: ☎ *800-835-0796, 264-497-6111; fax 264-497-6011*
www.malliouhana.com
$$$

This intimate, 56-room hotel is perched on cliffs overlooking a tranquil sea and another perfect Anguillian beach. Guest rooms here are secluded, spread among 25 manicured acres. We especially liked the décor of this elegant resort, which highlights items from around the world, including Asian artwork and Brazilian furniture.

Special Features/Activities: beachfront, waterskiing, cruises to nearby cays, windsurfing, Sunfish, Prindle catamarans, tennis, two pools, hot tubs, fitness facilities.

♥ Sonesta Beach Resort

Rendezvous Bay West
Reservations: ☎ *800-SONESTA; fax 264-497-6899*
www.sonesta.com
$$$

This is one of the island's most beautiful properties as well as one of the most memorable resorts in the Caribbean. Styled like something right out of *1,001 Arabian Nights,* this lavish resort dazzles with mirrored tiles, elaborate mosaics, and a unique Moroccan architecture. It is perched right on the edge of a three-mile-long beach.

The Islands

Kicking back island-style.
Courtesy of Sonesta Beach Resort.

One hundred guest rooms have private balconies, marble baths, televisions, mini-bars, hair dryers, safes, and cool tile floors. A beautiful décor continues the Moroccan theme in pastel Caribbean shades throughout. Oceanfront rooms have spectacular views of the long beach and the hills of St. Martin in the distance.

Special Features/Activities: beachfront, fine and casual dining, spa, use of snorkel gear, sea kayaks, windsurfers and Sunfish, tennis, fitness center, gift shops, freshwater pool.

Tables for Two

Price Chart

Restaurant prices are for dinner per person, including a drink, appetizer or salad, and entrée.

$..........................	under $15
$$	$15 to $30
$$$	$30 to $45
$$$$........................	over $45

♥ *Casablanca*
Sonesta Anguilla
☎ *264-497-6999*
Dress code: casually elegant
Reservations: suggested
$$$

This open-air restaurant serves continental cuisine in an elegant atmosphere. Offerings include Anguilla crayfish, Black Angus tenderloin, shellfish pepperpot, and several pasta dishes. We found this restaurant, with its Moroccan décor and a sea view, one of the island's most romantic. This is a unique night out you won't soon forget.

♥ *Koal Keel*
The Valley
☎ *268-497-5075*
Dress code: dressy
Reservations: required
$$$

One of the Caribbean's finest restaurants, Koal Keel is an attraction and a fine restaurant rolled in one. The menu features island pea soup, a purée of pigeon peas and Caribbean sweet potatoes. Entrées include coconut shrimp, "Drunken Hen" (Cornish hen baked and blazed with 151 Bacardi) and grilled crayfish. The wine list here is a veritable book; the restaurant has its own wine cellar with climate-controlled rooms. You make all dining decisions at once, including dessert, which is made to order. Vanilla crème brûlée, mango tarte soufflé and mango sorbet make the perfect end to a meal. Enjoy a walk around the historic site followed by a free rum tasting.

Gorgeous Scilly Cay
Island Harbour
☎ *264-497-5123*
Dress code: casual
Reservations: not needed
$$-$$$

This offshore restaurant features Anguillan lobster as well as grilled fish, chicken, and ribs. Just walk up to the dock in Island Harbour and wave; a boat will come over to transport you to Scilly Cay. Visitors can also enjoy a swim or a snorkel around the reefs, as well as live music on Wednesdays, Fridays, and Sundays.

The Islands

Johnno's
Sandy Ground
☎ *264-497-2728*
Dress code: casual
Reservations: not needed
$-$$

You may hear the name of this local hotspot if you ask where to go to enjoy music and to dance the night away, but before the night gets going, this is a great place to get fresh seafood.

Romantic Activities

Island Sights & Museums

If this is your first visit to the island, invest in an island tour led by one of the tour companies or a taxi driver. Guided island tours are available from most taxi drivers for $40 for one or two people ($5 for each additional person), and they will help give you a good overview of the island. From there, you can rent a car and motor around to the beaches and natural attractions scattered around the island (remember, though, driving is on the left).

Anguilla is home to several small museums. The National Trust is currently at work on a museum in **The Valley**, and several privately owned collections already welcome visitors. **The Heritage Collection**, Pond Ground, ☎ 264-497-4440, is the work of Colville Petty, an authority on Anguilla's rich history. Housed in part of Petty's home, the museum spans the entire range of the island's history, from its Amerindian days to the 1967 Revolution. Kids enjoy the collection of Arawak artifacts, including an Arawak shell necklace; a hollowed conch shell that served as an early drinking vessel; and spindle whorls, used to spin cotton to make hammocks and religious symbols for the Arawaks. This fascinating museum is open Monday through Saturday, 10 to 5 pm, and Sunday by appointment. Talking to Colville Petty about the island's history is well worth the modest price of admission.

Anguilla enjoys a rich West Indian culture. Have a look at the traditional song and dance with a visit to the **Mayoumba**

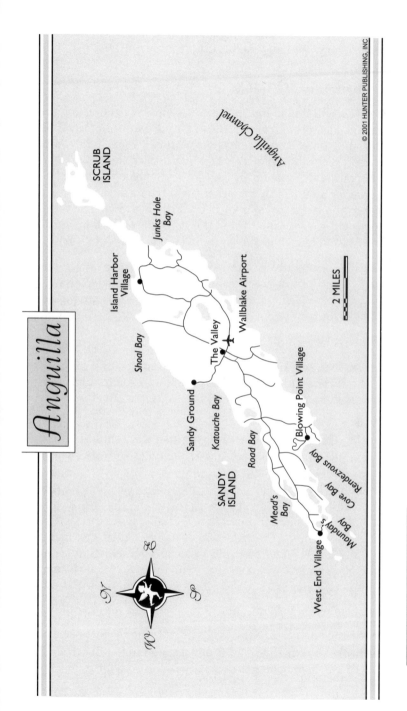

Anguilla

SCRUB ISLAND

Anguilla Channel

Junks Hole Bay

Island Harbor Village

Wallblake Airport

Shoal Bay

The Valley

Sandy Ground

Katouche Bay

Blowing Point Village

Road Bay

Rendezvous Bay

Cove Bay

SANDY ISLAND

Mead's Bay

Maunday's Bay

West End Village

2 MILES

© 2001 HUNTER PUBLISHING, INC.

The Islands

Folkloric Theatre, La Sirena Hotel, ☎ 264-497-6827. A group plays every Thursday night. Call for reservations.

Underwater Delights

Couples will find many opportunities for snorkeling and there's a marked snorkel trail off **Shoal Bay East**. Maintained by the National Trust, the site has been mapped and can be easily followed by most snorkelers. Stop by the National Trust office at the National Museum in The Valley or ask your hotel's concierge for a map of this snorkel trail. Laminated for use underwater, the maps are available from the National Trust for a $5 deposit; $4 is returned when the map comes back to the office. To obtain a map, call the National Trust, ☎ 264-497-5297.

Certified scuba divers can enjoy a look at one of seven wrecks that lie in the waters off Anguilla. Four were sunk in 1990 as part of an ecological program and all the wrecks are intact and upright on the ocean floor.

The wrecks include:

- ♥ The *Ida Maria*, 60 feet. Deliberately sunk in 1985, this 110-foot freighter is home to many schools of fish, and Anguilla's famous lobsters are often spotted here.

- ♥ The MV *Sarah*, 80 feet. Deliberately sunk in June, 1990, this 230-foot vessel is home to a wide variety of marine life.

- ♥ The MV *Meppel*, 80 feet. Also sunk in June 1990, this ship is intact and sits just inside the sail reef system.

- ♥ The MV *Lady Vie,* 80 feet. Another vessel sunk in June 1990, also located near the sail reef system.

- ♥ The MV *Commerce*, 45-80 feet. Sitting on a gently sloping bottom, this 1986 wreck has an abundance of fish life; rays are often spotted here.

Anguilla has two dive operations, located in Sandy Ground and Island Harbour. Contact these dive operators for information:

The Dive Shop, The Valley, ☎ 264-497-2020; fax 264-497-5125. Located in Sandy Ground, this is a five-star PADI international training center.

Anguillian Divers Ltd., Island Harbour, ☎ 264-497-4750; fax 264-497-3723.

Beaches

Anguilla's best asset is its beaches. Miles of shining sand pave the perimeter of this island, which is often cited as one of the top beach destinations in the Caribbean (with good reason).

The atmosphere at the various beaches varies from playful to placid. Regardless of which beach you select, the mood is friendly. A few beach vendors are found on the island's busiest stretch of sand, **Shoal Bay**, but even here the sales are very low-key and you'll be able to enjoy undisturbed sunbathing all afternoon.

Shoal Bay is a classic Caribbean beach, one of the best in the Caribbean. Nearly chalk-white sand stretches for two miles.

Shoal Bay has the most typical "beach" atmosphere in Anguilla, with casual eateries sprinkled along the sand. Beach chairs and umbrellas are rented by the day for a few dollars. This beach is a terrific choice for a family day of fun in the sun. Young swimmers generally find the water calm, and snorkeling is excellent on the northeast end of the beach.

Other good beach choices include **Sandy Ground**, stretching alongside the community of Sandy Ground (a favorite with boaters, windsurfers and water-skiers); **Rendezvous Bay**, at the Sonesta Anguilla (great for beachwalking); **Maundays Bay**, at Cap Juluca (also good for beachwalking).

One romantic adventure is to take a boat out to one of the many cays and islets surrounding Anguilla.

Check with boat operators for a day-trip to **Prickly Pear Cays** or **Sandy Island**, both known for their snorkeling, or for a

The Islands

unique experience take a day-trip to one of the uninhabited islands: **Anguillita Island, Sombrero Island,** or **Dog Island.** A boat can drop you for a full day's excursion, most departing from Sandy Ground. For information on excursions, call **Sandy Island Enterprises** (☎ 364-497-5643; **Cheers Charter Boats** (☎ 247-497-8079); or **No Mercy** charter boat (☎ 264-235-6283).

Shopping

Shopping is not one of Anguilla's strong points. The **Sonesta Anguilla** resort has several good gift shops; both the clothing store and general store have reasonably priced items. A good option is an afternoon of shopping in **St. Martin.** Take a ferry ride to Marigot, St. Martin for a day at the market. The ferry departs from the village of Blowing Point; the cost is US $10 (US $12 for journeys after 5 pm). There is also a US $2 departure tax. The ride takes 20-30 minutes each way. Travelers should also be sure to bring their passports. Kids of all ages find trinkets, clothes, jewelry, shells, carvings, and other goodies in all price ranges. The market is colorful, fun, and friendly.

Anguilla does tempt shoppers with one good opportunity: art. This tiny island is home to numerous artists, both Anguillian and relocated from around the globe, who work in oils, wood, and other mediums. One of the best known is Cheddie Richardson, a self-taught carver who sells his work at **Cheddie's Carving Studio** on the Main Road in The Cove (near the Sonesta turnoff). Working in mahogany, walnut, and especially driftwood, the artist portrays birds, dolphins, fish, and humans.

Other artists on Anguilla include **Lucia Butler** (specializing in wooden house plaques); **Marj Morani** (scenes of island life and hand-thrown pottery), **Jo-Anne Saunders** (sculpture, fabric, murals); **Susan Graff** (island scenes); **Tanya Clark** (Japanese woodblock prints); and **Courtney Devonish** (sculpture and pottery). For more information on Anguilla artwork, contact the Tourist Board on island in The Valley, ☎ 264-497-2710.

Nightlife

Nightlife, to put it mildly, is pretty darn quiet in Anguilla. This island has a lot of things, but a hopping night scene is not one of them. Plan to spend a night over on St. Martin for some casino action, dancing, and shows. For most Anguilla visitors, evenings are spent enjoying a gourmet meal at a luxurious pace, perhaps followed by an after-dinner liqueur or a moonlit walk.

Some beach bars and restaurants do offer evening entertainment, however. Here are a few places where you'll find evening fun (double-check with the properties for the night's entertainment before making your evening plans as changes occur frequently).

The Dunes Preserve, Rendezvous Bay. No phone. Located on the south end of the island near Sonesta Resort. Reggae musician Bankie Banx plays on Friday nights and during full moons.

Johnno's Beach Stop, Sandy Ground, ☎ 264-497-2728. From Wednesday through Sunday nights, this hopping beach spot offers live performances, usually starting between 8 and 9 pm (4 pm on Sundays).

La Sirena Hotel, Meads Bay, ☎ 264-497-6827. On Monday nights, this hotel offers the sounds of a steel drum band at 7:30. Thursday nights mark the Mayoumba Folkloric Theatre at 7:30 pm, featuring traditional songs and costumes.

Scilly Cay, off Island Harbour, ☎ 264-497-5123. Wednesday, Friday, and Sundays live music is offered at this offshore cay. Visitors take a boat from Island Harbour.

Just the Facts

Entry Requirements: Upon arrival in Anguilla by either ferry or plane, visitors must show proof of citizenship. Passports are the easiest way to prove citizenship; official photo ID along with a birth certificate with a raised seal can also be shown. A return or onward ticket is also necessary.

The Islands

Getting Around: If you'll be traveling around the island very much, by far the most economical transport is a rental car. Prices vary with agency and model, but a typical mid-size or a jeep runs about US $35 per day. A three-month Anguillian permit is required of all drivers. The fee is US $6; this license can be obtained from the rental car companies. Driving is on the left.

Taxis are readily available but not cheap. You can ask for a taxi to be dispatched at the airport or the ferry port in Blowing Rock. All taxis are on a call basis. Public transportation is not offered on the island.

Language: English

Currency: The Eastern Caribbean (EC) currency is legal tender. Value is set at $US 1 = EC 2.68. US dollars are also accepted.

Electricity: 110 volts/60 cycles

Information: For more information on Anguilla, contact the Anguilla Tourist Board, ☎ 800-553-4939, or write Anguilla Tourist Information Office, The Wescott Group, 39 Monaton Drive, Huntington Station, NY 11746. While on the island, stop by the Tourist Board office in The Valley at Factory Plaza, ☎ 264-497-2710. Website: http://net.ai.

Antigua & Barbuda

Antigua (pronounced an-TEE-ga) doesn't have the quaint shopping zones of islands like St. Thomas or St. Croix. And it doesn't have the lush tropical beauty of islands such as Jamaica or St. Lucia.

What Antigua has are beaches: 365 of them, a beach for every day of the year. Stretches of white sand that border turquoise waters teeming with marine life. Beaches where the two of you can walk hand in hand and hardly see another soul. Beaches where you can shop for local crafts and buy a burger at beachside grill. And beaches where you can just curl up under a tall coconut palm and sit until the sun sinks into the sea and marks the end of another perfect Caribbean day.

This 108-square-mile limestone and coral island is somewhat scrubby, with rolling hills, especially on the southern reaches. The capital city is **St. John's,** home of most of the tourist shopping and the cruise port.

The south shore of the island is favored by yachties, who call into **Nelson's Dockyard** at English Harbour.

For lovers in search of real peace and quiet, tiny Barbuda may just be the answer. This exclusive island is a jetsetter's hideaway, but it's also a nature lovers' island. Accessible as a day-trip from Antigua or as a vacation destination of its own, this small island is much less developed than its larger sister. Outside the lavish resorts, the island belongs to the wildlife, primarily the feathered variety. It's also noted for its spectacular beaches, long stretches of either pink or white sand that divide the sea from the land.

Festivals

The hottest event of the year is **Antigua Sailing Week**, held each year in April. During this time, Antigua hotel rooms can be hard to come by (in fact, many hotels continue their high season prices just to include this busy week). During this week, **Nelson's Dockyard** at English Harbour comes to life with the color and pageantry of the largest regatta in the Caribbean. Parties, barbecues, races, Lord Nelson's Ball, and more highlight this annual event, now in its third decade.

Other special events include the **Culinary Exposition** in late May and **Independence Day** on November 1st. **Carnival** is the hottest summer activity, held each year from late July to early August with musical entertainment, parades, and Antiguan cuisine.

In late October and early November, the **Hot Air Balloon Festival** lights the skies. Close to a dozen hot air balloons schedule launches at English Harbour, Newfield, Jolly Harbour, St. John's, Curtain Bluff, and other sites around the island. To celebrate Antigua's independence, British skydivers jump from 2,000 feet carrying the Antiguan flag. Other festivities include

The Islands

parades, gun salutes, and dancing in St. John's. A night flight over English Harbour is a spectacular scene to witness. Contact the Antigua and Barbuda Department of Tourism for more information on any of these events. ☎ 212-541-4117.

Sweet Dreams

Price Chart

Rates reflect high winter season (prices are as much as 40% lower during the off season) for a standard room for two adults for one night; prices are in US dollars.

$ . . . . under $150
$$ . . . . between $150 and $300
$$$ . . . . between $300 and $450
$$$$ . . . . over $450

Antigua

The Admiral's Inn
PO Box 713, St. John's
☎ 268-460-1027; fax 268-460-1534
$

Located right in Nelson's Dockyard, this 17th-century building now offers 14 guest rooms (each with twin beds). Each is decorated with antiques, wrought-iron chandeliers, and hand-hewn beams; some rooms feature air conditioning. This inn is a favorite with lovers of historic B&Bs.

Special Features/Activities: restaurant, transportation to beaches.

> *TIP: Be sure to book early during the peak time of April's Sailing Week. Hotels fill up early at this time of year.*

Curtain Bluff Hotel

PO Box 288, St. John's
☎ *268-462-8400; fax 268-462-8409*
Reservations: ☎ *800-672-5833*
www.curtainbluff.com
$$$$

This exclusive hotel, home of one of the Caribbean's best wine cellars, is located on a private peninsula with two beaches. The all-inclusive property includes meals, drinks, afternoon tea, watersports, tennis, golf, and even mail service so you can send those postcards home.

Special Features/Activities: beachfront, casual and fine dining, watersports, dive shop, tennis, golf, squash, croquet.

Hawksbill Resort

PO Box 108, St. John's
Reservations: ☎ *800-223-6510*
☎ *268-462-0301; fax 268-462-1515*
www.hawksbill.com
$$$

Located just a few minutes from St. John's, this resort is our favorite kind: quiet, restful, and located on not one, but four superb beaches. With a primarily British contingency, the resort is somewhat reserved, but just a few minutes from the action of St. John's. Nudists can wander over to the fourth beach to seek the total tan at the only nude beach in Antigua.

Special Features/Activities: beachfront, fine and casual dining, watersports, freshwater pool, nude beach.

Jumby Bay

PO Box 243, St. John's
☎ *268-462-6000; fax 268-462-6020*
Reservations: ☎ *800-327-3237*
www.elegantresorts.com
$$$$

One of the Caribbean's most exclusive resorts, Jumby Bay recently reopened under the ownership of Jamaica's Half Moon Golf, Tennis, and Beach Club. The resort offers junior suites

The Islands

and two- and three-bedroom villas, some with private plunge pools.

> *This exclusive resort is located on a 300-acre private island. Guests enjoy the best of everything: gourmet meals, fine wines, sports.*

Special Features/Activities: beachfront, all-inclusive, casual and fine dining, pools, watersports, tennis, massage and reflexology.

Strolling on the beach at Jumby Bay.
© Douglas G. Ashley

♥ Sandals Antigua Resort and Spa
PO Box 149, Dickenson Bay, St. John's
☎ *268-462-0267; fax 268-462-4135*
Reservations: ☎ *800-SANDALS*
www.sandals.com
$$

Like the other couples-only resorts in this popular chain, Sandals Antigua offers an array of activities that can keep even the most restless vacationer happy. Activity coordinators, or "Playmakers," keep things going for those who want to stay busy. For couples preferring inactivity, two-person hammocks and "love baskets" (swinging wicker baskets), offer quiet afternoons beneath shady palapas.

Many visitors are honeymooners or couples getting married on their honeymoon. During our late May visit, we counted three weddings on one afternoon alone.

This Sandals has low-slung buildings spread along a wide swath of white beach. We stayed in a rondoval room, an octagon-shaped cabin with a tall conical ceiling, louvered windows, and a true Caribbean atmosphere. Guests in the upper category rooms enjoy Suite Concierge Service for booking restaurant reservations or assistance with island tours, a fully-stocked, complimentary in-room bar, daily *New York Times* fax, and terry cloth robes.

Another romantic feature here is the excellent spa, although spa services are not part of the all-inclusive package.

The resort has many restaurants from which to choose: an open-air main dining room offering international fare in the evenings served à la carte, an Italian restaurant (with an excellent sunset view – get there early for a beachside table), and a Japanese restaurant where active chefs will prepare your meal right at the table amid flurry of flying knives and implements.

Special Features/Activities: beachfront, all-inclusive, couples-only, spa, watersports, fine and casual dining at five restaurants, five freshwater pools, five hot tubs, tennis.

Sunsail Colonna Club
Hodges Bay, St. John's
Reservations ☎ *800-327-2276*
www.sunsail.com
$-$$

If the two of you love the water and sailing, then you'll love Sunsail. This international company, with clubs as far away as Turkey, is a favorite among the sailing world. Here you'll find an array of vessels to take out and enjoy and, if you don't know stern from bow, you can take expert lessons here as well, part of the all-inclusive plan.

Sunsail isn't fancy, but it is one of the best bargains in the Caribbean. All rooms are air conditioned and include satellite TV, telephone, mini-refrigerator, and tea-and-coffee-making facilities. There are numerous twin and double rooms as well as apartments and two- and three-bedroom villas.

But the real attraction here comes in the form of watersports. The resort hugs a small cove where instruction is available in dinghy, catamaran, and yacht sailing as well as water-skiing and windsurfing. If your skills are up to par, you can take a vessel out or participate in one of the resort programs such as a yacht regatta or dinghy regatta. Waters are most challenging during the winter months; summer usually brings milder trade winds and conditions better suited to beginners.

Special Features/Activities: restaurant, pool, extensive watersports program, tennis.

Barbuda

♥ K Club

☎ 268-460-0300; fax 268-460-0305
Reservations: ☎ 800-223-6800
E-mail: k-club@candw.ag
$$$$

This is one of the Caribbean's most secluded resorts, the spot where the late Princess Di once went to get away from it all. The resort includes 40 guest rooms on the beach with kitchenettes, gardens showers, and air conditioning. All meals are included. The rates are pricey, even by high Caribbean standards.

Special Features/Activities: championship nine-hole golf course, two lighted tennis courts.

Coco Point Lodge

Coco Point, Hodges Bay
☎ 268-462-3816; fax ☎ 268-462-5340
Reservations: ☎ 212-986-1416
$$$$

On the southern end of Barbuda lies this small resort (complete with its own private airstrip) with 32 rooms, each with bath and beachfront patio. Small cottages offer kitchenettes. The resort is tucked on a private, expansive property with plenty of beach to explore. The rates here, although high, are all-inclusive and offer three meals daily with beverages available anytime.

Special Features/Activities: fishing, tennis, windsurfing, and more.

Palmetto Beach Hotel

☎ 268-460-0442; fax 267-460-0440
Reservations: ☎ 866-BARBUDA; fax 212-242-4768
www.palmettohotel.com
Email: info@palmettohotel.com
$$$$

Also a pricey property, Palmetto Beach Hotel does offer a lot for the money. Prices range from about US $170-250 per person, with all rates including breakfast, lunch, and dinner but not drinks. Children under 12 sharing a room with parents stay for free. The resort is closed from September through November, the island's slowest season.

Recently refurbished, the 24-junior suite resort is located on a great stretch of beach which all rooms overlook. A reflection of its Italian owners, the meals have a Mediterranean flair. When it's time to work off some of those calories, guests find plenty of sporting options.

Special Features/Activities: scuba diving, snorkeling, excursions to the bird sanctuary, horseback riding, tennis, windsurfing, and more.

Tables for Two

At the resort restaurants, you'll find familiar dishes on the menu as well as a few island specialties such as **christophine,** a type of squash; **pepperpot,** a spicy stew; **afungi,** a pudding of cornmeal and okra; and **ducana,** a pudding made from grated sweet potato and coconut, sugar, and spices boiled in a banana leaf. Save a little room to finish off your meal with a taste of the sweet **Antigua black pineapple.** The most popular beer on the island is **Wadadli,** made locally.

Price Chart

Restaurant prices are for dinner per person, including a drink, appetizer or salad, and entrée.

$..........................	under $15
$$	$15 to $30
$$$	$30 to $45
$$$$........................	over $45

Antigua

♥ *Admiral's Inn*
Nelson's Dockyard, St. John's
☎ *268-460-1027*
$-$$

This inn is home to a very popular eatery with outdoor dining near the yachts that come to this dockyard from around the Caribbean. Along with great people-watching, the restaurant offers breakfast, lunch, and dinner.

> *T IP: Save time before dinner for a stop by the lounge area filled with yacht club flags.*

Hemingways Veranda Bar and Restaurant
St. Mary's Street, St. John's
☎ *268-462-2763*
$$

Located near Heritage Quay, this informal, second-story restaurant is located in a West Indian-styled building constructed in the early 1800s. Start with a Hemingways' fruit punch or pineapple daiquiri, then move on to an entrée of Caribbean seafood or steak. This is a wonderful spot to dine at before walking over for a little casino action in town.

Redcliffe Tavern

Redcliffe Quay, St. John's
☎ *268-461-4557*
$-$$

Just steps from the shopping district of St. John's, this restaurant is housed in a former red brick warehouse that dates back to the 19th century. Enjoy quiche, sirloin steak, smoked salmon, or seafood in a casual atmosphere.

Vienna Inn

Hodges Bay
☎ *268-462-2300*
$-$$

Austrian food in Antigua? Why not? When you're ready for a break from island fare, stop by for Swiss schnitzel or veal filled with ham and cheese and topped with egg.

Barbuda

Palm Tree Restaurant

Park Area, Codrington
☎ *268-460-0092*
$

This casual restaurant serves up traditional cuisine, especially seafood. The restaurant is a favorite with locals and a great spot to feel a part of the island scene.

Romantic Activities

Beaches

Antigua's most romantic activity is a trip to one of its splendid beaches. Some of the most popular spots are **Dickenson Bay**, where you'll find beach bars and watersports action; **Hawksbill beaches** on **Five Island peninsula,** home of a clothing-optional beach; and **Runaway Beach,** also lively with watersports activities.

The Islands

If it's beach seclusion you're after, then consider a visit to Antigua's sister island, **Barbuda.** Day-trips to this un-commercialized island, popular with bird watchers because of its population of frigate birds, are available from several opera-tors.

Barbuda lies about 30 miles north of Antigua. To take advan-tage of Barbuda's beautiful beaches, you'll find guided daytrips available from several tour operators in Antigua. **Barbuda Tours/Earls Tours,** located in St. John's, offers a guided look at the island's top sights including Martello Tower, the Bird Sanctuary, and more. To arrange a tour, call ☎ 268-461-7388 or 268-462-0742. You'll also find several Barbuda residents who offer guided tours. Call **George Burton** (☎ 268-460-0103) or **Hilroy Thomas** (☎ 268-460-0015) for information on setting up a tour of the island sights customized to your interests.

You can also book with **Carib Airlines** (☎ 869-465-3055; www. candoo.com/carib). The airline offers charter flights to the is-land, with four- , five- , or seven-passenger planes.

Another option is to arrive via powerboat. The 1½-hour trip from Antigua is offered by **Adventure Antigua** (☎ 268-727-3261 or 268-560-4672; www.adventureantigua.com; adven-tureantigua@yahoo.co.uk). This day-trip departs from the west coast of Antigua early in the morning for a day of snorkeling and exploring in Barbuda, along with a visit to the bird sanctu-ary. Tours cost US $150 per person.

Underwater Delights

Nature lovers will find plenty of activity on Antigua. Scuba div-ing and snorkeling are popular activities. Certified divers can enjoy a variety of dives, from walls to wrecks. Some of Antigua's top scuba sites include:

♥ **Sunken Rock:** Advanced divers appreciate this deep site, with a maximum depth of over 120 feet. The dive begins at 40 feet in a coral canyon that de-scends a sandy ledge. Divers then proceed down a drop-off to the bottom of the ocean. Barracuda, amberjack, and rays are usually found here.

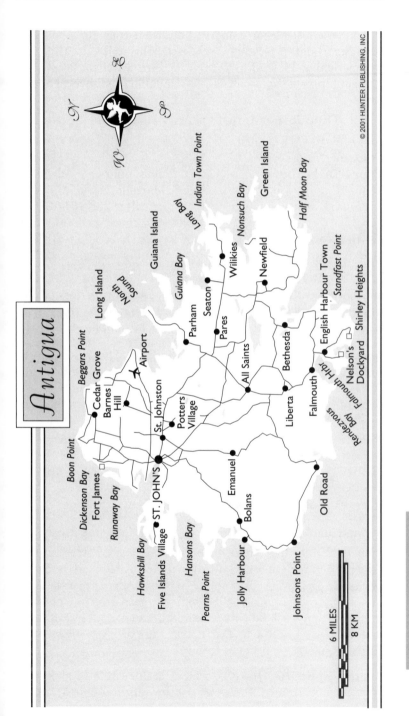

Antigua

Boon Point
Dickenson Bay
Fort James
Runaway Bay
Hawksbill Bay
Five Islands Village
Hansons Bay
Pearns Point
Jolly Harbour
Johnsons Point
ST. JOHN'S
Emanuel
Bolans
Old Road
St. Johnston
Potters Village
Barnes Hill
Cedar Grove
Beggars Point
Airport
Long Island
North Sound
Guiana Island
Guiana Bay
Long Bay
Indian Town Point
Parham
Pares
Seaton
Wilikies
Nonsuch Bay
Newfield
Green Island
Half Moon Bay
All Saints
Bethesda
Liberta
Falmouth
Rendezvous Bay
Falmouth Hrbr.
English Harbour Town
Nelson's Dockyard
Shirley Heights
Standfast Point

6 MILES
8 KM

♥ **The Chimney:** Located southwest of Antigua, this dive features a small cave at a depth of 60 feet, with sponge-filled gullies descending to 80 feet. Look for large parrotfish, lobsters, eels, and nurse sharks in the vicinity.

♥ **Thunderhead:** Just a short boat ride from the west coast hotels, this shallow site lies in 35 feet of water, making it popular with beginning divers. This wreck-strewn site features artifacts (medicine bottles and chamber pots have been found here) as well as hard corals.

Island Sights & Museums

Antigua is rich in historic attractions as well. The most visited is **Nelson's Dockyard National Park**. Built in 1784, this dockyard was the headquarters for Admiral Horatio Nelson. Today you can retrace its history at the **Dow's Hill Interpretation Centre** or at the complex's two museums: **Admiral's House** and **Clarence House** (☎ 268-460-1026). The latter was the former home of Prince William Henry, later known as King William IV.

Shopping

The primary shopping area on the island is in **St. John's**, near the cruise ship terminal. This area doesn't have the charm of many Caribbean shopping districts, and is somewhat littered, smelly, and dirty. Still, it's worth a two- or three-hour excursion to have a look at the goods offered in the small boutiques.

Along the waterfront you'll find the most tourist-oriented shopping, with duty-free wares such as fine jewelry, perfumes, and liquor. Look for **Gucci, Colombian Emeralds, Little Switzerland,** and other fine shops at **Heritage Quay**. Besides these pricey gift items, you'll also find a good selection of tropical prints and batik fabric sportswear (made on the island) sold in this area. **Caribelle Batik** has an excellent selection of shirts, skirts, and shorts in tropical colors.

Nearby, **Redcliffe Quay** is a more scenic place to shop and have a drink or lunch. You won't see the duty-free shops of Heri-

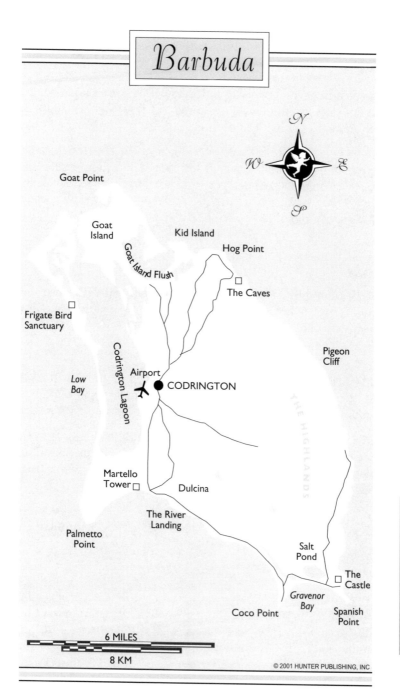

Barbuda

Goat Point

Goat Island

Kid Island

Hog Point

The Caves

Goat Island Flush

Frigate Bird Sanctuary

Codrington Lagoon

Pigeon Cliff

Low Bay

Airport

CODRINGTON

THE HIGHLANDS

Martello Tower

Dulcina

The River Landing

Palmetto Point

Salt Pond

The Castle

Gravenor Bay

Coco Point

Spanish Point

6 MILES

8 KM

© 2001 HUNTER PUBLISHING, INC

The Islands

tage Quay, but you will find plenty of cool shade, brick court-yards, and restored buildings where you can shop for Caribbean items or enjoy a cold beer in a charming atmosphere.

If you'd like to get away from the tourist center, take a walk up to **Market Street** for shops aimed at the local residents, including many fabric stores offering beautiful tropical prints.

Outside of St. John's, head to **Harmony Hall** in **Brown's Bay Mill.** This art gallery, which originated in Jamaica, features work by many Caribbean artists. Original works as well as prints and posters are for sale, accompanied by crafts, books, and seasonings that capture the spice of the island.

Nightlife

Casino gambling is a popular nightlife activity, with several casinos from which to choose. They are, by casino standards, fairly small and casual.

Casinos

Joe Mike's Downtown Hotel Plaza, St. John's, ☎ 268-462-1142/3244. Slot machines, table games and a good restaurant and bar with live music make this a favorite stop for visitors.

King's Casino, St. John's, ☎ 268-462-1727. Not only does this casino hold the record for the largest casino on the island, but also boasts the largest slot machine in the world. What better reason to visit?

St. James's Club Casino, St. James's Club, ☎ 268-460-5000. Table games and slot machines are available to visitors at this newly renovated casino.

Live Music

Most resort hotels offer evening entertainment, which might range from a Caribbean night with traditional music and dance, to local performers singing the latest reggae or soca tunes. You'll also find a fun nightlife atmosphere at these bars which frequently feature live music.

Abracadabra Bar and Restaurant, English Harbour, ☎ 268-460-1732. This local hot-spot has it all: dancing, sports, piano bar, live music; a great place to spend an evening.

Big Banana, Historic Redcliffe Quay, St. John's, ☎ 268-480-6985. Live music twice a week and a great selection of CDs for the other five nights of the week, along with great food.

Coconut Grove Beach Restaurant, Dickenson Bay, ☎ 268-462-1538. This beachside bar has a great menu and live music on the weekends.

Millers By The Sea, Fort James, St. John's, ☎ 268-462-9414. Each night of the week comes with a different style of live music. Be sure to stop by on Sundays for Caribbean Night.

O'Grady's Pub, Redcliffe Street, St. John's, ☎ 268-462-5392. A local favorite, the pub combines their impressive menu with live music on Wednesday nights.

Just the Facts

Entry Requirements: US and Canadian visitors must show a passport or a birth certificate and photo ID as well as an onward or return ticket.

Getting Around: Taxi travel is the most common means of transportation, especially for couples not comfortable with driving on the left side of the road. Taxi fares from the St. John's area to Nelson Dockyard on the far side of the island run about US $50 round trip.

Rental cars are available; a temporary Antiguan driver's license is required. We found that some roads are a little bumpy, and that a full tank of gas (as well as a spare tire) is recommended for visitors traveling away from the major destinations.

Language: English

Currency: Eastern Caribbean dollar (US $1 = EC $2.70)

Electricity: Part is 110 volts; part is 220. Bring an adapter just to be safe.

The Islands

Information: Contact the Antigua and Barbuda Department of Tourism, 610 Fifth Avenue, Suite 311, New York, NY 10020 or call ☎ 212-541-4117. In Canada: the Antigua and Barbuda Dept. of Tourism and Trade, 60 St. Clair Avenue East, Suite 304, Toronto, Ontario MT4 1N5, ☎ 416-961-3085. In the UK, Antigua House, 15 Thayer Street, London, W1M 5LD or ☎ 0171-486-7073. Website: www.antigua-barbuda.org.

$\mathcal{A}$ruba

$\mathcal{A}$ ruba has its own special beauty. Don't look for mountains covered with tall palms, walkways lined with flowering bougainvillea, or roads shaded by willowy casuarina trees.

Instead, you'll have to dig a little deeper for the beauty of Aruba. Venture to the rugged Atlantic shore and watch the tumultuous waves carving the natural bridge, continually changing the demarcation line where the land meets the sea. Or you can hike to some of Aruba's highest hills, curious bumps on the landscape, and look out at the *cunucu,* or countryside, for traditional Dutch-style houses with their sun-baked, orange tile roofs.

But perhaps the best way to see the beauty of Aruba is to look into the faces of the Aruban people, the island's greatest asset. This tiny island, a mere 70 square miles, is truly a melting pot of cultures. Over 43 nationalities are represented here, and with them a mélange of languages. Arubans learn from an early age the benefits and necessity of working with other nations. Learning different languages is a skill that most young Arubans master. The language of the Aruban home is **Papiamento,** a mixture of Spanish, Portuguese, French, Dutch, Indian, English, and even some African dialects. When youngsters head to school, they receive instruction in Dutch, because of Aruba's continuing ties to the Kingdom of Holland. Once they reach third or fourth grade, instruction in English begins. Spanish is introduced during the junior high years, and in high school students select either French or German to study.

That familiarity with many languages translates into a welcoming atmosphere for visitors of any nationality. There is no hostility to tourists on this island; no language barrier to overcome. There is just a spirit of *bon bini*, or "welcome" which greets visitors from the moment they arrive in the airport and continues throughout their visit.

Papiamento is the language of the streets and it sounds a little like Spanish. Below are some common Papiamento phrases.

How Do You Say...

good morning	bon dia
good afternoon	bon tardi
goodnight	bon nochi
welcome	bon bini:
thank you	danki
how are you?	con ta bai?
sweetheart, wonderful	dushi
kiss	sunchi
I love you	my stim abo
with all my love	ku tur mi amor

Located just 12½ degrees from the equator, Aruba's climate is drier than that found on most Caribbean islands. Normal rainfall is less than 24 inches annually, resulting in a desert landscape of tall cacti, aloe, and windblown divi-divi or watapana trees, bent permanently at a 45° angle by the ever-present trade winds.

The rugged countryside is known as the cunucu, and it spans the length of the 20x6-mile island. The island is dotted by small communities, including **San Nicholas**, and the capital, **Oranjestad** (literally "Orange City"). Here, Dutch-style buildings punctuate the landscape with cool pastel hues and red roofs baked a pumpkin color by the sun. Streets are bathed in restful tones of ochre, pink, baby blue, and sea green – everything but white. Supposedly, an earlier leader of Aruba, plagued by migraine headaches, ordered that all buildings be painted a soothing shade to stop the glare.

The Islands

Festivals

Aruba's biggest blowout is **Carnival**, a colorful celebration that rocks the streets with dancing parades, steel bands, and a general party atmosphere similar to Mardi Gras. The culmination of the festival is the **Grand Parade**, always scheduled for the Sunday preceding Ash Wednesday.

Other special events include **National Anthem and Flag Day** on March 18, when the island shows its patriotic spirit. In June, the island jams to the **Aruba Jazz and Latin Music Festival**.

The **Bonbini Festival** is your best chance to join in the party spirit of the island; it happens every Tuesday night in Oranjestad's **Fort Zoutman**.

Sweet Dreams

Price Chart

Rates reflect high winter season (expect prices to be as much as 40% lower during the off season) for a standard room for two adults for one night; prices are in US dollars.

$ . . . . under $150
$$ . . . . between $150 and $300
$$$ . . . . between $300 and $450
$$$$ . . . . over $450

♥ *Allegro Americana Aruba Beach Resort & Casino*
J.E. Irausquin Boulevard #83, Palm Beach
☎ *297-8-64500; fax 297-8-63191*
Reservations: ☎ *800-447-7462*
www.allegroresorts.com
$$$

The swimming pool is the centerpiece of this 419-room resort. The pool has its own current, so you can just float along the stream or swim against it to work off that Aruban food and drink. The pool also features "Spa Island," which has two whirl-pools and a rock waterfall.

Special Features/Activities: beachfront, casino, casual and fine dining, tennis, watersports. freshwater pool.

Aruba Marriott Resort & Stellaris Casino

L.G. Smith Boulevard #101, Palm Beach
☎ *297-8-69000; fax 297-8-60649*
Reservations: ☎ *800-223-6388*
www.marriotthotels.com/auaar/
$$$

This 413-room hotel is one of the newest on Palm Beach, a flashy property with a free-form pool, oversize guest rooms, and just about any activity a couple could want. A special honey-moon package includes welcome gift and champagne, break-fast-for-two on your private balcony, a candlelight dinner along with a tableside serenade at the resort's northern Italian res-taurant, and more.

Special Features/Activities: beachfront, casual and fine dining, freshwater pool, casino, watersports, diving, tennis.

Aruba Sonesta Resort and Casino

Seaport Village, L.G. Smith Boulevard #9, Oranjestad
☎ *297-8-36000; fax 297-8-34389*
Reservations: ☎ *800-SONESTA*
www.arubasonesta.com or www.sonesta.com
$$

After a day of connecting flights, we arrived in Aruba late, very late. But in Aruba, and especially at the Aruba Sonesta Resort and Casino, the lateness of the hour was no problem.

Aruba and this lively downtown hotel come alive in the late night hours, a time to enjoy life with a roll of the dice, a walk through the open-air lobby in a glittery dress, or a stroll down the waterfront to enjoy the sound of live bands, the smell of fresh Italian food, and the gentle lap of waves. Crime is rare here, and the atmosphere is perfect for a couple in love.

The hotel is perfect for lovers, who will find comfortable rooms with views of the waterfront, an array of restaurants (including L'Escale, one of our romantic favorites), and a shopping center

The Islands

that features everything from the latest European fashions to Delft Blue china.

> *The Sonesta Resort's most romantic feature is Sonesta Island, located less than 10 minutes away by private launch. And this isn't just any boat ride. Venturing up into the hotel via a canal that slices into the shopping mall, guests are transported to a private world where they can primp and parade on a crowded adult (often topless) beach, play volleyball on the family beach, dine at the open-air restaurant, or, for the ultimate in togetherness, enjoy a day alone on a private honeymoon beach, served by a waiter.*

Special Features/Activities: casual and fine dining, casino, shopping mall, private island, watersports, freshwater pool.

Aruba Sonesta Suites and Casino

Seaport Village, L.G. Smith Boulevard #82, Oranjestad
☎ *297-8-36000; fax 297-8-34389*
Reservations: ☎ *800-SONESTA*
www.arubasonesta.com or www.sonesta.com
$$$

Ah, what a delightful dilemma: to choose the Sonesta Suites or the Resort? The Sonesta Suites is located just a block from the Resort, but it is a beachfront (albeit a small beach) property. This hotel includes suites with all the comforts of home: a full, furnished kitchen, dining area, and bedroom. As you might expect, it's an especially popular property for those traveling with kids. The free-form swimming pool is the focal point for the property, which also includes a slightly less elegant casino than its nearby cousin.

Special Features/Activities: beachfront, casual and fine dining, shopping mall, watersports, freshwater pool.

♥ Hyatt Regency Aruba Resort and Casino

J.E. Irausquin Boulevard #85, Palm Beach
☎ *297-8-61234; fax 297-8-65478*
Reservations: ☎ *800-233-1234*
www.hyatt.com
$$$

The 365-room Hyatt, located on the northern end of Palm Beach, is one of Aruba's most luxurious properties. Like other Hyatts, this property is for anyone looking for a body holiday: be pampered in the health and fitness facility, slice across the clear Caribbean on a sailboat at the watersports facility, or just luxuriate in the warmth of the sun at the three-level pool complex.

Special Features/Activities: beachfront, casual and fine dining, freshwater pool, casino, tennis, watersports.

La Cabana All-Suite Beach Resort and Casino
J.E. Irausquin Boulevard #250, Oranjestad
☎ *297-8-37208; fax 297-8-77208*
Reservations: ☎ *800-835-7193*
www.lacabana.com/resort
$$

Located across the street from Eagle Beach, this orange sherbet-tinted property has plenty of action, including a huge casino, one of the island's top showrooms (see *Nightlife*, page 99), a host of restaurants, and more. With 803 suites, the property is large, but bountiful services keep things moving smoothly. All guest rooms are suites – from studios for couples to three-bedroom suites for families, and all include a fully equipped kitchenette.

Special Features/Activities: across from beach, freshwater pool, watersports, racquetball, squash, casino, casual and fine dining.

Radisson Grand Aruba Caribbean Resort Spa and Casino
J.E. Irausquin Boulevard #81, Palm Beach
☎ *297-8-66555; fax 297-8-63260*
Reservations: ☎ *800-333-3333*
www.radisson.com
$$

This 372-room hotel has plenty to keep couples busy on the beach with water-skiing, WaveRunners, catamarans, scuba instruction, the list goes on and on.

The hotel offers a romantic adventure package with welcome drinks, souvenir T-shirts, champagne, breakfast in bed, candlelight dinner, and more.

Special Features/Activities: beachfront, watersports, diving, freshwater pool, shopping arcade, fine and casual dining, casino.

Enjoy a dip in the freshwater pool.
Courtesy of Radisson Aruba Caribbean Resort & Casino.

Tables for Two

As you would expect on an island that's home to 40 nationalities, Aruba offers cuisine from around the globe. Chinese, Indonesian, French, Japanese, Argentinean, Italian, Russian, Spanish, Mediterranean, Dutch, and American food are all available. Fast-food outlets are plentiful, especially along the Oranjestad waterfront. (And don't laugh – they can offer an interesting slice of Aruban life. We popped into McDonald's for an inexpensive breakfast one morning and, as in a small-town diner, eavesdropped on conversations over the Papiamento newspaper.)

But don't miss the Aruban dishes. Fried fish with **funchi** (cornmeal), stewed lamb with **pan bati** (pancake), and **keshi yena** (a hollowed wheel of Edam cheese filled with meat and baked to combine flavors) are popular local dishes.

Price Chart

Restaurant prices are for dinner per person, including an appetizer or a salad, an entrée, and a drink. All prices are given in US dollars.

$. . . . . under $15
$$ . . . . $15 to $30
$$$ . . . . $30 to $45
$$$$. . . . . over $45

♥ *L'Escale Restaurant*
Aruba Sonesta Resort and Casino
Seaport Village, L.G. Smith Boulevard, #9, Oranjestad
☎ *297-8-36000*
Dress Code: dressy
Reservations: recommended
$$$-$$$$

We think this is one of the most romantic restaurants in the Caribbean, thanks not only to its beautiful décor, harbor view, attentive staff, and excellent dishes, but also to its musical entertainment. Every night, from 8 to 10 pm, a Hungarian string quartet strolls through the eatery, taking requests from diners. We heard everything from Beatles to Brahms, all performed tableside under low romantic lighting by these outstanding musicians. Have them play your special song and relive your first date.

If that's not enough for lovers, the menu presents plenty of additional reasons to visit L'Escale. Baked Caribbean grouper, calypso chicken stuffed with king crab, chateaubriand, and pasta with shellfish are presented in style. There is also a fairly extensive wine list, with many Chilean vintages and other choices to please any discerning palate.

The Islands

The Old Cunucu House Restaurant

Palm Beach 150
☎ *297-8-61666*
Dress code: elegant
Reservations: recommended
$$$-$$$$

Housed in a restored 80-year-old Aruban homestead, this well-known restaurant features local cuisine. Entrées include specialties such as an appetizer of Aruban mezze, cheese pastiche, or Aruban fish soup. Follow up with keshi yena, fresh conch, or seafood Palm Beach, a dish of lobster, fish, scallops, and squid in a cream sauce with wine, flamed with pernod. Open for dinner Monday through Saturday.

Charlie's Bar

Zepperfeldstraat 56, San Nicholas
☎ *297-8-71517*
Dress Code: casual
Reservations: not needed
$$

Located in San Nicholas, about a 15-minute ride from downtown Oranjestad, lies Aruba's best known and loved bar. Charlie's is an institution known to generations of Caribbean travelers looking for a watering hole. Many visitors have left memorabilia – from yacht flags to pieces of clothing – on every available surface in the structure. After a drink, settle in for a meal of garlic shrimp.

♥ Pavarotti

Palm Beach 21A
☎ *297-8-60644*
Dress Code: dressy
Reservations: recommended
$$$

Operated by the same management as the Old Cunucu House, this Italian restaurant and American grill tempts diners with an extensive menu. Choose from Italian favorites such as pasta with clams, penne pasta with pink vodka sauce and shrimp and crab, or angel hair pasta with clams, scallops, calamari, shrimp, and octopus in marinara sauce. Grilled items include lamb chops, filet mignon, and T-bone. Open for dinner only, Monday through Saturday.

Le Petit Café
Emmastraat 1, Oranjestad
☎ *297-8-23166*
Dress code: casually elegant
Reservations: optional
$$

Located on a busy corner off Oranjestad's main street, this indoor-outdoor eatery specializes in meat prepared on hot stones. Waiters bring the sizzling dish to your table.

Romantic Activities

Island Sights & Museums

As home to both the cruise port and the airport, your first look at Aruba will probably be in the city of **Oranjestad**. This beautiful city, where nearly every building sports a fresh coat of paint and a distinct Dutch style, is home to several historic sites. **Fort Zoutman** is the city's oldest building, constructed in 1796. Today it's home to a small museum.

Although you'll want to schedule at least half a day in Oranjestad for some shopping, have a look at the rest of the island first. The biggest tour operator is **DePalm Tours** (☎ 297-82-4400), with desks in every major hotel. This firm offers an excellent half-day tour aboard air-conditioned motor coaches with hotel pick-up. At the conclusion of the tour, you can return to your hotel or get off in downtown Oranjestad for an afternoon of shopping.

Island tours reveal terrain with a windswept romantic beauty that couples ochre colors against the turquoise sea and rugged beauty. You'll have an excellent view of the cunucu, or countryside, atop **Casibari Rock Formation**. It's a fairly easy climb (although you'll find yourself bent over and squeezing between rocks a few times), but wear good shoes for this trek. The formation is located just north of Hooiberg.

The Islands

Couples also should visit the **natural bridge**; like the divi-divi tree, it is a symbol of Aruba. This bridge was carved by the tumultuous sea waves that continue to crash on the rocks and spray visitors. You'll always find a crowd at the natural bridge, which is somewhat touristy with a bar and souvenir shop, but it's still worth a visit, especially if you're doing some photography along the way. The natural bridge is on the northeast coast.

Sports

Golfers are in luck. Aruba has a championship course. **Tierra Del Sol** (☎ 297-8-60978, www.tierradelsol.com), designed by Robert Trent Jones II, combines sand dunes, cacti, rock formations, and views of the sea. Tennis buffs can also enjoy an extensive facility: the $1.4 million **Aruba Racquet Club** (☎ 297-8-60215). With eight courts, an exhibition center court, pro show, swimming pool, fitness center, and even a shopping center, the club attracts world-class events.

Guided horseback rides at **Rancho Del Campo** (☎ 297-8-20290), are popular with many couples. On tours, you can ride through Aruba's only national park: **Arikok National Wildlife Park**, home of Indian rock markings, gold digging ruins, and a restored cunucu home. Don't forget to bring long pants for the horseback ride!

Beaches

Much of Aruba's allure is the sea, both for its beaches and the action in the water. On the southwest end of the island, **Palm** and **Eagle** beaches are two of the most popular because of their proximity to the major hotels, but for the calmest waters head to **Baby Beach**, located on the far southern tip of the island near the town of **San Nicolas.** Swimmers should avoid the north shore, which is rough and often plagued by undertow.

Above the waves, Aruba offers some of the Caribbean's top windsurfing. **Fisherman's Hut**, located on the northern tip of the island, is an ideal beginner's site because of its calm, shallow waters, while experts head to **Boca Grandi's** rough waves, located 25 miles southeast of Oranjestad. Every year, the island hosts the **Aruba Hi-Winds Pro Am World Cup** in June, with the best competitors from the world of windsurfing.

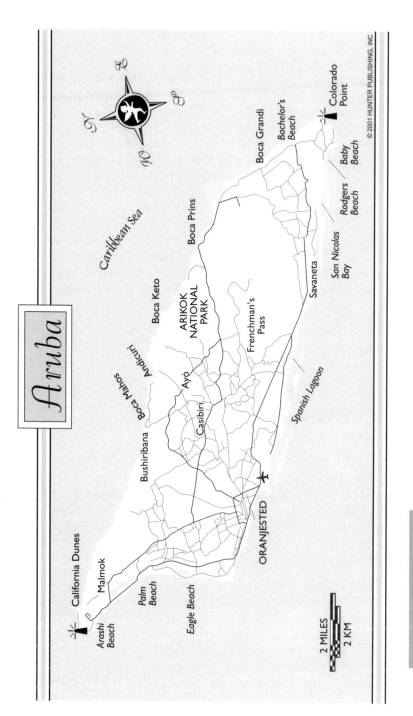

Aruba

California Dunes
Malmok
Arashi Beach
Palm Beach
Eagle Beach
ORANJESTED
Bushiribana
Boca Mahos
Andicuri
Casibiri
Ayó
ARIKOK NATIONAL PARK
Boca Keto
Caribbean Sea
Boca Prins
Frenchman's Pass
Spanish Lagoon
Savaneta
San Nicolas Bay
Rodgers Beach
Baby Beach
Boca Grandi
Bachelor's Beach
Colorado Point

2 MILES
2 KM

© 2001 HUNTER PUBLISHING, INC

The Islands

Underwater Delights

Below the surface, divers will find numerous sites in the 40- to 60-foot depth range, including the *Antilla*, a German freighter that's the largest wreck in the Caribbean, and the *California,* the ship that didn't respond to the distress signals of the *Titanic*. Both ships lie off the northwest tip of the island. For diving operators, call **Pelican Adventures** (☎ 297-8-72302) or **Red Sail Sports** (☎ 877-REDSAIL; www.redsail.com).

Shopping

Aruba definitely ranks as a top Caribbean shopping destination. International goods – perfumes, china, crystal, jewelry, cameras, and clothing – are best buys. Unlike the practice of many islands, bargaining is not customary in Aruba.

Most stores are open 8 am to 6:30 pm, Monday through Saturday, and usually close during the lunch hour. If a cruise ship is in port, you may find some shops open on Sunday.

The primary shopping district stretches along **Oranjestad's waterfront.** Malls as colorful as sherbet line this route, tempting shoppers with goods that range from T-shirts and Delft Blue salt and pepper shakers to European trés chic designer outfits and fine jewelry.

Seaport Mall and **Seaport Marketplace** have the lion's share of the mall business. The Mall is located adjacent to Sonesta Resort and includes high-priced shops on its lowest level. Upstairs, boutiques offer moderately priced resort wear, jewelry, china, and more, for a total of over 65 shops. At Sonesta Suites, the Seaport Marketplace is an outdoor gallery of nearly 60 shops specially targeted for vacationers.

If you forget someone special on your list, you'll also find shops at the **Queen Beatrix International Airport**. Fendi, Hummel, Gucci, Mont Blanc, and other top names are represented along with many liquors.

Nightlife

Nightlife is a hot topic on Aruba. The island sizzles when the sun sets and really heats up in the wee hours. Casino gambling is a favorite pastime with most visitors, with nearly a dozen casinos from which to choose. **Crystal Casino**, located downtown at the Sonesta Resort, is one of the most elegant, with Italian marble, Austrian crystal chandeliers, English carpet, and Spanish gold-leaf mirrors. Call ☎ 297-8-3600 for reservations.

Look for Las Vegas-type revues at the **Tropicana Showroom**, located at La Cabana's Royal Cabana Casino, ☎ 297-8-77000. The Tropicana features headliner acts as well as a female impersonator revue. **The Americana Showroom** at the Americana Aruba Resort (☎ 297-8-24500) and **Music Hall** at the Wyndham Aruba Beach Resort (☎ 297-8-64466) also offer lavish revues.

You can kick up your heels at the **Aladdin Theater** at Alhambra Casino, ☎ 297-8-35000, styled like a Moorish palace. If you get tired of dancing or run out of luck at the tables, you can always enjoy some late-night shopping at the arcade.

Just the Facts

Entry Requirements: American citizens need to present a current passport, official birth certificate, or voter registration card along with a photo ID.

Getting Around: Taxis are available in resort areas or you can have one dispatched by calling ☎ 22116 or 21604 on island. Rates are fixed (no meters), so check with your driver before the ride. Rental cars are widely available. The minimum age for driving a rental car is 21.

Language: Dutch and Papiamento, English spoken widely.

Currency: Aruban florin; (exchange rate fluctuates, but US $1 = about A.Fl. $1.77).

Electricity: 110 volts/60 cycles. Same as US.

Information: Call the Aruba Tourism Authority, 1000 Harbor Boulevard, Weehawken, N.J., ☎ 800-TO-ARUBA. In Canada:

The Islands

5875 Highway #7 Ste. 201, Woodbridge, Ontario L4L 1T9, ☎ 905-264-3434). Website: www.arubatourism.com.

The Bahamas

$\mathcal{T}$echnically, the Bahamas lie outside the boundaries of the Caribbean. But, except for a few days when the islands are cooled by winter's chill, you'll have a hard time telling the difference. These 700 islands, sprinkled like seashells across shallow water, share the same sun, sand, and festive atmosphere as their southern neighbors. Although there are many islands, only 20 of these landforms are populated.

A trip to the Bahamas can be as quiet or as active as the two of you choose. For privacy and a real island atmosphere, select one of the **Family Islands** like **Eleuthera**, tiny **Harbour Island** (where motorized transportation means a golf cart), or **San Salvador** (site of Columbus' first landfall in the New World). For a more active vacation, **Grand Bahama** offers golf, casino gambling, and even the chance to swim with dolphins.

But for most vacationers, a Bahama vacation includes a trip to **Nassau**, the capital city located on the island of **New Providence**. Nassau tempts travelers with glitzy shows, top duty-free shopping, and water that's as beautiful as any found in the Caribbean.

Just a half-hour flight from Miami, this island may be just a stone's (or a conch shell's) throw from the US mainland, but Nassau gives visitors a wonderful taste of Caribbean life. The atmosphere is a delightful combination of British and Caribbean.

Geography

Both locals and vacationers tend to use the term "Nassau" to identify the island of New Providence, but the city proper is located on the north side of the island. Nassau is compact, filled with activity, especially along **Bay Street,** where locals and visitors shop for duty-free items. Just blocks away, the seat of

The Bahamas

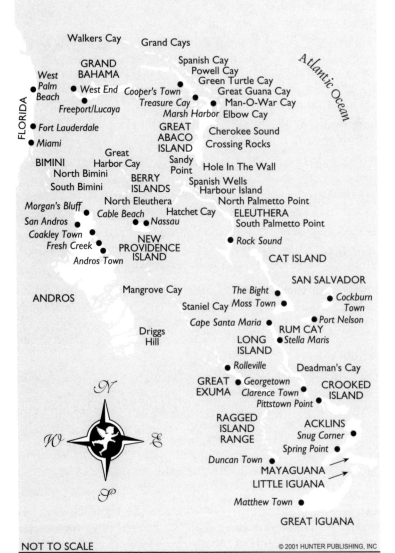

Walkers Cay   Grand Cays

GRAND BAHAMA   Spanish Cay
                     Powell Cay
West Palm Beach   West End   Green Turtle Cay
                  Cooper's Town   Great Guana Cay
Freeport/Lucaya   Treasure Cay   Man-O-War Cay
                  Marsh Harbor   Elbow Cay

FLORIDA

Fort Lauderdale   GREAT ABACO ISLAND   Cherokee Sound
Miami   Crossing Rocks
             Great Harbor Cay
BIMINI   Sandy Point   Hole In The Wall
North Bimini   BERRY ISLANDS
South Bimini   Spanish Wells
                                Harbour Island
Morgan's Bluff   North Eleuthera   Hatchet Cay   North Palmetto Point
San Andros   Cable Beach   Nassau   ELEUTHERA
Coakley Town   South Palmetto Point
Fresh Creek   NEW PROVIDENCE ISLAND
Andros Town   Rock Sound

                                       CAT ISLAND

                                       SAN SALVADOR
ANDROS   Mangrove Cay   The Bight   Cockburn Town
              Staniel Cay   Moss Town
              Cape Santa Maria   Port Nelson
                            RUM CAY
              Driggs Hill   LONG ISLAND   Stella Maris

                            Rolleville   Deadman's Cay
              GREAT EXUMA   Georgetown   CROOKED ISLAND
                            Clarence Town
                            Pittstown Point
                     RAGGED ISLAND RANGE   ACKLINS
                                           Snug Corner
                                           Spring Point
              Duncan Town   MAYAGUANA
                            LITTLE IGUANA
              Matthew Town

                            GREAT IGUANA

Atlantic Ocean

N
W   E
S

NOT TO SCALE   © 2001 HUNTER PUBLISHING, INC

The Islands

the Bahamian government operates in buildings the color of a conch shell. Downtown Nassau offers several inexpensive hotels that utilize nearby public beaches.

Prince George Dock always bustles with cruise ship passengers enjoying the city for the day. From the cruise port you'll also see a tall, curving bridge, which leads to **Paradise Island**. Nicknamed the "Monaco of the Bahamas," this is the most luxurious area of New Providence Island. It's an $8 taxi ride from the city (plus a $2 bridge toll when entering Paradise Island). Once named Hog Island, this area was revitalized by the investment of Donald Trump, Merv Griffin and South African businessman Sol Kerzner, who recently renovated the **Atlantis** hotel at the cost of $1 million a day – every day – in a six-month renovation and building spree.

Tourists also flock to **Cable Beach**, located 10 minutes west of downtown Nassau. This stretch of sand is lined with high-rise hotels and some of the island's hottest nightspots. Shuttles run between these resorts and Nassau several times daily.

Beyond these two resort areas, the island moves at a quieter pace. If you crave tranquillity, head to the south shore, about a 30-minute ride from downtown. Here, beneath willowy casuarina trees, couples can enjoy privacy and beautiful beaches that give way to a shallow sea. You can hire a taxi to explore the island, but it's cheaper to rent a car. The quieter roads of the south side are good for travelers new to driving on the left side of the road.

You may want to book your visit in spring, summer, or fall to be assured of a warm weather vacation. Winter temperatures are usually balmy, but occasionally a cold front reaches its chilly fingers into these waters and drops temperatures to spring-like levels. On an early March visit, we dug into our luggage for sweatshirts and, although temperatures were perfect for island touring, we found it too chilly for comfortable swimming.

While we're warning you, be careful of March and April bookings for another reason: spring breakers. Those low-cost downtown properties (and even some of the Paradise Island and Cable Beach resorts) swell with students during these weeks. Because of charter packages, Nassau is the Caribbean for the masses and, during this time, that means raucous students.

For a quiet, romantic getaway, consider an alternate month or a different destination.

Festivals

The biggest blowout of the year is **Junkanoo**. Junkanoo dates back to the island's slavery days and a time when slaves were given permission after Christmas to celebrate with African traditions. No one quite knows the origin of the term Junkanoo. Some believe it came from John Canoe, an African leader who demanded the right to celebrate even after he was brought to the island as a slave. Other people believe it comes from a French term used for the parade masks.

Fortunately, what really matters is fun, and everyone agrees on that during Junkanoo. Starting on **Boxing Day** (December 26) and continuing until New Year's Day, Junkanoo is filled with parades, partying, and lots of noise.

The Bahamas has many mega resorts.
Courtesy of Sandals Royal Bahamian.

The Islands

Sweet Dreams

Price Chart

Rates reflect high winter season (expect prices to be as much as 40% lower during the off season) for a standard room for two adults for one night; prices are in US dollars.

$ . . . . under $150
$$ . . . . between $150 and $300
$$$ . . . . between $300 and $450
$$$$ . . . . over $450

Nassau-New Providence Island

Atlantis, Paradise Island

Paradise Island
☎ *242-363-3000; fax 242-363-2493*
Reservations: ☎ *800-ATLANTIS*
www.atlantis.com
$$$

This resort transforms Paradise Island into Fantasy Island. Along with an elegant hotel, it brings to the Bahamas a water park that's unequaled in the Caribbean. The tunnel and water gardens surrounding it are the kinds of place travelers either love or hate. Don't expect to find peace and quiet here, or even a Caribbean atmosphere. This is Vegas-goes-to-the-Beach, but if you're into non-stop fun, it's the place to be on Paradise Island.

Special Features/Activities: 11 pools, seven waterslides, five marine habitats, spa, and golf.

Breezes Bahamas

PO Box CB 13049, Nassau
Reservations: ☎ *877-GO-SUPER*
☎ *242- 327-6153; fax 242- 327-5155*
www.superclubs.com
$

This may just be the all-inclusive bargain of the Caribbean. Part of the SuperClubs chain, Breezes is a moderately-priced property offering only slightly less than the others. Unlike the sprawling resorts of the SuperClubs chain, the Breezes properties (there are also two Breezes in Jamaica) are somewhat smaller and charge a fee for some premium activities. Breezes does offer all the amenities of SuperClubs, including excellent meals (one of our tastiest meals in Nassau was a buffet lunch at this property), watersports, bars and nightclubs, and even free weddings. (See *Wedding Packages*, page 50.)

The 400-room resort emphasizes fun and relaxation. Breezes is decorated in bright tropical pastels, from its open-air lobby to the rooms located in the lemon yellow hotel.

Special Features/Activities: beachfront, all-inclusive, adults over 16 only, tennis, buffet dining and Italian restaurant, watersports, Rollerblade and jogging track, circus workshop.

Club Med Paradise Island
Paradise Island
☎ *242-363-2640; fax 242-363-3496*
Reservations: ☎ *800-CLUB MED*
www.clubmed.com
$$-$$$

This recently renovated property offers double rooms with queen or two twin beds and a two-story villa called House in the Woods. The villa has a living room with TV and stereo, fully equipped and stocked kitchenette, bedroom with queen-size bed, wraparound porches, and more. "No facilities in Nassau or Paradise Island offer the kind of privacy, space, luxury, and pizzazz that Club Med's House in the Woods does," says Kamal Shah, president of Club Med North America. The villa was built as a set for the 1978 movie *Le Sauvage,* starring Yves Montand and Catherine Deneuve, and later brought to Paradise Island and renovated. Three restaurants are located on property and guests enjoy a full menu of activities as well: billiards, deep-sea fishing, fitness center, golf, kayaking, sailing, scuba diving, 18 Har-Tru tennis courts, windsurfing and more. All ages are welcome, although special children's programs are not offered.

Special Features/Activities: beachfront, watersports, all-inclusive, fine and casual dining.

The Islands

❤ *Compass Point*
PO Box C.B. 13842, Nassau
☎ *242- 327-4500; fax 242- 327-3299*
Reservations: ☎ *800-OUTPOST*
www.islandoutpost.com
$$-$$$

You won't find many resorts that list "state-of-the-art recording studio" among their features, but here's one, thanks to owner Chris Blackwell. The creator of Island Records has a string of small, fine hotels in the Caribbean, including Jamaica and Young Island in St. Vincent and the Grenadines.

Located about 25 minutes west of Nassau, Compass Point is removed from the hustle and bustle of Cable Beach on a quiet stretch of the island. It's near the upscale Lyford Cay, where stellar residents such as Sean Connery and Mick Jagger have residences in the private no-visitors-allowed compound. (You might get lucky and spot a familiar face at Compass Point, however. There's a dock for Lyford Cay residents to cruise up to the restaurant for a night out.)

Compass Point has only 18 rooms, but you can't miss the rainbow property. Look for the festive colors of the Junkanoo festival: vibrant tones of purple, blue, yellow and red. Each individual cottage is decorated in a style that might be described as Caribbean kitsch meets Gilligan's Island. Guests can choose from five cabana rooms (the only air-conditioned accommodations) or the larger, more private huts and cottages (which include a downstairs open-air kitchen and picnic-table dining room). Every room is hand-crafted and faces the sea. The two of you can complete your day in the rocking chairs on your private porch that looks out to the sea, then come in to sleep beneath a ceiling fan in a handmade bed covered with a Bahamian batik spread.

Special Features/Activities: oceanfront (next to Love Beach), watersports, dive shop, freshwater pool, casual restaurant.

❤ *Graycliff Hotel*
West Hill Street, Nassau
☎ *242-322-2796; fax 242-326-6110*
www.graycliff.com
$$-$$$

This historic building is located next to Government House and offers 14 luxurious guest accommodations and spacious pool cottage suites. The building dates back to Nassau's swashbuckling days. The mansion was originally built by Captain John Howard Graysmith, a pirate who commanded the schooner *Graywold* and plundered treasure ships along the Spanish Main. In 1776, the mansion became the headquarters for the American Navy when Nassau was captured by the soldiers. In 1844, Graycliff became Nassau's first inn.

The home has a rich history of celebrity visitors. During Prohibition, Graycliff was owned by Mrs. Polly Leach, a companion to Al Capone. Later Graycliff was purchased by Lord and Lady Dudley, Third Earl of Staffordshire, who hosted many dignitaries, including Duke and Duchess of Windsor, Lord Beaverbrook, Lord Mountbatten, and Sir Winston Churchill. In 1973, Enrico and Anna Maria Garzaroli purchased Graycliff and turned the mansion into a hotel and restaurant.

Guests can choose from old or new décor. Those with a yen for historic furnishings will like the Pool Cottage, where Winston Churchill used to stay, or the Baillou, the original master bedroom in the main house. Travelers with a taste for modern décor find it in the Mandarino Cottage, which has an extra-large bathroom and whirlpool tub. All rooms are air-conditioned and include a private bath. Breakfast is served to hotel guests only.

Special Features/Activities: fine dining, saltwater Olympic-sized lap pool, hot tub, sauna, fitness center.

Hilton British Colonial

One Bay Street, Nassau
Reservations: ☎ *800-445-8667*
☎ *242-322-3301; fax 242- 302-9010*
www.hilton.com
$$-$$$

This historic hotel sits at the head of Bay Street, a reminder of Nassau's early hotel days. It's a warm reminder of our early hotel days as well, as the scene of our first visit to the Caribbean. Following a recent renovation, the hotel is now one of the top business properties in the islands but offers a convenient address for the leisure traveler as well; it's just steps from the duty-free shops of Bay Street. The 291 guest rooms include sat-

The Islands

ellite TV, desk with modem and power outlet, mini-bar, voice mail, and more. Business and executive floors are available.

Special Features/Activities: downtown location, small beach, full health club, dive shop, four restaurants.

Marriott Crystal Palace

PO Box N-8306, West Bay Street, Nassau
Reservations: ☎ 800-222-7466
☎ 242-327-6200; fax 242-327-6818
www.marriotthotels.com-NASBS
$

Cable Beach's largest hotel is tough to miss. The property literally glows in the dark, with colored lights over each balcony giving the hotel the look of a seaside candy cane. This is one of the liveliest nightspots in town, thanks to its super-sized casino and glitzy revue. (See *Nightlife*, page 119.)

Special Features/Activities: beachfront, casino, fine and casual dining.

♥ The Ocean Club

Paradise Island Drive, Paradise Island
Reservations: ☎ 800-321-3000
☎ 242-363-3000; fax 242-363-3703
www.oceanclub.com
$$$

This ultra-elegant resort is the stuff of the rich and famous. Cindy Crawford married here and the small resort received worldwide attention, but the well-heeled have been coming here for many years. The resort has entertained Ronald Reagan, Sean Connery, Michael Caine, Sidney Poitier, Magic Johnson, and many other celebrities. The estate was first named Shangri-la, purchased in 1962 by Huntington Hartford, heir to the Great Atlantic and Pacific Tea Company fortune. The estate had formal Versailles-inspired gardens and statues of Napoleon's Josephine, FDR, David Livingstone, and more. Huntington built a 51-room resort and restaurant and renamed what was then called Hog Island to Paradise Island.

In 1994, Sun International (the same company that owns Atlantis as well as South Africa's Sun City) purchased Ocean

Club and totally renovated the resort. The hotel now offers 71 guest rooms including four suites and five two-bedroom villas, each with a private whirlpool. All accommodations in the main building have central air conditioning, indoor ceiling fans, outdoor ceiling fans on balconies or patios, mini-bars, safes, and 27-inch televisions.

Special Features/Activities: beachfront, gourmet dining, gardens.

Radisson Cable Beach

PO Box N4914, Nassau
☎ *305-932-0222; fax 305-932-0023*
Reservations: ☎ *800-432-0221*
www.radisson.com
$

Sporting a new renovation, the Radisson Cable Beach offers round-the-clock action both on and off the beach. Every room in the high-rise hotel offers an ocean view. For real luxury, splurge with a junior suite located at the end of each floor. We did and enjoyed sunrise from the bedroom balcony and sunset from the living room balcony. A shopping arcade (with surprisingly good prices) connects the Radisson with the Marriott Crystal Palace Casino.

The hotel's all-inclusive program is available for $100 per person, per day. Participants wear a wristband that allows them unlimited access to all sports, plus all meals, drinks, snacks, and tips.

Special Features/Activities: beachfront, casual and fine dining in six restaurants, adjoining casino, pools, shopping arcade, golf, tennis, watersports.

Sandals Royal Bahamian Resort and Spa

PO Box 39-CB 13005,Cable Beach, Nassau
☎ *242- 327-6400; fax 242- 327-6961*
Reservations: ☎ *800-SANDALS*
www.sandals.com
$$

This luxurious Sandals offers couples a romantic, elegant atmosphere with all the options of all-inclusives. Along with a full

The Islands

menu of watersports fun, a highlight of this resort is its excellent spa. Guests can purchase spa treatments à la carte or in packages, selecting from facials, massages, body scrubs, aromatherapy, and reflexology treatments. Amenities such as manicures, pedicures, paraffin hand and feet treatments, and more, are also available.

Special Features/Activities: beachfront, all-inclusive, couples-only, fine and casual dining, spa, watersports, freshwater pool.

Sheraton Grand Resort Paradise Island
6307 Casino Drive, Paradise Island, Nassau
☎ *242-363-3500; fax 242-363-3900*
Reservations: 800-782-9488
www.sheraton.com or www.sheratongrand.com
$$

Located just down the beach from Atlantis, this beachfront resort is well known in the world of business and meeting travelers but is also a good choice for families with children. There's plenty of activity here: banana boating, parasailing, jet skiing, windsurfing, and snorkeling. There are bike rentals and tennis courts available. The resort also features many daily complimentary activities such as snorkeling, native dance, arts and crafts demonstrations, and more.

Special Features/Activities: beachside, pool, restaurants, watersports.

Grand Bahama Island

Bahamia
Freeport
☎ *242-352-9661; fax 242-352-2542*
Reservations: 800-545-1300
www.bahamia.com
$$-$$$

Formerly the Bahamas Princess Resort, this sprawling resort includes 400 rooms in the 10-story Princess Tower and two- and three-story accommodations with 565 rooms at the Country Club. All rooms have two double beds, cable TV, direct dial telephone, and more. The resort has a wide array of dining options including Guanahani's, the Rib Room, and Morgan's Bluff, among others.

Special Features/Activities: casino, shopping, numerous dining options.

Our Lucaya
Across from Port Lucaya
☎ *877-ONE-LUCAYA*
www.ourlucaya.com
$$-$$$

The newest addition to Grand Bahama (formerly, The Lucayan) is this expansive resort. When completed, it will boast a full-service spa, two 18-hole championship golf courses, five tennis courts, 15 restaurants, a casino, three pools, and a 10,000-square-foot shopping complex. At press time, not all phases of this new resort had opened, so check in with the property for an update. We recently stayed in the first section to be opened, a 550-room complex with island-inspired décor, several restaurants, and the Sugar Mill Pool, a beautiful complex highlighted with a mock sugar mill and aqueduct.

Special Features/Activities: beachfront, golf, large pool complex; will include casino, spa, 15 restaurants, shopping complex.

Harbour Island

Pink Sands
Harbour Island
☎ *242-333-2030; fax 242-333-2060*
Reservations: ☎ *800-OUTPOST*
www.islandoutpost.com
$$$-$$$$

This 29-room resort offers 21 one-bedroom cottages and four two-bedroom cottages with a living room area. Located on, yes, a pink sand beach, the resort boasts a laid-back atmosphere. Guests find plenty of amenities such as a freshwater pool, three tennis courts (one lit for night play), exercise studio, club house, library, and more. The resort can arrange for golf cart and bicycle rentals as well. Two restaurants serve up local dishes with a gourmet flair. The Blue Bar serves lunch dishes right on the beach while breakfast and dinner are served in the main dining area.

Special Features/Activities: beachfront, fine dining, watersports, pool, tennis.

Tables for Two

Although you'll find any type of food in Nassau (including plenty of fast food), give Bahamian cuisine a try. One of the most popular dishes is **conch** (pronounced Konk), a shellfish served chopped, battered and fried in conch fritters. **Grouper**, a large fish caught in the waters just offshore, also appears on every menu, usually served with the ever-present side dish, peas and rice. For real traditional Bahamian food, give **johnnycakes** and **boiled fish** a try – for *breakfast*. You might have a tough time looking at the fish (usually grouper) so early in the morning, but sample the cornbread-like johnnycakes.

The popular beer in these islands is **Kalik**, (pronounced ca-LICK). For something a little stronger, a popular drink in the Bahamas is **gin and coconut water**.

Throughout the Bahamas, gratuities of 15% are usually added to your food and drink bills.

Price Chart

Restaurant prices are for dinner per person, including a drink, appetizer or salad, and entrée.

$	under $15
$$	$15 to $30
$$$	$30 to $45
$$$$	over $45

Nassau-New Providence Island

Café Johnny Canoe

Forte Nassau Beach Hotel, West Bay Street on Cable Beach
Dress code: casual
Reservations: not accepted
$-$$

This is one of our favorite Bahamian restaurants, both for its festive atmosphere and its excellent food and service. This is a diner-style restaurant decorated with Bahamian crafts and photos of the restaurant's long history. You can eat indoors or outside, a good choice on warm evenings. Share a drink beneath the multicolored Christmas lights and listen to live music.

Breakfast, lunch, and dinner are served in this popular eatery. We opted for an appetizer of conch fritters followed by grouper entrées. Prime rib, Bahamian fried chicken, fried shrimp, cracked conch, and burgers round out the extensive menu. Follow it all with a Bahamian guava duff with light rum sauce.

Café Matisse

Bank Lane, behind Parliament Square
☎ *242-356-7012*
Dress code: proper attire required for dinner
Reservations: suggested
$$

Why is this restaurant named for Matisse? Because you'll find prints of his colorful work decorating the walls of this charming café. The real art, though, is found on the plate in the form of Italian dishes, including homemade pasta, seafood, and pizza. Open for lunch and dinner.

Compass Point Restaurant

Compass Point, West Bay Street, Gambier
☎ *242-327-4500*
Dress code: casually elegant
Reservations: suggested
$$

This oceanfront restaurant serves up inventive cuisine using local ingredients. An open-air seaside eatery, it is as delightfully

casual as the resort itself, the perfect place to throw on a colorful sundress and enjoy a Bahamian meal, set to the sound of the
surf. Chef Stephen Bastian's talents are showcased on a menu
that features Californian-Caribbean cuisine. Breakfast, lunch
and dinner are served here.

Gaylords
Dowdeswell St.
☎ *242-356-3004*
Dress code: dressy, no casual attire
Reservations: requested
$$

Located in a 150-year-old Bahamian home, Gaylords is for
those looking for a taste of authentic Indian (not West Indian)
cuisine. Tandoori and Indian dishes fill the menu. A specialty
shop next door sells Indian food items.

♥ Graycliff
West Hill Street
☎ *242-322-2797*
Dress code: dressy, jacket and tie suggested
Reservations: required
$$$

The most famous gourmet restaurant in all of the Bahamas
(and some say the Caribbean), Graycliff has received numerous
awards and honors. A member of the Chaine Des Rotisseurs,
the oldest culinary association in the world founded in 1248 by
the king of France, this restaurant is reason enough to schedule
a trip to the Bahamas if you are serious about fine dining.

"The" place for visiting celebrities looking for an elegant place
to dine, Graycliff has drawn diners such as Sean Connery, King
Constantine, Princess Caroline, Barbara Mandrell, Paul
Newman, and Stevie Wonder.

The restaurant has also been named one of the world's 10 best
restaurants by *Lifestyles of the Rich and Famous*. Other acco-
lades include the Grand Award by *Wine Spectator* for its
180,000-bottle wine cellar. The award has been bestowed on
only 93 restaurants around the world. A quick look at
Graycliff's restaurant verifies the magazine's choice: if you're
feeling flush you can order up a bottle of 1865 Chateau Lafite

for $16,000 or a 1795 Terrantez for $17,200. The restaurant also features rare cognacs from the Charente region of southwest France including vintages such as 1788 Clos de Giffier Cognac, and 1872 Armagnac Janneau. It is also noted for having one of the best Cuban cigar collections in the world.

Gourmet Bahamian and continental dishes are served at gourmet prices; expect to spend about $150 for an average dinner for two. Chef Ashwood Darville's specialties include dishes such as Bahamian crawfish in puff pastry, grouper with cream and dijon mustard (featured in *Gourmet* magazine), roast rack of lamb marinated in Graycliff's secret recipe, and pepper filet with sweet, hot, white and black peppers, cream, onions, and cognac.

Historic Graycliff, part of the National Register of Historic Places, is also an inn. The setting is as exquisite as the cuisine, filled with antique charm and elegance from a Baccarat chandelier to photographs of King George VI at Buckingham Palace. Diners can enjoy their meal in the library dining rooms, which are filled with rare books.

Mama Loo's

Atlantis, Paradise Island
☎ *242-363-3000*
Dress code: casually elegant or dressy
Reservations: suggested
$$-$$$

This dinner-only eatery serves up unique Caribbean-Chinese dishes. Diners enjoy torchlight chandeliers and rattan wingback chairs.

Romantic Activities

Paradise Island

We looked up through the sea water, the sun filtering down in liquid shafts and illuminating the hundreds of fish around us. Suddenly, the light was blocked by an sinister silhouette – a shark.

Directly overhead, the six-foot predator swam with deliberate slowness, making schools of yellow grunts scurry closer to sheltering rocks.

But, unlike the school of fish and the large spiny lobster on the sandy floor below, we were not worried. Along with other visitors in the 100-foot-long clear tunnel, we just delighted in the view, surrounded by thousands of tropical fish, sharks, manta rays, and sea turtles in the world's largest open-air aquarium.

The tunnel and the water gardens surrounding it are found at the **Atlantis Hotel** on Nassau's Paradise Island. The resort is one of several changes that have brought glitz and glamour to what was formerly called "Hog Island." Thanks to investors, Paradise Island could now be renamed Fantasy Island – a place where high-dollar hotels meet gourmet dining and world-class shopping to create a lavish playground.

Investor Sol Kerzner is well known for themed resorts in South Africa (including one with a zoo), and his Sun International company worked to give visitors to this resort the feeling that they were discovering the lost city of Atlantis. Inclusion of marine life, or at least symbols of it, starts with dolphin fountains at the entrance and continues with conch shell carpet and even marine-themed slot machines in the casino.

Nowhere is the marine theme more evident than in the waterscape, now bigger and better than ever thanks to the most recent expansion. Here waterfalls splash and churn sea water into fish-filled lagoons that weave among walkways, open-air bars, and bridges. Guests flock to the **Predator Lagoon** for a close-up look at the half-dozen reef sharks that swim a constant pattern alongside barracudas and rays. Above the water's surface, guests watch for the shark's telltale fin to break the lagoon's surface; underwater, encased in the clear tunnel, they stand within inches of the sharks. The Predator Lagoon is popular with all ages of visitors, from small children who delight at the diving turtles and crawling spiny lobsters to the older visitors and non-swimmers looking for the sensation of scuba diving without getting wet.

Viewing in the tunnel and from the adjacent "sea grottos" (created from molds made of actual Bahamian sea grottos), visitors hear the sounds of the sea. Lighting in the grottos comes from flickering "whelk" lanterns, creating the mood of an underwater civilization.

Water activities continue above the surface as well. Near Predator Lagoon, a rope suspension bridge swings and sways over the water. Nearby water tricycles churn across **Paradise Lagoon**, a salt water lagoon that opens to the sea where the resort hopes to introduce tropical fish. The protected, calm waters will be used by beginning snorkelers as well as for scuba diving classes. And if the two of you are thrill seekers, you can plunge down the **Leap of Faith** slide on a replica of a Mayan temple. The slide takes an almost vertical 60-foot drop, plunging riders into an acrylic tunnel in a lagoon. The temple is also home to the **Serpent** slide, which spins through the interior of the dark temple before emerging into Predator Lagoon. For something a little quieter, hop an inner tube and set off on the quarter-mile journey pushed by a gentle current.

If you are not a guest of the hotel, you can purchase a day pass to the attractions for $25.

Island Sights & Museums

The heart of Nassau is **Rawson Square**. Make your first stop here at the Visitors Information Center, ☎ 242-332-7500, for brochures and maps before starting off on busy **Bay Street**, the shopping district. Here gold and gems are sold down the street from straw baskets and T-shirts at the **Straw Market**, one of the most popular souvenir stops. Be sure to look behind the Straw Market for a glimpse at the cruise ships that dock at **Prince George Dock**.

At Rawson Square, horse-drawn surreys wait for passengers, who pay about $10 (be prepared to negotiate) for a two-person, half-hour ride along picturesque Bay Street.

Another popular attraction is the **Ardastra Gardens and Zoo**, located on Chippingham Road, off West Bay Street, ☎ 242-323-5806; www.ardastra.com. The only zoo in the Bahamas, Ardastra features 300 species of animals and 50 species of birds, including monkeys, iguanas, and marching pink flamingos. Stop here if you have time, but this is one site that can be cut from busy itineraries. The caged animals are depressing to view, and the personnel are far from friendly.

A better choice is the nearby **Botanical Gardens,** also on West Bay Street, ☎ 242-323-5806, where you can walk hand in hand along blooming paths that feature tropical plants and flowers.

History lovers should head over to **Fort Charlotte** for a free guided tour of the largest fort in the Bahamas. Perched high on a hill overlooking **Cable Beach**, this fort never saw action but today sees plenty of activity as tourists come to enjoy a bird's eye view and a look at the fort's dungeons, cannons, and exhibits. To reach the fort, travel west from Nassau on West Bay Street. At Nassua Street, turn left and continue to Deans Lane, turn right and continue until you reach the fort (☎ 242-322-7500).

Beaches

One of the most popular activities in Nassau is a day at **Blue Lagoon Island**, ☎ 242-363-3577. This "uninhabited" island lies about half an hour from the dock at Paradise Island and offers some beautiful beaches, hammocks beneath towering palms, and plenty of watersports activity. Visitors can parasail, swim with stingrays, or meet dolphins (make reservations early for this choice). One option includes feeding, petting, and swimming with the friendly mammals. The dolphin encounters can also be booked as a separate attraction without a day at Blue Lagoon Island by calling ☎ 242-363-1653. Prices vary with activities.

For our money, Blue Lagoon Island is only for those looking for a party, not for peace and quiet or anything resembling privacy. If you do make this trip, bring a towel and, to save money, your own snorkel gear. A better choice is an excursion to the south side of the island, where wide beaches give way to shallow seas and warm water. Rent a car or hire a driver for a half-day excursion to this quiet getaway.

> *On Grand Bahama, a favorite stop with lovers is the Garden of the Groves botanical garden. This 12-acre garden is home to over 10,000 varieties of flowers, trees, and shrubs from around the world. Quiet, shaded paths wind through the gardens; you can take time and sit by a waterfall and hear the call of native birds. For information, call ☎ 242-373-5668.*

We also enjoyed the **Lucayan National Park**, Grand Bahama Highway, ☎ 242-352-5738. This 40-acre park is filled with mangroves, pine, and palm trees. Six miles of charted caves are also found here, as well as a secluded beach, hiking trails, and picnicking spots. This park is home to an enormous network of underwater caves, although diving is prohibited without a permit from UNEXSO (☎ 242-373-1244; fax 242-373-8956), and even swimming in the caves is a no-no. If you want to swim, cross the highway and visit **Gold Rock Beach**. This wide swath of sand, located 20 miles east of Freeport, is edged with pine trees (perfect for hanging your clothes on) and is a great place to walk hand in hand in peace and quiet. The waters here are warm and shallow and great for a romantic dip. There are no facilities, so bring along something to drink.

Shopping

Bay Street is the Fifth Avenue of the Bahamas, a boulevard lined with shops stocked with names like Gucci, Lalique, Cartier, and Baccarat. Inside, display cases gleam with gold, diamonds, and emeralds, and travelers look for duty-free bargains.

> *T IP: Perfume prices are regulated by the government, so you will find the same prices at any of the "perfume bars," which are plentiful in Nassau. Everything from French to American perfumes, colognes and after-shaves are sold in the perfume bars, as well as in many clothing stores.*

For authentic Bahamian souvenirs, head down Bay Street to the frenzied, open-air **Straw Market**. Every imaginable straw good is sold, and if you don't see it, the nimble-fingered women will make it for you. Expect to haggle over the cost, but overall, prices and goods vary only slightly from booth to booth. Upstairs, woodcarvers chip away at logs to produce sculptures of animals, birds, and anything else you might request.

Nightlife

The most popular nightlife on Nassau is probably its casinos. You can find them at the **Nassau Marriott Crystal Palace**

Casino and Resort and **Atlantis** on Paradise Island. The largest is found at Atlantis (make that the largest in the Caribbean) with over 1,000 slots and 80 gaming tables. The casino has a nautical theme and spectacular glass artwork.

If you're in the mood for a Bahamian show, check out the **Kings and Knights Club**, ☎ 242-327-5321, at Forte Nassau Beach Hotel on Cable Beach. For over 35 years, this delightful show has entertained visitors with Bahamian songs, dances, steel bands, fire eaters, limbo dancers, comedians, and even a few baudy calypso tunes.

In a dancing mood? There are several discos on the island. At Atlantis, dance the night away at **Dragons**, ☎ 242-363-3000. Located in the Royal Towers, this nightclub is high-tech and high-energy. The bandstand is elevated 10 feet above the floor and the whole atmosphere is fanciful, from dragon sculptures to video montages of fire dancing and voodoo.

Another high-energy nightspot is **The Zoo**, located on West Bay Street at Saunders Beach, ☎ 242-322-7195. With a name like The Zoo, you'd expect wild nightlife, and you're right. This dance club doesn't open until 8 pm and really gets rolling after midnight, with die-hard partiers staying until 4 am.

> *T IP: There's a hefty cover charge ($20-$40 depending on the night) but you can get find coupons in many giveaway publications during your stay.*

 Just the Facts

Entry Requirements: US and Canadian citizens need to show proof of citizenship in the form of a passport or a birth certificate. Visitors must also show a return airline ticket. Voter registration cards are not accepted as a proof of citizenship. Visas are not required for stays shorter than eight months.

You will be issued an immigration card when entering the Bahamas. Hold onto it; you will need to present the card upon departure. When departing, you'll clear US Customs and Immigration in Nassau or Freeport, a real time saver.

Getting Around: With driving on the left, taxi and limo service are the best way to get around. Rates are set by the government at $2.20 for the first quarter-mile for one or two passengers. Every additional quarter-mile will be charged at 30¢ per mile. Extra passengers pay $3 per person. On New Providence Island, expect to pay about $15 to get from the airport to Cable Beach; $20 for a ride downtown; or $24 (plus a $2 bridge toll) to reach Paradise Island. Car rental desks are available at the airport and major hotels. Plan on plenty of traffic within Nassau, however, and don't forget that you'll be driving on the left.

Language: English

Currency: The currency is the Bahamian dollar, which is on par with the US dollar. US currency is also widely accepted.

Electricity: 120 volts. US compatible.

Information: Call toll-free ☎ 800-4-BAHAMAS within the United States. From Canada, the toll-free number is ☎ 800-667-3777. While on island, contact the Bahamas Ministry of Tourism from 9 am-5:30 pm daily at ☎ 242-377-6833 for hotline help. After 5:30 pm, call ☎ 242-377-6806. Websites: For more information on the Islands of the Bahamas, check out www.bahamas.com. For specifics on the Out Islands, see www.bahama-out-islands.com.

Barbados

George Washington slept here. Really. This tiny island has been welcoming tourists since the days before the American Revolution. George himself came to enjoy the healthful climate (much needed by his tuberculosis-stricken brother, Lawrence) back in 1751, and visitors have been coming to this island in the far eastern Caribbean ever since.

The reasons are easy to see. An idyllic climate. An atmosphere that combines tropical casualness with British formality, where high tea on a hot afternoon makes perfect sense. A history that

The Islands

includes not only presidents but pirates, and great houses that recall the days of vast plantations and a jungle of sugarcane.

Today, Barbados exudes the most British atmosphere found in the Caribbean. As you drive through the island, look for both men and women in cool white suits on the cricket fields. In the afternoons, take time to enjoy high tea. And listen to the voices of the Barbadians or Bajans (rhymes with Cajun): their accent is almost British.

If the two of you like to maintain a regular exercise routine, you'll feel right at home on Barbados. When the sun's first rays peek out over the Atlantic (around 5 am), Barbadians hit the roads for some early morning jogging, power walking, or just strolling to enjoy this special time before the day's heat sets in.

Barbados is a pear-shaped island with gentle rolling hills. Agriculture still rules much of the landscape, and cane is still king. Although sugar prices have dropped severely in recent years, the crop is a Barbadian mainstay. A drive through the island will take you through a jungle of cane, often with nothing but the road before and behind you visible during the peak of the growing season.

Festivals

The biggest blowout of the year is the **Crop Over Festival,** held late June through the end of August. This island-wide celebration includes six weeks of competitions and festivities that exhibit Barbadian arts, foods, music, and dance. Look for the calypso and steel band competitions, folk concerts, and craft exhibitions and markets.

Music lovers head to the island in mid-January for the **Barbados Jazz Festival,** where world-class artists such as Ray Charles, Roberta Flack, and others have headlined. Other major events include February's week-long **Holetown Festival** to celebrate the arrival of the first settlers on the island, and April's **Oistins Fish Festival** with fish-boning competitions, boat races, dances, and crafts. Or, jump in the Caribbean's longest conga line at **DeCongaline Carnival,** an 11-day street festival held in late April.

Sweet Dreams

Price Chart

Rates reflect high winter season (expect prices to be as much as 40% lower during the off season) for a standard room for two adults for one night; prices are in US dollars.

$ . . . . under $150
$$ . . . . between $150 and $300
$$$ . . . . between $300 and $450
$$$$ . . . . over $450

♥ ## Almond Beach Club and Spa
St. James Parish, 6 miles north of Bridgetown
☎ *407-872-2220; fax 407-872-7770*
Reservations: ☎ *800-425-6663*
www.almondresorts.com
$$$$

You have your choice between two resorts: Almond Beach Village (see below) and Almond Beach Club. The Club is a couples-only resort, so it's favored by honeymooners and lovers looking to spend time together.

The full-time wedding specialist at Almond Beach can help couples arrange weddings during their stay.

The all-inclusive offerings here are extensive: meals, watersports, golf, squash, room service for lunch and dinner, beverages, weekly picnic, shopping excursion, the list goes on and on. The resort is home to the Salud Spa, which offers a full menu of treatments for additional fees.

Special Features/Activities: beachfront, all-inclusive, spa, watersports, fine and casual dining, freshwater pools and hot tubs.

The Islands

Almond Beach Village

St. Peter Parish, 11 miles north of Bridgetown
☎ *407-872-2220; fax 407-872-7770*
Reservations: ☎ *800-425-6663*
www.almondresorts.com
$$$$

Similar in many ways to its sister property above, the Village, however, caters to both families and couples. You can still enjoy a romantic vacation while traveling with your family, thanks to the children's program here, where the little ones can have supervised fun while the two of you play a round of nine-hole golf, enjoy watersports right on property, or just lounge around the long expanse of sand. The Village also has a romantic wedding site: a stone sugarmill. We watched a wedding in this historic setting during our stay.

Special Features/Activities: beachfront, all-inclusive, watersports, fine and casual dining, freshwater pools and hot tubs, golf.

♥ ## Glitter Bay

Porter's Street, St. James Parish
☎ *246-422-5555; fax 246-422-1367*
Reservations: ☎ *800-283-8666*
www.fairmont.com
$$$

You'll feel the elegance and refinement of Barbados and Britain at Glitter Bay, constructed as the home of shipping magnate Sir Edward Cunard. The Mediterranean-style structure, with white stucco walls and Spanish clay roofs, is located on a half-mile long beach. Glitter Bay's sister resort is the Royal Pavilion (see below), so guests enjoy reciprocal privileges and services at both resorts. You can also golf at the island's newest golf course, the Royal Westmoreland.

Special Features/Activities: beachfront, casual and fine dining, freshwater pool, watersports, dive center, tennis, golf, fitness and massage center.

♥ Royal Pavilion

Porter's Street, St. James Parish
☎ 246-422-5555; fax 246-422-3940
Reservations: ☎ 800-283-8666
www.fairmont.com
$$$$

This elegant property is designed for guests looking for the finest money can buy: from a grand entrance lined with the exclusive boutiques such as Cartier, to the 72 junior suites that overlook the sea. In your room, you'll be pampered with twice-daily maid service, a private terrace or patio, and a décor that combines elegance and tropical splendor. Children aren't permitted at Royal Pavilion during high season. The sister property of this resort is Glitter Bay, and guests at both resorts share facilities and services. Guests also enjoy golf privileges at the Robert Trent Jones, Jr.-designed course, the Royal Westmoreland.

Special Features/Activities: beachfront, casual and fine dining, watersports, dive center, tennis, golf.

♥ Sam Lord's Resort

St. Phillip Parish, SE coast
Reservations: ☎ 800-223-6388
☎ 246-423-7350; fax 246-423-5918
www.barbados.org/hotels/samlords/index.htm
$$

This 248-room, all-inclusive resort is more than a hotel, it's a regular tourist attraction. Built in the 19th century, this castle was the property of pirate Sam Hall Lord, who, according to legend, lured passing ships onto the east coast rocks. Of course, no real castle would be complete without its resident ghost, and at Sam Lord's they say his truly still rests on his four-poster bed.

Special Features/Activities: beachfront, casual and fine dining, health club.

The Islands

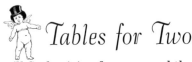

Tables for Two

Although you'll find cuisine from around the world represented on Barbados (especially at the luxury resorts), make time for a meal of local favorites like **flying fish**, **cou-cou** (a cornmeal and okra dish), **pepperpot stew**, and **jug-jug** (a dish made of Guinea corn and green peas).

The most popular drinks are **Banks** beer and **Mount Gay Rum**, both local products.

Price Chart

Restaurant prices are for dinner per person, including a drink, appetizer or salad, and entrée.

$......................... under $15
$$ .... $15 to $30
$$$ .... $30 to $45
$$$$....................... over $45

♥ Olives Bar and Bistro
2nd Street, Holetown
☎ 246-432-2112
Dress code: casually elegant
Reservations: not required
$$

This casually elegant eatery offers indoor and courtyard dining in a two-story Barbadian structure. Choose from entrées ranging from potato rösti with smoked salmon and sour cream to Jamaican jerk pork to gourmet pizza. Follow it all up with an espresso at the upstairs bar.

Ragamuffins
1st Street, Holetown
☎ 246-432-1295
Dress code: casually elegant
Reservations: recommended
$$

West Indian and European cuisine highlight the menu of this restaurant and bar, which has been recommended by many US gourmet publications.

♥ The Cliff
Derricks, St. James
☎ *246-432-1922*
Dress code: casually elegant
Reservations: recommended
$$$

A view of the sea competes with the bounty of the menu at this west coast restaurant featuring fish, steaks, and pastas.

Nico's Champagne and Wine Bar
Derricks, St. James
☎ *246-432-6386*
Dress code: casual
Reservations: not needed
$$$

This informal restaurant (with a menu chalked on blackboards) features starters such as Martinique pâté, and continues with favorites such as Caribbean lobster, lasagna, and deep-fried blue brie with passion fruit sauce.

Romantic Activities

Beaches

Barbados is home to many romantic beaches where couples can snorkel in calm Caribbean waters or enjoy windswept vistas on the Atlantic shoreline. Swimmers should definitely head to the Caribbean coast; precautions should be taken not to get over waist deep in the often-dangerous currents. These Atlantic waters are preferred by windsurfers and sailors. Swimmers are better off with the calm waters found on **Mullins Beach**, **Crane Beach**, and **Dover Beach**.

The Islands

Island Sights & Museums

The natural beauty of Barbados can also be enjoyed in many of its other attractions. Hold hands and enjoy a motorized tram ride into **Harrison's Cave**, where damp rooms reveal their hidden formations, waterfalls, and pools. A sea cave rather than a cavern, the **Animal Flower Cave**, ☎ 246-439-8797, is named for the sea anemones found in its pools.

History lovers should make plans to be in Barbados on a Sunday to participate in one of the walking tours sponsored by the **Barbados National Trust,** ☎ 246-426-2421. Starting at 6 am and 3:30 pm, the walks are a good way to learn more about the culture and history of this rich island. Call the Barbados National Trust for meeting points and to confirm times.

History buffs will also appreciate a tour of the greathouses. **St. Nicholas Abbey**, in St. Peter Parish, ☎ 246-422-8725, built in 1650, is one of only three houses of Jacobean architecture that remain standing in the Western Hemisphere. With Dutch gables and coral finials, the estate combines European and Caribbean styles and is well worth the meager admission price.

Sam Lord's Castle, ☎ 246-436-8929, located in St. Philip on the eastern shore, is another must-see. Now a hotel, the "castle," built in 1820, is rich with tales of piracy on the high seas and stories of Sam Lord allegedly luring ships onto the eastern shore's rocky coastline. With elaborate plaster ceilings created by the same artist who crafted the ceilings of Windsor Castle, gilt mirrors, and fine mahogany furniture, this is a Caribbean gem of a home, now a hotel.

Underwater Delights

If you're wondering what lies beneath the ocean's depths, take a cruise aboard the **Atlantis Submarine**, ☎ 246-436-8929, which dives to 150 feet below sea level. It's an excellent way for non-divers to see the rich marine life and the wrecks that surround this island. For diving, call **Coral Island Divers** (Cavers Lane, Bridgetown, ☎ 246-434-8377) or **One on One Scuba** (Husbands Heights, St. James, ☎ 246-233-5737).

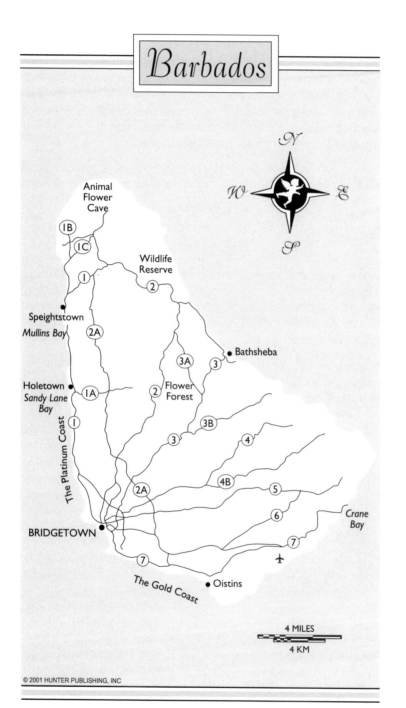

Barbados

Animal
Flower
Cave

1B
1C
1

Wildlife
Reserve

2

Speightstown
Mullins Bay

2A

3A
3

● Bathsheba

Holetown ●
*Sandy Lane
Bay*

1A

2
Flower
Forest

1

3B

The Platinum Coast

3

4

2A

4B
5

6

BRIDGETOWN

7

Crane
Bay

7

✈

7
The Gold Coast

● Oistins

4 MILES
4 KM

The Islands

© 2001 HUNTER PUBLISHING, INC

Golf

Golf lovers are in good shape; Barbados is home to a Robert Trent Jones, Jr.-designed course. **Royal Westmoreland**, ☎ 246-422-4653, an 18-hole championship course, is the best known on the island. Other popular choices are the 18-hole **Sandy Lane** course, ☎ 246-432-1311, and nine-hole courses at **Almond Beach Village** and **Club Rockley** hotels.

Rum Tours

And, if all this touring whets your thirst, take the **Mount Gay Rum Tour**, ☎ 246-425-8757, for a look at the place where the oldest rum in the world is produced. Luncheon tours include a Bajan buffet, transportation to and from your hotel, and, of course, a complimentary miniature bottle of the distillery's product. Regular 45-minute tours are offered on weekdays every half-hour and include a taste of Mount Gay Rum at the conclusion of the tour.

For a little different taste, stop by **Malibu Visitors Centre**, ☎ 246-425-9393, in St. Michael to tour the distillery that produces Malibu Caribbean White Rum with Coconut. After the tour, enjoy a Bajan barbecue or take a swim on the beach. Other local product tours include **Cockspur Rum**, ☎ 246-420-1977, or **Banks Breweries Tours,** ☎ 246-429-2113.

> *TIP: If the two of you will be enjoying many excursions, check out the **Heritage Passport Program,** ☎ 246-436-9033, sponsored by the Barbados National Trust. Sixteen sites are included on the pass, which offers about a 50% savings on admissions (a mini-passport is available for fewer stops). The passport includes admission to Harrison's Cave, St. Nicholas Abbey, Mount Gay, and many other sites.*

Shopping

The primary shopping area on the island is found in **Bridgetown** along **Broad Street**. Here the two of you will find fine goods of every variety: luggage, designer clothing, china, crystal, silver, cameras, the list goes on. Barbados is a tax-free haven, so you'll enjoy savings.

Nightlife

The **Barbados Museum** offers a folklore dinner show, "1627 and All That" every Thursday night. Along with dinner and an open bar, guests enjoy a show featuring the Barbados Dance Theater. The price of the show is US $57.50 and includes transportation, a tour of the Historic Museum, buffet dinner, complimentary bar, craft market, steel pan band, and cultural show. For reservations, call ☎ 246-428-1627; fax 246-428-3897; or email goldsand@caribsurf.com.

On Wednesday and Friday nights, the **Tropical Spectacular Dinner Show** takes place at the Plantation Garden Theatre, St. Lawrence, Christ Church. This long-running dinner show includes performers ranging from a fire-eater to a limbo dancer. The package includes transportation, a buffet dinner, and complimentary bar; tickets are US $75. For reservations, call ☎ 246-428-5048; fax 246-420-6317; e-mail plantationrest@ sunbeach.net; or see the online reservations form at www.barbados.org/tours/spectac/index.htm.

Just the Facts

Entry Requirements: A passport or birth certificate and driver's license or identification card is required of US citizens.

Getting Around: Taxis are prevalent but expensive. From the airport to the Speightstown-area will run you close to US $30.

Rental cars are available; a Barbados driver's license (US $5) is required. Many visitors rent "Mini-Mokes," a cross between a jeep and a dune buggy for about US $50 daily. And, don't forget, driving is on the left side of the road.

Language: English

Currency: US $1 = BDS $1.98

Electricity: 110 volts/50 cycles

The Islands

Information: Contact the Barbados Tourism Authority, 800 Second Avenue, New York, NY 10017; ☎ 800-221-9831; fax 212-573-9850. In Canada, the Barbados Tourism Authority can be reached at Suite 1010, 105 Adelaide St. West, Toronto, Ontario; ☎ 416-214-9880; and in the UK, at 263 Tottenham Court Road, London W1P 0LA; ☎ 0207-6369448. Website: www.barbados. org.

Bermuda

$\mathcal{A}$lthough technically not part of the Caribbean, Bermuda has all the sun, sand, and surf of its southern neighbors. It combines a slightly formal British atmosphere and its position as one of the world's richest countries with the island's semi-tropical climate, to create a setting where palm-lined roads connect Easter egg-colored houses.

Since the days of Mark Twain, Bermuda has attracted travelers seeking a luxurious retreat with warm summers and temperate winters, perfect for a round of golf or a game of tennis. Located 650 miles off the North Carolina coast, the island is a favorite getaway with honeymooners, golf buffs, and travelers looking for a safe, upscale island destination free from beach vendors.

This island is fast becoming a favorite with lovers. Couples will find a full range of activities both on and off the beach. Rent a scooter (there are no rental cars available, to keep traffic down) or hire a taxi driver for a few hours and tour the island, check out its historic sites, or stroll on its pink sand beaches.

Golf is also a favorite activity here. Note that proper golf attire is required, and that usually includes Bermuda-length shorts and shirts with collars and sleeves. Reseeding of the greens occurs throughout Bermuda for two to four weeks between late September and early November, and some courses use temporary greens during that time.

With weather that's often described as only two seasons – spring (69° average in January) and summer (85° average in July) – Bermuda is a golfer's delight. Boasting more golf courses per square mile that any other country in the world, Bermuda has eight courses among its 22 square miles.

Although many consider Bermuda to be one island, the country is actually formed by about 180 small islands. Seven of these islands are connected by causeways and bridges, and this forms the landmass referred to as "Bermuda." The broken shoreline means a plentitude of beaches, most found on the south side from **Southampton** to **Tucker's Town.**

Festivals

Bermuda special events include the **Bermuda Festival of the Performing Arts,** scheduled for February, and numerous golf tournaments, including the annual **February Couples Golf Tournament** at the Port Royal Course (☎ 800-343-4155). Regularly scheduled throughout the year, a romantic special event is the **Candlelight Walking Tour,** filled with tales about Bermuda's history (E. Michael Jones, Town Crier, ☎ 441-297-8000, e-mail towncrier@ibl.bm).

In early May, **International Race Week** brings sailors from throughout North America to the waters off Bermuda; for information, call ☎ 441-295-2214 or see www.rbyc.bm. Several other racing events are planned throughout the year.

In mid-June, the official celebration of the **Queen's Birthday** is a public holiday with a military parade through Hamilton. In August, lovers can take part in the **Sunset Jazz Dinner Cruise,** which departs from Albuoy's Point in Hamilton. The three-hour dinner cruise also includes entertainment; for information, call ☎ 441-234-0453.

Fall visitors find that September 3 is **Labour Day,** a public holiday that includes a march from Union Square in Hamilton to Bernard Park, where events include local music, games, raffles, and local foods. Later in the month, the **Bermuda Jazz Festival** draws internationally known names; for tickets, contact ☎ 212-921-2100 or the Bermuda Department of Tourism, ☎ 441-292-0023 or www.bermudajazz.com.

The Islands

Sweet Dreams

Price Chart

Rates reflect high winter season (expect prices to be as much as 40% lower during the off season) for a standard room for two adults for one night; prices are in US dollars.

$ .... under $150
$$ .... between $150 and $300
$$$ .... between $300 and $450
$$$$ .... over $450

♥ Elbow Beach Bermuda

60 South Shore Road, Paget
☎ 441-236-3535; fax 441-236-5882
Reservations: ☎ 800-223-7434
www.elbowbeach.com
$$$-$$$$

The island's largest hotel has a full menu of activity options: five championship tennis courts, a putting green, volleyball, a half-mile sand beach, kayaking, snorkeling, Olympic-sized climate-controlled pool, and more. Rooms here are deluxe with a full menu of options: dataports (hey, don't even think about it, though; remember, this is a romantic getaway!), mini-bars, 25 channel TV, bathrobes, bed slippers, and more.

Special Features/Activities: pool, exercise room with hot tub, kayaking, snorkeling, massage, horse and carriage rides.

Fairmont Hamilton Princess Hotel

PO Box HM 837, Hamilton
☎ 441-295-3000; fax 441-295-1914
Reservations: ☎ 800-441-1414
www.cphotels.com
$$-$$$

Located on the edge of Hamilton Harbour, this downtown hotel has a cooperative agreement with its sister hotel, the Fairmont Southampton Princess, so guests can enjoy both facilities. The guest rooms are decorated in soothing colors and have views of the gardens or Hamilton Harbour (our choice).

Special Features/Activities: two pools, beach club on secluded beach across the bay with golf and tennis.

Fairmont Southampton Princess Hotel
PO Box HM 1379, Hamilton
☎ *441-238-8000; fax 441-238-8968*
Reservations: ☎ *800-441-1414*
www.cphotels.com
$-$$$

This luxury resort stands on high above the sea with views of the island and includes golf course and a spa. This is a large resort with 564 guest rooms and 36 suites.

Special Features/Activities: tennis, beach club, spa, Dolphin Quest (a dolphin encounter program).

Pink Beach Club
PO Box HM 1017, Hamilton HM DX
☎ *441-293-1666; fax 441-293-8935*
Reservations: ☎ *800-355-6161 or 203-655-6161*
www.pinkbeach.com
$$$

Looking for peace, quiet – and privacy? Then the Pink Beach Club might be just the place for you. "Guests who celebrate at Pink Beach Club are afforded time alone to enjoy each other," said Michael Williams, managing director of the Pink Beach Club. "Our cottages are spacious, and most have breathtaking ocean views; our beaches are private and quiet; and we offer in-cottage breakfast service each morning and in-cottage massages for the ultimate in pampering."

The hotel is located on 16 acres of gardens with two pink sand beaches.

The Islands

The Pink Beach Club also offers destination weddings. Most couples exchange their vows under the hotel's "moongate." The wedding package is priced at $525 and includes the marriage license and certificate; minister and ceremony; bouquet for the bride; in-house photographer; bottle of champagne and a welcome fruit and cheese basket.

Special Features/Activities: massage, tennis, snorkeling, scooter rentals.

Enjoy an ocean view while relaxing.
Courtesy of the Pink Beach Club.

♥ Sonesta Beach Resort Bermuda
PO Box HM 1070, Hamilton
☎ *441-238-8122; fax 441-238-8463*
Reservations: ☎ *800-SONESTA*
www.sonesta.com
$$$

This sprawling resort is the only one in Bermuda that's right on the beach. We enjoyed our stay here.

The Sonesta is one of the most romantic properties in Bermuda, thanks in part to its many options for couples.

You'll find several beaches here (yes, look for that famous pink sand), and three swimming pools. There's also a spa, fitness center, and dive shop. The 400 rooms are decorated in tropical colors and include mini-bars, in-room safes, and hair dryers.

Special Features/Activities: pool, indoor pool, spa, restaurants, tennis, kayak tours, scooter rentals, paddleboat rentals.

Tables for Two

Price Chart

Restaurant prices are for dinner per person, including a drink, appetizer or salad, and entrée. Prices are in US dollars.

$. . . . . under $15
$$ . . . . $15 to $30
$$$ . . . . $30 to $45
$$$$ . . . . over $45

Frog and Onion
Royal Naval Dockyard
☎ *441-234-2900*
Dress code: casual
Reservations: not needed
$$

This genuine pub is great fun and a wonderful place for lunch if you're at the Dockyard. Its dark rooms are a great respite from the sun; dine on true pub fare, such as fish and chips.

Henry VIII
South Shore Road, just below Gibbs Hill Lighthouse
☎ *441-238-1977*
Dress code: casual
Reservations: optional
$$

This restaurant serves up English grill in a genuine pub atmosphere, from its dark oak furnishings to its brass railings. It makes a good stop after a look at the view at Gibbs Hill Light-house.

♥ *La Coquille*
Bermuda Underwater Exploration Institute
Pembroke Hall, 40 Crow Lane, Pembroke
☎ *441-292-8825*
Dress code: casually elegant
Reservations: suggested
$$$

We loved our evening meal at this waterside restaurant. From our window table, we watched the boats maneuver Hamilton Harbour as we dined on local seafood. Both indoor and outdoor dining are available.

Swizzle Inn
Baileys Bay
☎ *441-293-1854*
Dress code: casual
Reservations: not needed
$
Swizzle Inn is a Bermuda institution. As the oldest pub in Bermuda, this two-story restaurant also is home of the Rum Swizzle. You can dine inside or out on pub grub; there's also a cigar room here as well as pool and darts.

Romantic Activities

Island Sights & Museums

An excellent stop is the **Naval Royal Dockyard**. Recently restored, these extensive dockyards offer a half-day of activity with a shopping mall housed in a historic structure, a crafts market and, best of all, the **Bermuda Maritime Museum,** ☎ 441-234-1418. Save at least two hours for a visit to this extensive collection, which is located in the island's largest fort.

If it rains during your stay, there's always one place that's got perfect weather: the **Crystal Caves,** ☎ 441-293-0640. This limestone cavern was found in 1907 by two boys playing cricket, and since that time has been open to the public. You'll enjoy a

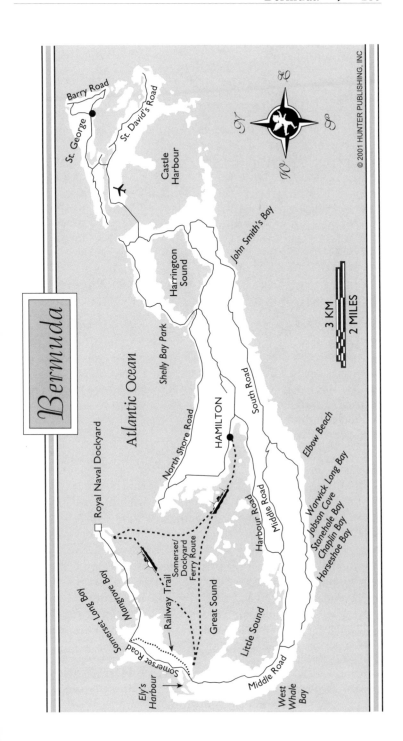

Bermuda

Atlantic Ocean

Royal Naval Dockyard

Barry Road

St. George

St. David's Road

Castle Harbour

Harrington Sound

John Smith's Bay

Shelly Bay Park

North Shore Road

HAMILTON

South Road

Somerset/ Dockyard Ferry Route

Railway Trail

Harbour Road

Middle Road

Elbow Beach

Warwick Long Bay
Jobson Cove
Stonehole Bay
Chaplin Bay
Horseshoe Bay

Great Sound

Little Sound

Monroe Bay

Somerset Long Bay

Somerset Road

Ely's Harbour

Middle Road

West Whale Bay

3 KM
2 MILES

© 2001 HUNTER PUBLISHING, INC

The Islands

look at cave formations and small pools in this underground wonderland.

One of the island's most popular attractions is the **Bermuda Aquarium and Zoo,** in Flatts Village, halfway between St. George's and Hamilton, ☎ 441-293-2727. This site is an excellent stop for travelers looking for a break from the beach. From the moment you step from the sunny outdoors into the dark, cool interior of the aquarium, you'll be transported into the undersea environment that lies just off Bermuda's pink beaches. The well-kept tanks each feature local marine life ranging from green morays to gray triggerfish. Free audio handsets allow visitors to hear more about the tank's residents.

The aquarium is just the introduction to the large complex, however. Outside, harbor seals play in their tanks or laze in the sunshine. Nearby, the **Natural History Museum** houses exhibits on everything from whaling to undersea exploration.

Outside stands the zoo. Along with free-ranging peacocks and exhibits of lemurs and sloths, the zoo is especially noted for its Australasia exhibit. Animals are separated from visitors by flowing water to provide an unobstructed view. Matschies Tree Kangaroos, tree shrews, Murray river turtles, and binturongs (bearcats) are found in the display.

Shopping

Whether you've come to Hamilton to buy a wedding ring or just to pick up a souvenir of your romantic getaway, you'll find that this waterside community is a shopper's dream. Goods run the gamut, but look primarily for imported items such as Swiss watches, English china, Scottish tweeds, Italian leathers, and more. Most shops sell high-ticket items but, if you are a savvy shopper and familiar with price tags at home, you'll see that they often come at substantial savings. One of the largest stores in Hamilton is Trimingham's (☎ 441-295-1183, www.triminghams.com), located on Front Street. Here you'll find duty-free jewelry, perfumes, china, crystal, and more. This shop has served Bermuda shoppers since 1842.

Another favorite shopping area is the Royal Naval Dockyard. This enclosed mall includes numerous small boutiques selling everything from T-shirts to souvenirs.

A few purchases are unique to Bermuda. Many stores sells gold or silver charms of Bermuda's longtailed tropic birds, which are often seen in pairs flying near the sea cliffs. Another favorite local item is Bermuda's famous black rum, used to make rum cakes as well as the island's favorite drink: Dark and Stormy.

Just the Facts

Entry Requirements: US and Canadian citizens need to bring a passport, or Green Card, US Naturalization certificate, or Canadian certificate of citizenship, or birth certificate with a photo ID. Citizens of other countries need a passport and possibly a visa; check with the Department of Tourism (below).

Getting Around: The best way to get around Bermuda is by motor scooter. To rent a scooter, you must be over 16 and wear a helmet (most outfitters will provide this). Contact **Wheels Cycles Ltd.,** ☎ 441-292-2245, for rentals.

Language: English

Currency: The legal currency is the Bermuda dollar, pegged equally to the US dollar. US currency is widely accepted throughout the country.

Electricity: 110 volts; American appliances need no adapters.

Information: For more on Bermuda, call the Bermuda Department of Tourism office, ☎ 800-223-6106 or write the Bermuda Department of Tourism North America Sales Office, 310 Madison Avenue, Suite 201, New York, NY 10017. Website: www.bermudatourism.com.

British Virgin Islands

Hoist the sails and gather way. Grip the wheel in your hands and cut a feather through aquamarine waters to a quiet Caribbean cove. Drop anchor and motor a small launch to an empty beach for a gourmet picnic on the white sand.

The Islands

Sound like a boating fantasy? It is, but in the British Virgin Islands, it can also be a reality. Year-round, old salts and would-be skippers come from around the world to sail these calm waters and take advantage of a group of 50 islands called "Nature's Little Secrets." These Virgins are loved for their quiet getaways, empty beaches, and a romantic maritime atmosphere.

More than any other Caribbean destination, you'll find that the British Virgin Islands (or just "the BVI" if you want to sound like a real salt) is a great destination for those who want to divide their vacation with a stay on land and on water. The island of **Tortola** is the home of the largest charter yacht company in the world, **The Moorings,** and many properties offer packages combining resort rooms with a few days on a crewed or bareboat yacht. You can set sail for paradise from just about any point in the BVI.

Tortola will probably be your first taste of these islands. It's the most active destination in this island chain, but don't expect big resorts, duty-free shopping or cruise ship crowds. Here traffic comes from a goat in the middle of the road or from boaters coming ashore for a full moon party at a side-of-the-road joint called **Bomba's Shack**. These are, as the tourist office likes to say, the Virgin Islands that are still virgin.

Semi-arid and hilly, Tortola is home to two primary communities: **Road Town,** which is the capital, and **West End.** With such no-nonsense names, you'd expect no-nonsense places, and that's exactly what these towns are. You won't need a road map to locate West End, a community that's visited by yachtsmen who come in to provision their vessels and to enjoy the local flavor at **Soper's Hole,** a marina splashed in shades of pink, sea green, and turquoise. This pastel shopping center offers Caribbean arts, crafts, and also one of the most picturesque photo spots in the islands where waterfront buildings are as colorful as Easter eggs.

Another popular provisioning area is **Road Town,** logically named because most roads converge here. Government offices and banks line the streets of the capital city, along with a few shops and restaurants of special interest to travelers. In either town you can catch a water taxi to other islands in the chain.

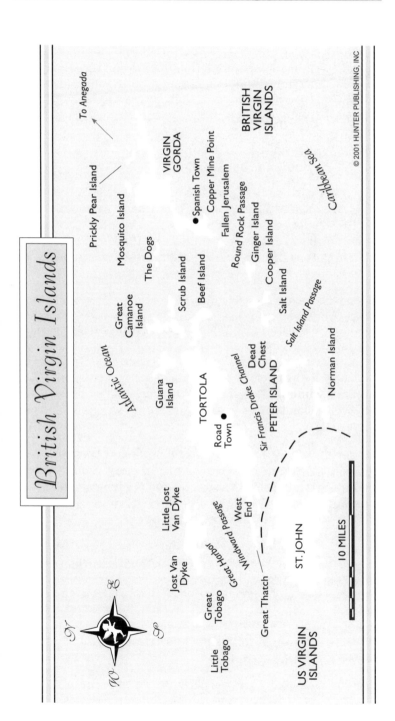

British Virgin Islands

The Islands

Tortola, with only 21 square miles, is the largest of about 50 scattered islands and cays, many of which are uninhabited. Don't let distance fool you, however. Because of steep hills, a car trip around or across the island is a slow undertaking. The other prime destination is **Virgin Gorda,** home to both resorts and marinas. Separated from Tortola by the Sir Francis Drake Channel, Virgin Gorda is an even quieter version of Tortola. Equally hilly, most activity and lodging here is clustered around the **Spanish Town** region and marina area.

The other islands are even less visited. **Jost** (pronounced "Yoast") **Van Dyke** was named for a Dutch pirate, and today the tiny island is a getaway for those seeking true tranquility, beautiful snorkeling waters, and a sometimes rollicking atmosphere. **Peter Island** is almost totally owned by a single resort operated by the Amway Corporation.

If you read the tabloids you may have heard of **Necker Island,** a hideaway for the rich and famous, like Princess Di and Oprah. And there's **Anegada,** a quiet destination that rises barely 27 feet over sea level. Between these islands, tiny landforms dot the horizon. Look for **Dead Chest,** a tiny islet of bare rock where legend has it Blackbeard marooned his men to fight over a single bottle of rum. (Remember "Fifteen men on a dead man's chest, Yo ho ho and a bottle of rum"? Now you know where that got started.)

All the islands in the BVI are semi-arid, sprinkled with cacti and succulents, but also dotted with tropical blooms. A drive around Tortola reveals numerous coconut palms and flowering hibiscus, mixed with tall organ and squat barrel cacti. The islands receive only about 16 inches of rain a year.

The British Virgin Islands are different from their American cousins. Life is quieter here and more attuned to the sea. Days aren't spent shopping, but **limin'**, as the locals say. meaning hanging out and doing nothing at all. Nights are even quieter, beneath the stars that guided explorers here over 500 years ago. And when morning comes, if you've stayed at one of the small inns for which the BVI is known, your alarm clock may well be the rooster next door.

For some couples, this is true paradise. This was one of our first Caribbean destinations, and it remains one of our favorites.

Festivals

Not surprisingly, many BVI special events are boat races. One of the biggest is the **BVI Spring Regatta** in early April. Sailors from around the globe come to compete in this yachting event.

In late June, windsurfers take the stage at the **Hook-In-Hold-On** (HIHO), which is billed as the world's greatest windsurfing adventure.

For fun out of the water, drop by the **BVI Summer Festival**, held in late July and early August. We were lucky enough to be in Tortola during this special event held in Road Town. We danced in the moonlight to steel pan bands and watched locals betting on a game of chance we never could understand. With all the atmosphere of a small town festival, this event is popular with locals and visitors alike and shouldn't be missed.

Long Bay Beach.

The Islands

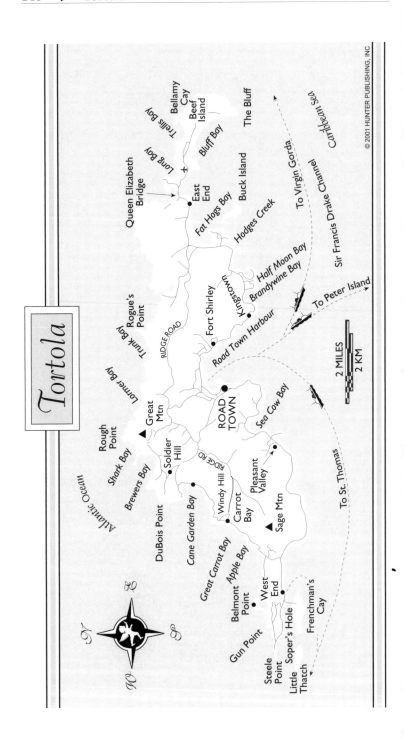

Tortola

Sweet Dreams

Price Chart

Rates reflect high winter season (expect prices to be as much as 40% lower during the off season) for a standard room for two adults for one night; prices are in US dollars.

$	under $150
$$	between $150 and $300
$$$	between $300 and $450
$$$$	over $450

♥ Sugar Mill

PO Box 425, Road Town
☎ *284-495-4355; fax 284-495-4696*
Reservations: ☎ *800-462-8834*
www.sugarmillhotel.com
$$-$$$

If you're a cooking aficionado, you may already be familiar with the Sugar Mill's owners, Jinx and Jeff Morgan. These *Bon Appétit* columnists and cookbook authors have brought their expertise to the Caribbean in the Sugar Mill Restaurant (see *Tables for Two*, page 149).

But part of this former California couple's recipe for happiness included not just a restaurant, but a complete resort. Since 1982, the Morgans have operated this 21-room inn and made it a prime destination for couples looking for peace and privacy.

The Sugar Mill is one of the finest small inns in the Caribbean, offering visitors a chance to enjoy a spectacular setting while at the still feeling part of island life. The rooms are nice but not distinctive. In our second-floor room, air conditioning was pro-

The Islands

vided by nature. We enjoyed a balcony and kitchen facilities and a simple room with a view of the lush grounds.

It's those grounds that draw visitors to this Tortola site. This hotel is located on the ruins of the Appleby Plantation, which dates back to this island's days of sugar and slaves. Little remains of the early buildings except the ruins of a 360-year-old sugar mill, which today is part of the hotel's elegant restaurant. Another reminder of the location's sugar history is the swimming pool. This circular tank is built on the site of a treadmill where oxen once powered the machinery to crush the sugarcane, which eventually was made into rum.

> *Honeymooners will find a seven-night package that includes a deluxe room, bottle of champagne, massages for two, a castaway beach picnic for two, a daysail to neighboring islands, car rental, and more.*

Special Features/Activities: beachfront, freshwater pool, casual and fine dining.

Long Bay Beach Resort

PO Box 433, Road Town
☎ *284-495-4252; fax 284-495-4677*
Reservations: ☎ 800-729-9599
$$

They call this resort Long Bay, but we found that they might as well change the name to Long Beach. A mile-long white sand beach is the focal point of this 105-room resort located near West End. All rooms, both hilltop and beachside, have views of the beach and the quiet waters of Long Bay.

Special Features/Activities: two restaurants, two bars, shopping center, tennis, spa.

The Moorings

PO Box 59, Road Town
☎ *284-494-2332; fax 284-494-2226*
Reservations: ☎ 800-521-1126
www.moorings.com
$ and up

Ahoy mates, here's your chance to take to the seas on your own yacht. Well, maybe the yacht's not technically yours, but for a few days it will be home to you and usually two or three other couples. You can rent a stateroom aboard a yacht and enjoy a luxurious trip around the islands (or, for true luxury you can rent the entire boat, complete with the services of a captain and a cook). The Moorings is the world's largest charter yacht company, an operation that started right in tiny Road Town.

Special Features/Activities: beachfront, casual and fine dining, tennis, freshwater swimming pool, sailing.

Tables for Two

Price Chart

Restaurant prices are for dinner per person, including a drink, appetizer or salad, and entrée.

$.	under $15
$$	$15 to $30
$$$	$30 to $45
$$$$	over $45

Garden Restaurant
Long Bay Estates
☎ *800-729-9599 or 284-495-4252*
Dress code: elegant
Reservations: recommended
$$$-$$$$

This restaurant serves what is said to be the most elegant fare in the British Virgin Islands. Seated near the Long Bay Estates tropical gardens, diners feast on fresh seafood and choose from an extensive wine list featuring the best labels from Europe and North America. This acclaimed restaurant is not to be missed by any visitor.

The Islands

♥ *Sugar Mill Restaurant*
Sugar Mill
☎ *284-495-4355*
Dress code: casually elegant
Reservations: suggested
$$

This restaurant is housed in the remains of a former sugar mill. The stone walls form a backdrop for Haitian artwork and for couples enjoying a candlelight dinner.

> *This is our choice for the BVI's most romantic restaurant.*

The menu changes daily, starting with appetizers such as smoked conch pâté or scallops, followed by roasted corn soup or West Indian tania soup. Entrées range from tropical game hen with orange-curry butter to fresh fish in banana leaves with herb butter.

Virgin Gorda

 Sweet Dreams

Price Chart

Rates reflect high winter season (expect prices to be as much as 40% lower during the off season) for a standard room for two adults for one night; prices are in US dollars.

$	under $150
$$	between $150 and $300
$$$	between $300 and $450
$$$$	over $450

Biras Creek

PO Box 54
☎ *284-494-3555; fax 284-494-3557*
Reservations: ☎ *800-608-9661*
www.biras.com
$$$$

Biras Creek makes a mighty tempting offer to lovers: they'll maroon you on a deserted beach for the day. Just the two of you, a picnic basket and paradise.

Problem is, it's pretty tough to leave Biras Creek itself. This luxurious resort on Deep Bay is part beach resort and part yacht club. The 32-suite property recently was purchased by Bert Houwer, who had vacationed at the hotel for 14 years. You can't get a much better guest recommendation than that.

> *Biras Creek offers a complete wedding package with marriage license, registrar's fee, floral arrangement, wedding cake, champagne toast, and photographer. Pick from an outdoor ceremony or an intimate exchange of vows on a 47-foot luxury yacht.*

Special Features/Activities: beachfront, FAP (all meals included), watersports, tennis, fine and casual dining, freshwater pool.

Bitter End Yacht Club

PO Box 46, North Sound
☎ *284-494-2746; fax 284-494-4756*
Reservations: ☎ *800-872-2392*
www.beyc.com
$$$$

This 100-room resort is located at the "bitter end" of the BVI on the North Sound. Reached only by boat, you have the real feeling of staying at a yacht club, where days are spent in close connection with the sea.

Bitter End boasts 150 vessels, the largest fleet of recreational boats in the Caribbean. Many guests arrive via their own craft and simply dock at the marina for their stay. Those without a boat can stay in a resort room or aboard one of the club yachts. Spend the day in your "room" boating among the islands, then return to port at night and enjoy a quiet meal in the resort's elegant restaurant.

> *Lovebirds will find a seven-night honeymoon package here that includes a beachfront villa, a refrigerator stocked with orange juice and champagne, a sunset sail on the North Sound, a daysailer or outboard skiff to explore quiet coves, and more. Call the resort for other special offers.*

Even if you don't take the package, there's plenty of romance at this resort, from mornings spent on the hillside hiking trails among orchids and island birds, to afternoons spent learning to sail together.

Special Features/Activities: beachfront, FAP (all meals), marina, casual and fine dining, sailing school.

♥ Little Dix Bay

PO Box 70, The Valley
☎ *284-495-5555; fax 284-495-5661*
Reservations: ☎ *800-928-3000*
www.littledixbay.com
$$$$

We have fond memories of our stay at Little Dix: lazing beneath a palm palapa, snorkeling just offshore, enjoying our rondoval guest room with a wonderful view in every direction, dining outdoors to the music of whistling tree frogs.

Apparently plenty of other couples also have good memories of Little Dix; it boasts a wonderful repeat business. Many customers have been coming since the days Laurance Rockefeller first developed this property in 1964.

> *Today the hotel still provides the same attention to service as it did in its Rock resort days; the ratio of employees to guests is one to one.*

Special Features/Activities: casual and fine dining, tennis, watersports, dive shop, Sunfish sailboats and kayaks.

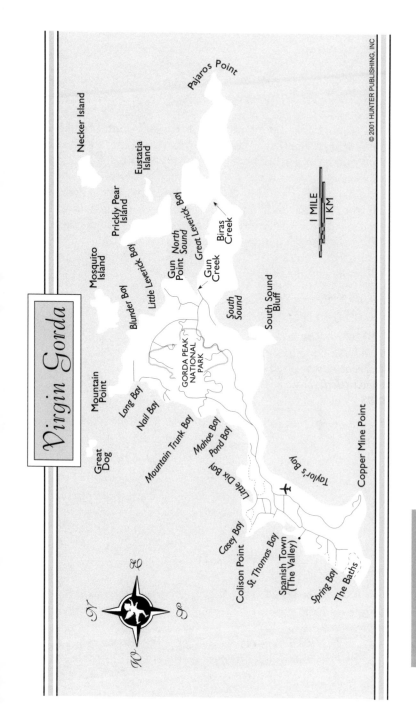

Virgin Gorda

Pajaros Point

Necker Island

Eustatia Island

Prickly Pear Island

Mosquito Island

Great Leverick Bay

Little Leverick Bay

Blunder Bay

Gun North Point Sound

Biras Creek

Gun Creek

South Sound

South Sound Bluff

Mountain Point

Long Bay

Nail Bay

Great Dog

Mountain Trunk Bay

GORDA PEAK NATIONAL PARK

Mahoe Bay

Pond Bay

Little Dix Bay

Casey Bay

Colison Point

St. Thomas Bay

Taylor's Bay

Copper Mine Point

Spanish Town (The Valley)

Spring Bay

The Baths

1 MILE

1 KM

© 2001 HUNTER PUBLISHING, INC

The Islands

Toad Hall

PO Box 7
☎ *284-495-5397; fax 284-495-5708*
www.toadhallvg.com
$$$$

This elegant inn offers its guests privacy and one-of-a-kind rooms where you'll truly feel like you're living outdoors. Scattered among the 6½ acres are three guest suites, bath cottages with stone showers tucked into screened gardens (and one with a whirlpool bath), dining room, kitchen, and living room. The real treat is the location: perched just above The Baths, this inn has the only private access to the park beach. The atmosphere of The Baths is felt here at the inn as well; granite boulders tumble from the sides of the swimming pool, mimicking the natural pools just down the hill.

Special Features/Activities: freshwater pool, music system and video players.

Tables for Two

Price Chart

Restaurant prices are for dinner per person, including a drink, appetizer or salad, and entrée.

$	under $15
$$	$15 to $30
$$$	$30 to $45
$$$$	over $45

The Clubhouse Steak & Club

Bitter End Yacht Club
☎ *284-494-2746*
Dress code: casual elegant
Reservations: required for dinner
$$$

For any meal, this eatery offers a top-notch menu and great food. For breakfast, choose from homemade pastries, traditional breakfast foods or the buffet, which has a little of both. The lunch menu offers seafood, hamburgers and another buffet for those visitors who can't decide. The dinner menu is a bit more elegant and gives diners fresh fish, pastas or soups.

♥ *Biras Creek Resort*
☎ *800-223-1108 or 284-494-3555*
Dress code: casual elegant
Reservations: suggested
$$$$

One of the most elegant restaurants on the island, Biras Creek offers diners an extensive menu of gourmet meals and delicious desserts. We recommend the Caribbean lobster medallions for starters, then move on to the pan-roasted chicken leg stuffed with avocado. For dessert, try the iced white chocolate parfait or the warm berries served with champagne sauce.

Peter Island

Sweet Dreams

Price Chart

Rates reflect high winter season (expect prices to be as much as 40% lower during the off season) for a standard room for two adults for one night; prices are in US dollars.

$ . . . . under $150
$$ . . . . between $150 and $300
$$$ . . . . between $300 and $450
$$$$ . . . . over $450

♥ Peter Island Resort

PO Box 211, Road Town, Tortola
☎ *284-495-2000; fax 284-495-2500*
Reservations: ☎ *800-346-4451*
www.peterisland.com
$$$$

This is true luxury: a resort that occupies an entire island. Owned by the Amway Corporation (a fact that most visitors are unaware of except for the can of Amway spot remover in the closet), Peter Island is truly a place where romance can flourish like the bougainvillea, hibiscus, and sea grapes that dot its hills. The 1,800-acre island is paradise for couples. It starts with your arrival by private launch from Tortola, and continues as you check in and see your guest room: a combination of Scandinavian and Caribbean styles.

Lovers can try the special Island Romance package, which includes a day sail to The Baths in Virgin Gorda, champagne on arrival, and a photo album. Other packages include scuba diving, a combination land and sea stay with two nights on your own private yacht with guide, crew and cook.

For us, though, Peter Island's most memorable feature is its beach. Here we lazed away one afternoon in a hammock built for two beneath the shade of some of the most impressive coconut palms we've ever seen in the Caribbean. They were planted by the daughter of an early island family, and today they stand in tall, straight rows looking out on the turquoise waters dotted with nearby islands.

> *The most isolated spot is Honeymoon Beach, perfectly named and outfitted with nothing but two lounge chairs and a single thatch hut.*

Special Features/Activities: beachfront, casual and fine dining, freshwater pool, tennis, yacht harbor, watersports center and dive shop, fitness center and massage center.

Tables for Two

Price Chart

Restaurant prices are for dinner per person, including a drink, appetizer or salad, and entrée.

$........................	under $15
$$	$15 to $30
$$$	$30 to $45
$$$$.......................	over $45

Tradewinds
Peter Island Resort
☎ *800-346-4451 or 284-495-2000*
Dress code: casually elegant
Reservations: not necessary
$$-$$$

The main restaurant on Peter Island, Tradewinds keeps visitors guessing with its weekly changing menu of Caribbean food with a fusion flair. The restaurant itself offers a breathtaking view of Drake Channel and has a wine room next door for private dinners. Musicians entertain at sunset with reggae or calypso music to make the evening truly memorable.

Romantic Activities

Island Sights

A top destination in the BVI (or, for that matter, in the Caribbean) is **The Baths.** This 682-acre park is located on **Virgin Gorda,** and it's so unique that once you visit it you'll be able to spot this park in any Caribbean video or magazine. Unlike most Caribbean beaches, which are generally flat, this site is scattered with massive granite boulders. As smooth as river-bed stones, these gargantuan rocks litter the sea and the beach. They also form shadowy caves, where you can swim in water that's lit by sunlight filtering through the cracks. This unique

The Islands

site is unspoiled (just one or two concessionaires and no hagglers) and a fun snorkeling spot as well.

Hikers should save time for a visit to **Sage Mountain National Park,** ☎ 284-494-3134, on Tortola. The BVI's highest point has an altitude of 1,780 feet and is lush with greenery that can be viewed from its many gravel walkways.

Underwater Delights

Divers will find plenty of activity in the waters off any of the British Virgin Islands. The best known dive spot is the wreck of the **RMS *Rhone,*** a mail steam packet that broke up in a storm. You may be familiar with this wreck – it was used in filming the movie *The Deep.* Located off Salt Island, the bow lies just 80 feet below the surface, making it an easy wreck dive (and it's usually even visible to snorkelers). Other top dive sites include **Alice in Wonderland,** a deep dive with mushroom-shaped corals, the ***Chikuzen,*** a 246-foot fish-filled wreck just 75 feet below the surface, and **Santa Monica Rock,** located near the open ocean and a good place to spot large fish. For dive information, call **Dive BVI** (Virgin Gorda, ☎ 284-495-5513) or **Sunchaser Scuba** (Bitter End, Virgin Gorda, ☎ 284-495-9638).

BVI Shopping

Unlike the "other" Virgin islands, shopping is not a major attraction of the BVI. However, you will find a good variety of shops in Tortola in **Road Town** and **West End** at **Soper's Hole.** Look for **Pusser's Rum,** spiced rum, or guavaberry liqueur; you may bring back one liter duty free. Spices are also popular buys, from hot sauces to West Indian mustards to chutney.

For inexpensive buys, visit the open-air market on **Main Street**. Here you can haggle for jewelry, T-shirts, calabash bags, and straw hats. The mood is friendly, and you'll be entertained most days by steel band musicians.

Another popular Road Town stop is **Pusser's Company Store**, located near the ferry dock. Here you'll find plenty of Pusser's Rum as well as souvenirs bearing the name of this local drink.

Nightlife

One of the BVI's best nightspots is also a good place during the day, albeit a little quieter. On Jost Van Dyke, **Foxy's Tamarind Bar,** ☎ 284-495-9258, is a legend throughout the Caribbean, thanks to the boats that frequent this beach bar and pass the word on to other boaters. The yachties so love this joint that many have removed clothing – shoes, T-shirts, even bras – and stapled them to the posts and the underside of the palm-thatched roof.

Whether you come by for lunch or dinner, you'll have your choice of West Indian specialties like curried chicken rotis or burgers and plenty of drinks. But the real treat is Foxy himself.

Foxy, aka Philicianno Callwood, is a one-man show, greeting incoming guests with impromptu songs that may feature a political viewpoint, the president of the US, the person at the next table, or Foxy himself. Sung to a calypso beat, these off-the-cuff tunes bring Foxy's loyal fans back for more. Every year in earely September, Foxy's really celebrates with the **Foxy's Wooden Boat Regatta.**

Over in Tortola, the hottest spot is **Bomba's Shack,** ☎ 284-495-4148, home of the famous full moon parties. These blowouts are some of the best-known parties in the Caribbean – don't be surprised to see some wild action at these bashes.

Just the Facts

Entry Requirements: US, UK, and Canadian citizens must bring a current passport or original birth certificate with photo ID. You'll also have to show a return or onward ticket.

Getting Around: Island-hopping is a way of life in the BVI and the most common way is aboard ferries. One-hour service from St. Thomas is available daily to Road Town and West End in Tortola aboard **Smith's Ferry Service,** ☎ 284-495-4495.

Language: English

Currency: US dollar

Electricity: 110 volts

The Islands

Information: Contact the British Virgin Islands Tourist Board at 370 Lexington Ave., Suite 313, New York, NY 10017, ☎ 800-835-8530 in the eastern US, or ☎ 800-232-7770 in the western US. In Canada, at 801 York Mills Rd. #210, Don Mills, Ontario, ☎ 800-835-8530; and in the UK, at 110 St. Martin's Lane, London WC2N 4DY, ☎ 0171-240-4259, fax 0171-240-4270. Website: www.bvigovernment.org.

Cayman Islands

*F*or the American traveler, perhaps no other Caribbean islands offer the comforts and the "This is almost like back home" feeling of the Cayman Islands, especially the most popular destination: **Grand Cayman.** This island, together with its smaller cousins, **Cayman Brac** and **Little Cayman**, enjoys the highest per capita income in the Caribbean. It is friendly, safe, and tailor-made for couples looking for a slice of home on their vacation. Here you'll find all the comforts of the US, as well as an American standard of service in many restaurants, bars, and hotels from many stateside ex-pats who make their home in these lovely isles. For some visitors, this Americanized atmosphere is as welcome as eating a Big Mac in Paris; for others it is a comforting way to experience the islands.

All that comfort comes at a price, however. The Cayman dollar is stronger than its US equivalent, so at present the US dollar is worth only 80¢ CI. Prices in hotels, restaurants, shops, and attractions reflect that unfavorable exchange rate and high standard of living; we've paid as much as US $36 for breakfast for two in a hotel restaurant.

These lofty price tags don't deter the nearly 300,000 US vacationers and business people who visit every year. The vacationers are drawn by protected waters as clear as white rum, teeming with marine life, offering one of the best snorkeling and scuba vacations in the region. The business world is attracted to these small islands for an entirely different reason: tax-free status. (Remember *The Firm*? Portions of that movie, based on the John Grisham book, were filmed right here.)

Located in the westernmost reaches of the Caribbean, about 180 miles west of Jamaica, the Cayman Islands are composed of three islands: Grand Cayman, Cayman Brac, and Little Cayman. Grand Cayman is the largest of the trio, spanning 76 square miles. Called the **sister islands**, Cayman Brac and Little Cayman are located about 80 miles east-northeast of Grand Cayman, separated by seven miles of sea.

The three islands are actually the peaks of a submarine mountain range, the **Cayman Ridge**, part of a chain running from Cuba to near Belize. They are actually limestone outcroppings with little soil, so vegetation is not as lush as on some islands. Most of the rain is quickly absorbed in the porous limestone, so there are no rivers. That means little runoff and therefore greater visibility in the waters surrounding the islands. Divers rave about the visibility, often 100 to 150 feet.

Each island is surrounded by coral reefs, producing some of the best snorkeling and scuba diving in the Caribbean. The deepest waters in the Caribbean are found between this nation and Jamaica, depths that plunge into inky blackness over four miles beneath the ocean's surface.

The Cayman Islands have taken strict measures to protect the marine life of these waters. Today the sea turtle is protected and no one may disturb, molest, or take turtles in Cayman waters without a license. Other marine conservation laws prohibit the taking of any marine life while scuba diving or damaging coral with anchors. Over 200 permanent boat moorings have been installed to prevent further coral damage by anchoring.

Festivals

The Cayman Islands observe special holidays throughout the year. The month of June is **Million Dollar Month,** when fishermen from around the globe come to try their luck. Mid-June is also the **Queen's Birthday,** a date observed with bands and colorful parades.

At the end of October, it's shiver-me-timbers time during **Pirates Week.** The islands celebrate their buccaneering history with treasure hunts, parades, and plenty of excuses to dress as pirates and wenches.

The Islands

Sweet Dreams

Most visitors to Grand Cayman stay along **Seven Mile Beach** just outside of **George Town**. Okay, it's only 5½ miles long, but with this kind of beauty, who's counting? Along this busy stretch you'll find luxurious hotels, fine restaurants, nightclubs, and most of the activity on the island.

The sister islands of Little Cayman and Cayman Brac are far quieter than Grand Cayman, although you'll find an array of accommodations on these islands as well. Don't look for branded, expansive hotels on the scale of Grand Cayman's Hyatt Marriott, but there are several resorts, condominiums and villas on each island.

Price Chart

Rates reflect high winter season (expect prices to be as much as 40% lower during the off season) for a standard room for two adults for one night; all prices are in US dollars.

$	under $150
$$	between $150 and $300
$$$	between $300 and $450
$$$$	over $450

Grand Cayman

Cayman Villas
PO Box 681
☎ 345-945-4144; fax 345-949-7471
Reservations: ☎ 800-235-5888
www.caymanvillas.com
$-$$$$

Cayman Villas manages numerous properties on Grand Cayman as well as on the sister islands, many aimed at middle to upper level travelers. "More and more private houses and exclusive condos are being built," notes Penny Cumber, managing director for Cayman Villas. "Both houses and condos are becoming more deluxe, many of which have a private pool, some with hot tub and gym."

Aside from its most luxurious properties, Cayman Villas also offers properties for the average traveler. Over 100 properties, some starting at US $99 a night, are represented. "Cayman Villas specializes in beachfront condos and private houses ranging from economy to deluxe, from studios to seven bedrooms. Most condos are on Seven Mile Beach. Most private houses are at Cayman Kai but there are many other quiet beaches around Grand Cayman, Cayman Brac and Little Cayman on which we also have villas. Guests can be on their own private beach and in the midst of all the action." Do a little research to decide what kind of property would best suit your needs.

Be sure to ask about the complimentary bottle of champagne for honeymooners! You can celebrate as soon as you arrive.

Grand Cayman Marriott Beach Resort
West Bay Road
☎ 345-949-0088; fax 345-949-8088
Reservations: ☎ 800-228-9290
www.marriotthotels.com
$$

Located two miles from George Town and about four miles from the airport, this convenient property sits on a beautiful stretch of Seven Mile Beach. Swimmers and snorkelers can enjoy calm waters and a small coral reef just offshore. You can even learn to scuba dive or book dive trips through the on-site shop. Oceanfront rooms include private balconies with good beach views and are worth a somewhat long walk to the elevators in this 305-room hotel.

Special Features/Activities: beachfront, casual and fine dining, pool and hot tub, dive shop, WaveRunners, windsurfing, shopping arcade, full service spa.

The Islands

♥ *Hyatt Regency Grand Cayman*
PO Box 1388
West Bay Road, Seven Mile Beach
☎ *345-949-1234; fax 345-949-8528*
Reservations: ☎ *800-233-1234*
www.hyatt.com
$$$

For lovers looking for a full menu of hotel amenities, the Hyatt Regency Grand Cayman fits the bill. The longtime favorite recently underwent an expansion to offer rooms directly on Seven Mile Beach and to increase its recreational facilities.

A cross between a country club and an island resort, the hotel flows from a great main house to grounds dotted with royal palms and ponds filled with colorful koi. A free-form swimming pool, with bridges and pool bar, is found here. Blocks of guest rooms circle this central area; Britannia Villas lie beyond the guest rooms adjacent to the Britannia golf course. Shuttle service is available from the main house to the villas and spa.

> *A romantic spot for a drink is the Hyatt's* **Aquas Pool Bar.** *It just might look familiar: this is where Jeanne Tripplehorn's character in the movie* The Firm *shows up to surprise Avery (Gene Hackman).*

Many guest rooms overlook the Britannia Golf Course, designed by Jack Nicklaus, or the private marina. Standard rooms, each carpeted and featuring a soft Caribbean color scheme, include a mini-bar, satellite TV, coffee makers, electronic room card, direct dial telephones with voice mail, in-room safe, ironing board, and hairdryer. The property also has 50 one-to-four-bedroom villas and 10 bi-level suites.

The $15 million expansion added 53 beachfront suites on Seven Mile Beach. These include a separate living room with a dining area, wet bar, work station (with two phone lines), and other upgraded amenities. The seaside suites are served by a dedicated concierge. A landscaped pool complex includes bronze sea turtle sculptures, waterfalls, and three freshwater pools.

Red Sail Sports opened a 2,000-square-foot state-of-the-art diving center as part of the beach addition. The center serves as Red Sail's main on-island training facility with dedicated classroom space, an on-site eight-foot training pool, a locker room and a retail shop that includes photo-video editing and developing facilities. Red Sail offers a range of watersports options including catamaran cruises on two 65-foot vessels for dinner sails, cocktail cruises, and luncheon snorkel excursions to Stingray City. Dive boats offer one- and two-tank trips as well as night dives. Sea kayaking, waverunners, waterskiing, parasailing, and underwater photography are also available as well as deep-sea, bone, and reef fishing.

Special Features/Activities: casual and fine dining with three restaurants and four bars, some units beachfront, beach club, pools, dive shop, tennis, 24-hour room service.

Westin Casuarina Resort
West Bay Road, PO Box 30620
☎ *345-945-3800; fax 345-945-3804*
Reservations: ☎ *800-228-3000*
www.westin.com
$$

The newest hotel in Grand Cayman is built on a strip of beach bordered by willowy casuarina trees. It has 340 guest rooms, most with breathtaking views of the sea from balconies. The hotel has the feel of a conference property, with a slightly dressed-up atmosphere in the main lobby.

Special Features/Activities: beachfront, casual and fine dining restaurants, pools, whirlpools, tennis, fitness facilities, beauty salons, massage

Little Cayman

♥ ## Little Cayman Beach Resort
PO Box 51, Blossom Village
☎ *813-323-8727; fax 813-323-8827*
Reservations: ☎ *800-327-3835*
www.littlecayman.com
$$

Little Cayman Beach Resort brings together the amenities of a Grand Cayman resort with the privacy of a getaway on Little Cayman. The island's largest property is specially tailored for

The Islands

couples who want luxury. This two-story conch-shell-pink resort overlooks a shallow area inside the reef on the south side of the island. Just outside the reef lie top scuba spots accessible through Reef Divers, the on-site operator. Beginners can learn with a resort course or obtain open water certification. Underwater photographers can see their shots the same day; an underwater photo and video center has E-6 processing and rentals. Non-divers also enjoy this resort for its laid-back atmosphere. Hammocks sway just yards from the shoreline; chaise loungers line the edge of the freshwater pool just steps from the bar. All rooms include air conditioning, balcony or patio, color TV, ceiling fan, and beach. New oceanfront rooms include wet bars, microwaves, and coffeemaker.

Special Features/Activities: restaurant, bar, gift shop, freshwater pool, dive shop, underwater photo center, fitness center, spa, and hot tub.

Pirates Point Resort
Box 43, Preston Bay
☎ *345-948-1010; fax 345-948-1011*
$$

This 12-room resort is a favorite with divers and it's easy to see why. Four dive instructors reveal the secrets of Bloody Bay Wall, from sheer cliffs to delicate sponges and coral formations.

Non-divers find plenty of activity (or non-activity, if they so choose) at Pirates Point as well. Owner Gladys Howard is active in eco-tourism. The lobby of Pirates Point is filled with nature guidebooks, and Gladys also has a nature trail guide and fishing guide to take visitors out for a day or half-day of fishing, birding, or just to learn more about the island's indigenous species.

The resort offers plenty of temptation to just laze the day away on the powdery white beach as well. Guest cottages are simple and light, decorated in Caribbean colors. Rooms include ceiling fan, tile floors, and private baths. Drinking water is produced by the resort's own reverse-osmosis plant.

After a day in the sun, guests can relax in the island's most unique bar, furnished with artwork created by previous guests. (The grounds of Pirates Point also feature guest-donated artwork, charmingly produced out of everything from coconut shells to driftwood.)

But there's no doubt that dining ranks as one of the top attractions of Pirates Point. Along with her expertise in natural history, Gladys Howard is also a Cordon Bleu-trained chef. While guests may enjoy roughing it during the day, at night they enjoy gourmet meals as elegant as those found at any of the Caribbean's finest resorts. Gladys boasts "My kitchen never closes."

Special Features/Activities: restaurant, dive shop, bicycles, hammocks, beach.

Cayman Brac

♥ Brac Reef Beach Resort
West End
☎ *813-323-8727*
Reservations: ☎ *800-327-3835*
www.braclittle.com
$

This 40-room resort is located off Channel Bay on the island's southeast shore. Guest rooms include air conditioning, ceiling fans, telephones, televisions, and porches or patios.

Special Features/Activites: beach, pool, hot tub, restaurant, bar, scuba, dive shop, snorkeling, fishing, tennis, underwater photo center and gift shop.

Tables for Two

Grand Cayman is filled with restaurants of every description, from fast food joints to fine dining. Dining is more limited on Cayman Brac and Little Cayman but you will find both excellent Caribbean eateries and continental dining on each island.

> *Check your bill before paying, as some restaurants automatically add a 15% gratuity to the total.*

The Islands

Price Chart

Restaurant prices are for dinner per person, including a drink, appetizer or salad, and entrée.

$............................	under $15
$$	$15 to $30
$$$	$30 to $45
$$$$........................	over $45

♥ *Casa Havana Restaurant*

Westin Casuarina
West Bay Road, Seven Mile Beach
☎ *345-945-3800*
Dress code: casually elegant
Reservations: suggested
$$$

The Casa Havana is the signature restaurant of the Westin, and comes complete with white-glove service and a romantic atmosphere. Look for favorite menu items such as glazed swordfish, roast pork tenderloin, and filet mignon.

♥ *Grand Old House*

South Church St., George Town
☎ *345-949-9333*
Dress Code: dressy
Reservations: required
$$$

The Grand Old House is one of Grand Cayman's most lauded restaurants, and with good reason. We dined here one evening as a wedding reception took place under a huge tent set up on the grounds. The Grand Old House is indeed both grand and old, dating back to 1908 when it was built by a merchant and lawyer from Boston. Once surrounded by a coconut plantation, the house was used for entertaining and lavish parties in its early days; later the structure became a hospital for soldiers wounded in World War II and a storm shelter during hurricanes.

Today the home showcases the work of Chef Kandathil Mathai, who has cooked for Prince Charles, Princess Diana, Margaret Thatcher, Princess Anne and the Reagan family. The menu includes entrées such as tenderloin of Black Angus beef, Caribbean broiled lobster tail and more. Specialties include lobster tail sautéed with shallots, mushrooms, fresh tomatoes and beurre blanc, and baked shrimp "Grand Old House." They offer an extensive wine list.

The restaurant is open for lunch Monday through Friday from 11:45 am to 2 pm, and dinner, Monday through Saturday from 6 to 10 pm.

Hemingway's
Hyatt Britannia Beach Club
West Bay Rd., Seven Mile Beach
☎ *345-945-5700*
Dress Code: casual
Reservations: optional
$$

This is a delightfully fun eatery, located right on the beach with indoor and outdoor seating. Start with pepperpot soup or conch and clam chowder, but don't miss the Cayman-style conch fritters with chipotle tartar sauce. Entrées range from Caribbean spiny lobster tail to roasted rack of lamb to pan-fried snapper.

Lantanas
West Bay Rd.
☎ *345-945-5595*
Dress code: casually elegant
Reservations: suggested
$$

This elegant restaurant has an excellent menu featuring spicy Cuban black bean soup, jerk pork tenderloin, and grilled yellowfin tuna with cilantro linguine, followed by tropical coconut cream pie with white chocolate shavings and mango sauce or frozen Cayman lime pie with raspberry sauce and whipped cream. Need we say more?

The Islands

♥ Lighthouse at Breakers

Breakers
☎ *345-947-2047*
Dress code: casual
Reservations: optional
$$

On the south shore about 25 minutes from George Town, this picturesque restaurant offers good seafood and Italian cuisine and an even better view. We dined on the open-air back deck, a romantic spot for dinner or lunch.

Lobster Pot

North Church Street, George Town
☎ *345-949-2736*
Dress Code: casually elegant
Reservations: recommended
$$$

We enjoyed a dinner of, what else, Caribbean lobster tail, at this casually elegant restaurant overlooking the sea. Other popular dishes include cracked conch, island seafood curry with shrimp, and Cayman turtle steak.

> *Save this restaurant for your most special night out. An excellent view, an attentive staff, and a good wine list make this a romantic favorite.*

Lone Star Bar

West Bay Rd., Seven Mile Beach
☎ *345-945-5175*
Dress code: casual
Reservations: not needed
$

This bar, located by the Hyatt Regency entrance, was recently named one of the "World's Top 100 Bars" by *Newsweek* magazine. The atmosphere is rollicking and fun, a mix of both locals and vacationers who come to enjoy a drink and some conversation in this T-shirt decorated bar. The restaurant specializes in Tex-Mex food. Monday and Thursday are all-you-can-eat fajita nights; on Thursday lobster is the specialty of the house.

Wednesday brings in steak lovers; Friday is a favorite with prime rib buffs; and Saturday is barbecue night.

Rum Point Restaurant

Rum Point
☎ *345-947-9412*
Dress code: casually elegant
Reservations: optional
$$-$$$

Open for dinner only, this restaurant features island favorites like shrimp, lobster, and conch as well as pasta dishes, prime rib, and chicken.

The Wharf

West Bay Rd.
☎ *345-949-2231*
http://wharf.ky
Dress code: casually elegant
Reservations: suggested
$$$

Just past George Town at the start of the beach, The Wharf is a favorite with couples. This seaside restaurant and bar is open for lunch on weekdays and dinner nightly with a menu featuring continental and Caribbean cuisine, but the Wharf is best experienced as a sunset spot.

> *Located right on the water's edge, The Wharf's open-air bar offers an uninterrupted view of the setting sun.*

A school of huge tarpon linger below the deck, waiting for scheduled handouts, and live music is offered most evenings.

The Islands

Romantic Activities

Grand Cayman

Underwater Delights

There's no doubt that one of the top draws of the Cayman Islands is the unparalleled scuba diving in the clear waters. With visibility often exceeding 100 feet, this is a diver's paradise, with over 130 sites to select from near Grand Cayman. Many wall and reef dives are less than half a mile from shore. There are many operators, including **Bob Soto's Diving** (☎ 800-BOB-SOTO); **Don Foster's Dive Cayman** (☎ 800-83-DIVER); **Red Sail Sports** (☎ 877-RED-SAIL); **Treasure Island Divers** (☎ 800-872-7552); **Tortuga Surfside Divers** (☎ 800-748-8733), to name a few.

The top attraction on Grand Cayman is **Stingray City,** the place for you to act out your Jacques Cousteau fantasies. It's an area where numerous operators introduce vacationers to one of the most unique experiences in the Caribbean.

Following a short boat ride, visitors don snorkel gear and swim with the stingrays just offshore on a shallow sandbar. Accustomed to being fed, the stingrays (which range in size from about one to six feet across) are docile and friendly, brushing against swimmers and even allowing themselves to be held and petted. About 30 stingrays frequent this area.

But you don't even have to get wet to enjoy the underwater sights of the Caribbean. Based in George Town, the *Atlantis* submarine, ☎ 800-253-0493, offers hourly dives six days a week. For 50 minutes, you'll feel like an underwater explorer as you dive to a depth of 100 feet below the surface. It's a unique opportunity to view colorful coral formations and sponge gardens, and identify hundreds of varieties of tropical fish. The submarine has individual porthole windows for each passenger, plus cards to help you identify fish species. A pilot and co-pilot point out attractions during the journey.

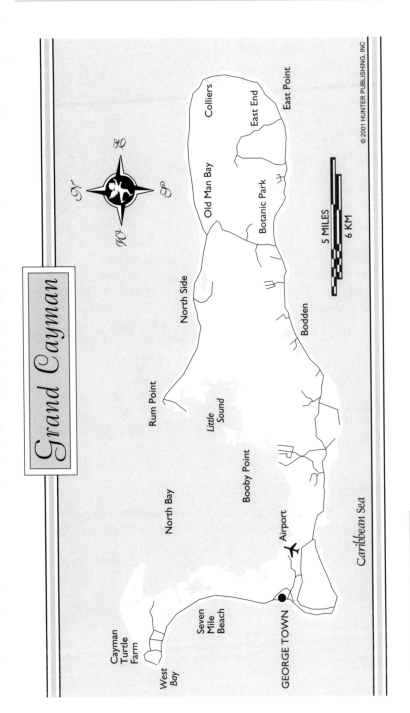

Grand Cayman

Island Sights & Museums

Outside the city of George Town on Grand Cayman, the population is sparse and the atmosphere is rural. The least populated region is called **North Side**. Located about 25 minutes from George Town, this remote area is home to the **Queen Elizabeth Botanic Park** (☎ 345-947-9462; fax 345-947-7873; www.botanic-park.ky), a 65-acre park filled with native trees and wild orchids, as well as birds, reptiles, and butterflies. Here we enjoyed a self-guided tour and a quiet look at the flora and fauna that make the Cayman Islands special. To reach the gardens, travel east from George Town on the south side road, turning north on Frank Sound Road. The gardens will be on your right.

From the North Side, travel to the **East End,** home of the **Blow Holes.** Park and walk down to the rugged coral rocks that have been carved by the rough waves into caverns. As waves hit the rocks, water spews into the air, creating one of the best photo sites on the island. To reach the blowholes, travel east of George Town on the south side road. The blowholes are on this road, east of the Frank Sound Road turnoff.

Just under 30,000 people populate Grand Cayman and almost half live in the capital city of George Town. Save a few minutes for a tour of the **Cayman Islands National Museum,** ☎ 345-949-8368. This excellent two-story museum traces the history of the Cayman Islands, including their natural history. George Town bustles with life any time of day as a center for shoppers and diners. Among historic government buildings, you'll find plenty of shops selling Cayman souvenirs and restaurants featuring both Caribbean cuisine and international dishes.

Continuing north on West Bay Road, past George Town lies the world's only **Turtle Farm,** ☎ 345-949-3894, www.turtle.ky. Here you'll have a chance to get up close and personal with green sea turtles, viewing them as eggs, hatchlings, and in various sizes as they work their way up towards adulthood. Some reach 600 pounds, and can be viewed slowly swimming in an open-air tank in the center of the farm.

One of Grand Cayman's top tourist spots is pure **Hell**. This odd attraction is actually a community named Hell, a moniker derived from the time an English commissioner went hunting in the area, shot at a bird, missed, and said "Oh, hell." The name must have seemed appropriate for the devilishly pointed rocks near town, a bed of limestone and dolomite that, over millions of years, eroded into a crusty, pocked formation locally called ironshore. Today, Hell trades upon its unusual name as a way to draw tourists to the far end of West Bay. **The Devil's Hangout Gift Shop** (open daily) is manned by Ivan Farrington, who dresses as the devil himself to greet tourists who come to buy the obligatory postcard and have it postmarked from Hell.

Golf

The Links at SafeHaven, ☎ 345-949-5988, off West Bay Road, Seven Mile Beach, is the only championship 18-hole golf course in the Cayman Islands. Rates average about US $100 for 18 holes. Shoe and cart rentals are available.

Sailing

Another good option for couples are the many sunset and dinner cruises that sail along Seven Mile Beach. **Red Sail Sports,** ☎ 345-945-5965, offers a sunset cruise from Rum Point on Sundays and other days from Seven Mile Beach. The two-hour sunset cruise departs at 5 pm during the winter months and 5:30 pm during the summer. Complimentary appetizers are served; a full cash bar is available. Dinner cruises are also available with three courses.

The ***Jolly Roger,*** ☎ 345-949-8534, is another option and a favorite with couples. On Saturdays, Sundays, Tuesdays and Thursdays, this replica of a 17th-century galleon sails at dusk. Admission includes complimentary rum punch and appetizers; a full bar is also available. The *Jolly Roger* also offers dinner cruises on Monday, Wednesday, and Friday evenings. Dinner includes complimentary rum punch and appetizers, and Caribbean entrées with wine, dessert and coffee. Reservations must be made by 2 pm the day of the cruise. The cruise leaves from the Jewelry Factory, located in George Town on the waterfront, across from the Hard Rock Café.

The Islands

Shopping

Duty-free shopping is especially popular in **George Town** where you can choose from china, perfumes, leather goods, watches, crystal, and more. Jewelry (mostly gold) is a popular buy and available at stores such as **24 K-Mon Jewellers** (Treasure Island Resort); **Savoy Jewellers** (Fort St. and Church St, George Town); and **The Jewelry Center** (Fort Street in George Town). For china and crystal, check out the **Kirk Freeport Centre** (Albert Panton St., George Town). And don't miss the oldest bookstore on the island, **Hobbies and Books** (Piccadilly Centre, Elgin Avenue).

If you're looking for something uniquely Cayman, check out **Caymanite** jewelry. Made from a stone found only on the eastern end of Grand Cayman and on Cayman Brac, Caymanite somewhat resembles tiger's eye and is often sold in gold settings.

Another popular island purchase is the **Tortuga Rum Cake,** made using five-year-old Tortuga Gold Rum. The cake is the product of a 100-year-old family recipe. Or, if you just want to skip the cake, take home a bottle of **Tortuga Rum, Blackbear,** or **Cayman Gold.**

Little Cayman

On Little Cayman, attractions are primarily related to the sea. Couples will find a romantic picnic and sunworshipping spot at Point of Sand, also known as **Sandy Point**. To reach this remote beach, turn right off the main road where you see a stop sign at the approaching road. The sand is packed for the first half of the drive, but stop at the wide section. Do not attempt to take vehicles down to the beach because of deep sand. It's a long walk back to town and there are no facilities or telephones in this park. This beach, luminescent with beautiful pink sand, is one of the island's prettiest and also most secluded. You very well might spend the entire day on this stretch of beach and never see another person (although on weekends visitors from Cayman Brac often come over to enjoy the beach). A covered picnic table invites you to enjoy a quiet lunch with the sound of the sea as background music.

Little Cayman is also home to one of the Cayman Islands's top scuba (and snorkel) sites: **Bloody Bay Wall.** One of 57 dive sites marked with moorings around this island, the wall drops off just a short swim from the shore at a depth of only 20 feet. For diving excursions, call **Pirates Point Resort** (☎ 345-948-1010); **Reef Divers** (☎ 800-327-3835 or 345-327-3835); **McCoy's Diving and Fishing Lodge** (☎ 800-626-0496, 345-948-0026); or **Southern Cross Club** (☎ 800-899-2582, 345-948-1099).

If the two of you enjoy birding, don't miss the **Booby Pond Visitors Centre.** Operated by the National Trust, Booby Pond, a 1.2-mile-long brackish mangrove pond, is the home of the Caribbean's largest breeding colony of red-footed boobies (*Sula sula*) and a breeding colony of magnificent frigate birds. Approximately 30% of the Caribbean's population of red-footed boobies resides at this pond. Even without the help of telescopes or binoculars, you can view the large white birds (or their large, gray offspring) in the trees surrounding the brackish pond. Over 7,000 of the birds make their home here. The Visitors Centre includes exhibits on the island's many indigenous species, from the common crab to the seed shrimp to the pond's many resident birds. Friendly volunteers staff the center and welcome questions about the wildlife and about island life.

Cayman Brac

Cayman Brac isn't known for its beaches (Little Cayman is the best choice for that) but this island has some incredible topography. Don't miss the 140-foot-high **Bluff,** the highest point in the Cayman Islands. A trail weaves its way to the edge of the Bluff and provides excellent photo opportunities. Rocky paths snake their way along the Bluff; wear hiking boots for this challenge.

Another excellent stop on Cayman Brac is the **Parrot Reserve.** Located in the center of the island, this trail is great for self-guided tours. It is a mile long and takes hikers through the home of the endangered Cayman Brac parrot. There is no charge to enter the reserve and trails are always open. Bring your own water; there are no facilities on the trail. You'll also want to wear long pants and good shoes for the trek, which traverses ironshore.

The Islands

To reach the Parrot Reserve, travel either the North Side Road or the South Side Road to the center road called Ashton Reid Drive (but known as Bluff Road). Take this road to the intersection of the gravel Major Donald Drive (a.k.a. Lighthouse Road) and continue to the Parrot Reserve and the Lighthouse. The gravel road is well graded and can be manuevered by bicycles (just watch out for the stray cow or two!). For more information, contact Wallace Platts, chairman of the trust's district committee, at ☎ 345-948-2390.

Nightlife

Mention Cayman and nightlife in the same sentence and Seven Mile Beach's best-known performer comes to mind: the **Barefoot Man.** George Now, a.k.a. the "Barefoot Man," has been entertaining Cayman audiences for years, and his music was heard in *The Firm*. For years the Barefoot Man performed at the Holiday Inn Grand Cayman. Today he can be found at the **Royal Palms Beach Club**, ☎ 345-945-6358, Thursday through Saturdays starting at 8 pm.

Caribbean music and fun is the theme of the **Caribbean Dinner Party,** ☎ 345-949-1234, ext. 5208, held on Tuesday and Friday nights at the **Hyatt Regency Grand Cayman** from 6:30-9:30 pm. This show features limbo dancers, fire eaters, and a steel pan musician. The evening includes a dinner of pepperpot soup, spicy conch stew, salads, Jamaican barbecued fish, jerk mahi mahi, and more.

Seven Mile Beach is also home to several nightclubs, favorites with young, energetic travelers. In The Falls Shopping Centre, **Legendz,** ☎ 345-945-5288, features the sound of live rock. **Sharkey's Niteclub,** ☎ 345-945-5366, in Cayman Falls Shopping Centre, is known for its dancing with live rock-and-roll Tuesdays, comedy on Wednesdays, Thursdays, Saturdays and Sundays, and big screen music theme nights.

Two comedy clubs pack in crowds looking for laughs. **Coconuts Comedy Club,** ☎ 345-949-NUTS, at the Legendz nightclub in The Falls Shopping Centre, features traveling comics on Wednesday, Thursday, Saturday and Sunday nights at 9 pm. **Chuckles Comedy Club**, ☎ 345-945-5077, moves between the

West Bay Polo Club and Sharkey's, depending on the night of the week.

Sports buffs have several bars to catch up on sporting action. At the **Lone Star Bar and Grill,** ☎ 345-945-5175, all major games are televised in the bar. **West Bay Polo Club Sports Bar and Grill,** ☎ 345-949-9892, located in Seven Mile Shops, has over 15 television screens broadcasting just about any sporting event available. Pizza is served nightly until midnight.

For couples looking for something a little quieter, the **Loggia Lounge,** ☎ 345-949-1234, ext. 5209, at the Hyatt Regency Grand Cayman, is a good choice. The lounge has a piano player tinkling out quiet favorites as well as a humidor filled with Cuba's finest.

Nightlife on Cayman Brac and Little Cayman is far quieter, usually spent over a leisurely dinner. The perfect end to a day is often a quiet walk hand in hand.

Just the Facts

Entry Requirements: US, UK, and Canadian citizens need to show proof of citizenship in the form of a passport, birth certificate or voter registration card. Visitors must also show a return airline ticket.

Getting Around: Transportation around Grand Cayman is easy. Take your pick from taxis and group tours as well as rental cars, vans, jeeps, and scooters (a scary option to us, considering the left side driving and considerable traffic in George Town). Jeeps and taxis are also available on the Sister Islands.

Language: English

Currency: Cayman dollar, fixed at US $1 = CI $.80

Electricity: 110 volts

Information: For general information and brochures, call the Cayman Islands Department of Tourism at ☎ 800-346-3313. Or, contact your nearest Cayman Islands Department of Tourism Office. In Miami, 6100 Blue Lagoon Drive, Suite 150, Miami, ☎ 305-266-2300; New York, 420 Lexington Ave., Suite 2733, NY, ☎ 212-682-5582; Houston: Two Memorial City Plaza, 820

The Islands

Gessner, Suite 170, Houston, ☎ 713-461-1317; Los Angeles, 3440 Wilshire Boulevard, Suite 1202, Los Angeles, ☎ 213-738-1968; Chicago, 9525 W. Bryn Mawr, Suite 160, Rosemont, ☎ 708-678-6446. In Canada, c/o Travel Marketing Consultants, 234 Eglinton Ave. East, Suite 306, Toronto, ☎ 416-485-1550. In the United Kingdom, 6 Arlington Street, London, SW1A 1RE, England; ☎ 0171-491-7771. When on Grand Cayman, visit the Cayman Islands Department of Tourism office at Elgin Avenue in George Town, or call ☎ 345-949-0623. Website: www.caymanislands.ky.

Curaçao

*J*ust the name Curaçao – derived from the Portuguese word for the heart – speaks of romance. Add to that a historic capital city with tiny twinkling lights and picturesque European-style structures, fine cuisine from around the globe, and both tranquil beaches and rugged coastline, and you have all the ingredients for a romantic getaway.

Geography

Curaçao is part of the **Netherlands Antilles,** along with the islands of **Sint Maarten, Bonaire, Saba,** and **St. Eustatius.** The Netherlands Antilles, the island of Aruba, and Holland comprise the **Kingdom of the Netherlands.** Ruled by a governor appointed by the Queen, each island has autonomy on domestic affairs. Curaçao is the capital of the Netherlands Antilles, and here you'll find most of the governmental, financial, and industrial institutions.

Tucked into the far southern reaches of the Caribbean, less than 40 miles from the coast of South America, Curaçao is very much an international destination. **Dutch** is the official language, and you'll hear many Dutch-speaking vacationers. South Americans also enjoy the island, where most residents speak also Spanish. We found that most Curaçao residents actually speak an amazing total of five languages: Dutch, Spanish, English, Papiamento, and either French or German.

Papiamento is the local language spoken on the streets, a veritable cocktail of tongues. Spanish, Portuguese, French, Dutch, Indian, English, and some African dialects combine to form the *lingua franca* of the Netherlands Antilles. Even between the islands the language varies slightly, each with its own slang and accent.

That ease with multiple languages seems to translate into a comfort with many cultures as well. Over 70 nationalities are represented on the island and, with such a true melting pot on this 184-square-mile piece of land, there's a true welcoming spirit for tourists, wherever their homeland. When Curaçaoan says *Bon Bini*, they mean "welcome."

Some say the island of Curaçao looks like a bikini top, pinched in the center. On one side lies the capital of **Willemstad,** by Caribbean standards a major metropolitan area, with a harbor consistently rated about the fifth busiest in the world. This truly international city boasts streets lined with Dutch-style architecture as colorful as a candy store.

The city is divided into two sides: **Punda,** the original settlement, and **Otrobanda,** literally the "other side." Both sport picturesque harborfront buildings, and are connected by the largest bridge in the Caribbean, a free ferry, and the **Queen Emma Pontoon Bridge** for pedestrians, locally known as the "Swinging Old Lady" because of the way it moves out of the way for harbor traffic.

Festivals

Curaçao parties with special events such as **Carnival,** which starts New Year's Day and comes to a feverish pitch the day before Ash Wednesday. Every month, Willemstad throws a giant block party called the **Ban Tupa Street Fair**, which has with a rollicking island spirit.

The Islands

Sweet Dreams

Price Chart

Rates reflect high winter season (expect prices to be as much as 40% lower during the off season) for a standard room for two adults for one night. Prices are in US dollars.

$ . . . . under $150
$$ . . . . between $150 and $300
$$$ . . . . between $300 and $450
$$$$ . . . . over $450

♥ *Marriott Beach Hotel and Casino*
PO Box 6003, Piscadera Bay
☎ *599-9-7368800; fax 599-9-4627502*
Reservations: ☎ *800-223-6388*
www.marriotthotels.com
$$

This elegant hotel holds the position as the island's best, stretched along a wide swath of beach just a short ride from either the airport or the city. Built in 1992, the 248-room property is designed in the style of the Netherlands Antilles architecture. Cool lemon walls contrast with chile-pepper-colored roofs, all framed by stately palms. The property is a veritable oasis on this dry island, just down the beach from the desalinization plant (the world's largest), where unsightly smokestacks distract slightly from the view but don't interfere with the enjoyment of this romantic property

We especially liked the low-rise, open-air quality of this resort, starting with the lobby, where you'll arrive to a view of a cascading fountain across the palm-shaded pool and out to the sea. Every room includes either a balcony or patio (ask for a ground floor room for direct beach access) and at least a partial view of the ocean.

Special Features/Activities: beachfront, freshwater pool, hot tub, casino, casual and fine dining, tennis, shopping arcade, watersports.

Princess Beach Resort and Casino
Dr. Martin Luther King Boulevard 8
☎ *599-9-7367888; fax 599-9-4614131*
Reservations: ☎ *800-327-3286*
www.princessbeach.com
$$

Located near the Seaquarium, this resort is nestled along a wide stretch of beach protected by a man-made breakwater. The three-story resort features rooms in Caribbean colors, as well as three restaurants, four bars, and a casino.

Special Features/Activities: beachfront, casual and fine dining, casino, freshwater pools, shopping arcade, watersports, dive shop.

Lion's Dive Hotel and Marina
Bapor Kibra
☎ *599-9-4618100; fax 599-9-4618200*
Reservations: ☎ *888-546-6734*
www.lionsdive.com
$

Especially popular with divers, this hotel has everything scuba enthusiasts could want: a five-star dive center, dive courses, snorkel and boat dive trips, rentals, and a complete dive shop. Its 72 guest rooms are all air conditioned, each with a balcony or a patio. The hotel also operates a shuttle to Willemstad and offers free admission to Seaquarium.

Special Features/Activities: beachfront, fine and casual dining, dive shop.

Tables for Two

With its numerous nationalities, Curaçao enjoys many cuisines. Indonesian **rijstaffel,** or rice table, is especially popular. Local specialties include **stoba di cabrito** (goat stew), fried plantains, seafood, and conch or karko. Amstel beer, Dutch gin, and local rums such as San Pablo are choice drinks. For an after-dinner liqueur, try **Senior Curaçao's Blue Curaçao** (it comes it several other colors as well). Made from a bitter orange grown on the island, select from flavors including orange, chocolate, rum raisin, and coffee.

Price Chart

Restaurant prices are for dinner per person, including a drink, appetizer or salad, and entrée.

$............................	under $15
$$	$15 to $30
$$$	$30 to $45
$$$$........................	over $45

Old Market

Breede Straat (Punda), Willemstad
☎ *599-9-612178*
Dress code: casual
Reservations: not taken
$

Don't expect anything fancy at this cafeteria called "Grandma's Kitchen" by many locals. Located behind the post office and within walking distance of the Punda's shops, this is where residents come for Curaçaoan dishes like *kadushi* (cactus) soup and *giambo* (gumbo). Diners line up and order from the cooks, who ladle generous helpings out of gargantuan pots. Wash it all down with a glass of cold Amstel. Open for lunch only, daily except Sundays.

Fort Nassau

(Otrabanda) Willemstad
☎ *599-9-4613450*
Dress code: elegant
Reservations: suggested
$$$

Dine indoors or out on continental dishes by candlelight. Enjoy dishes as varied as saltimbocca (veal cutlets with sage and prosciutto) or fried sunfish breaded with pecan nuts, served with a choice of excellent soups such as mustard or rich coconut.

> *The* most romantic night view in Willemstad is from this historic fort.

Landhaus Brieguengat
☎ *599-9-8648087*
Dress code: casually elegant
Reservations: suggested
$$$

Rijsttafel, an Indonesian feast, is served in this historic country house. Diners sit outdoors beneath a web of tiny lights strung in the trees. Come with a big appetite to this spread. The meal begins with an appetizer of egg rolls followed by main courses such as *sateh ajam* (skewered chicken covered with a spicy peanut-flavored sauce), *kerrie djawa* (beef curry), *daging ketjap* (beef braised in soy and ginger sauce), and *telor* (egg in spiced coconut sauce). You can work off the calories on the dance floor, then return the next day to tour the landhaus which is furnished with period antiques.

Mambo Bar
Seaquarium Beach
Dress code: beachwear
Reservations: no
$

Casual fun is the order of the day at this beachside joint, where the tables are located right on the sand. Choose from pasta dishes or look for lighter fare like tuna, shrimp, and crab on a baguette.

Romantic Activities

Island Sights & Museums

Independent travelers love Curaçao. It's easy to get around and it's simple to move beyond the resort to experience the stream of

everyday life. This is an island without hasslers or pushy vendors, a place where the two of you can walk hand in hand along
the streets, dine at sidewalk cafés, and be greeted by friendly
Curaçaoans.

Start with a visit to **Willemstad,** a historic city that bustles
with activity but also takes a slower pace in its shopping district. Here you can take a guided tour aboard an open-air trolley
or a self-guided walk for a look at **Fort Amsterdam.** And you
can't miss the historic harborside shops, as bright as Easter
eggs.

While you're in the city, make time for a visit to **Seaquarium,**
☎ 599-9-4653160, one of the Caribbean's finest marine exhibits.
Along with tanks of local fish, coral, and sponges, the aquarium
also has several outdoor tanks with larger species – including
sharks, sea turtles, and stingrays. Divers and would-be divers
can take a dip here and feed the sharks through holes in an underwater wall. Complete instructions and equipment are provided. For those who want a drier look at these toothy denizens,
just walk down into the **Seaquarium Explorer,** ☎ 599-9-
4616666, a semi-submarine parked by the shark tank.

> *T*he Seaquarium has been the site of an underwater
> wedding as well as four deep-sea proposals. Divers
> popped the question by writing on underwater clip-
> boards.

Beaches

After seeing the exhibits, have a dip at the **Seaquarium
Beach,** a full-service beach with watersports, restaurant, bar,
and plenty of action. There's a small admission charge. This is
the beach where Curaçaoans and visitors come to see and be
seen, and topless bathing is popular. Waters as calm as a lake
make swimming inside the breakwaters easy and safe.

Curaçao has over three dozen additional beaches from which to
choose, all located on the Caribbean side of the island. Two of
the most popular are **Knip Bay,** located near Christoffel park
on the north coast and **Barbara Beach,** located on the southeast end of the island.

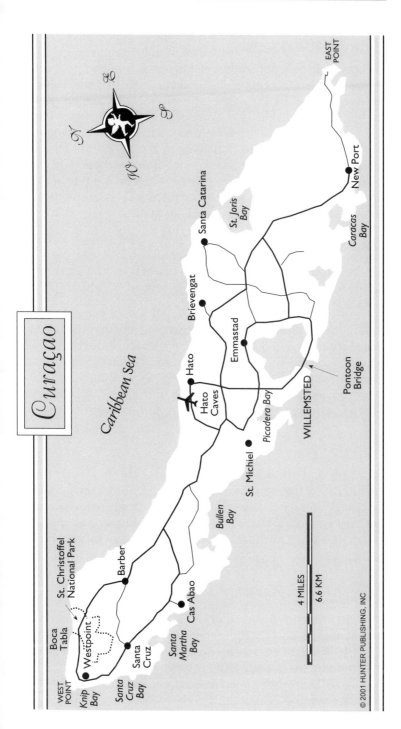

Curaçao

Caribbean Sea

The Islands

WEST POINT
Knip Bay
Santa Cruz Bay
Boca Tabla
St. Christoffel National Park
Westpoint
Barber
Santa Cruz
Cas Abao
Santa Martha Bay
Bullen Bay
St. Michiel
Hato
Hato Caves
Brievengat
Santa Catarina
Emmastad
Picadera Bay
WILLEMSTED
Pontoon Bridge
St. Joris Bay
Caracas Bay
New Port
EAST POINT

4 MILES
6.6 KM

© 2001 HUNTER PUBLISHING, INC

Natural Attractions

Curaçao may be a desert island, but you'll find plenty of other natural attractions. One of the most romantic is **Boca Tabla,** a sea cave carved by pounding Atlantic waves. Located on the road to Westpoint, the cave is a short walk off the road (wear sturdy shoes!) but it rewards lovers with one of the region's most breathtaking sights. Kneeling in the darkness of the sea cave, you'll watch the surge of crystal blue waves as they come within feet of you, roaring into the cave and back out to sea. After, take a walk above on the volcanic rock (stay on the pebble path) to the seaside cliffs for excellent photos.

If you'd like to venture into a cavern, take a tour of **Hato Caves,** located near the airport, ☎ 599-868-0379, open daily except Monday. Guided tours take the two of you through the stalactite and stalagmite filled rooms, several of which include pools or waterfalls.

Nature lovers should save time for a visit to **Christoffel National Park,** ☎ 599-864-0363, on the western end of the island. This wildlife preserve includes the island's highest point and 20 miles of trails that wind through local flora and fauna. Don't be surprised to see some native wildlife in the park; it is home to iguanas, donkeys, small deer, rabbits, and many bird species.

Tours

For a look at all these attractions, consider an island tour. Tours can be booked through hotel desks or call **Taber Tours,** ☎ 599-9-737-6637, for a rundown of their packages, which include east and west end tours; Hato Cave tour; jeep safari; and sailing and sunset cruises. On the web: www.curacao.com/tabertours/index.html.

Shopping

Curaçao's shopping opportunities keep many travelers busy, especially in downtown **Willemstad.** The prime shopping district is in **Punda,** just across the floating bridge. Cross the bridge and continue up **Breede Straat,** where you'll find most of the shops and boutiques aimed at vacationers, along with some charming sidewalk cafés.

The most obvious shop in Punda is the **J.L. Penha and Sons** department store, housed in a beautiful lemon-tinted colonial building constructed in 1708. You'll find just about everything, from perfumes to fine jewelry to collectibles.

For lower-priced purchases, take a turn off Breede Straat and enjoy a stroll down **Heeren Straat** or **Keuken Straat.** These streets are filled with electronics, inexpensive clothing, and housewares. It's a fun atmosphere where you'll have a chance to mix with residents.

Stroll through the streets and alleyways, then walk across the **Wilhelmina Bridge** to the **Floating Market,** one of Willemstad's most colorful sites. Venezuelans sell fresh fish and vegetables (a real commodity on an island without much agriculture). Stroll along the waterway booths and buy exotic tropical fruits or watch fishermen cleaning their catch for a buyer. Behind the stalls, colorful schooners make an excellent photo. Hours vary depending on the day's sales, but arrive early for the best selection. We highly recommend the market to enjoy a slice of island life and, for the photographers out there, to capture one of Curaçao's most colorful sights.

Nightlife

Discos, live music, and casinos offer nightlife to restless visitors, especially in the Willemstad area and in the major hotels. The **Sonesta Casino** offers one room of slots and table action.

The **Papaya Plantation House** is open Thursday and Friday nights with an open-air barbecue and music by local bands, ☎ 599-9-869-5850.

For those looking for a night out, there are several places to choose from on Curaçao. **Hook's Hut,** located at Las Palmas Beach (☎ 599-9-4626575), and **The Music Factory** (☎ 599-9-4610631) are local favorites. **Club Façade** (☎ 599-9-4614640), and **The Jail** (☎ 599-9-4656810) have dancing.

The Islands

Just the Facts

Entry Requirements: US, UK, and Canadian citizens need to offer proof of citizenship in the form of a passport or a birth certificate and a photo ID. Travelers also need to show a continuing or return ticket.

Getting Around: For most properties, rental jeeps are the best option. Hertz, Avis, Budget, National, and other firms offer rentals.

When traveling in the downtown Punda area, if you have questions or need directions, look for burgundy-suited men and women, members of the **Curaçao Hospitality Service.** Stationed throughout the shopping area, these friendly assistants provide help in many languages.

Language: Dutch is the official language, but English and Spanish are widely spoken, as well as Papiamento.

Currency: Antillean guilder (US $1 = ANG $1.77).

Electricity: 110-130 volts/50 cycles. Most 60 cycle appliances work, but bring an adapter to be safe.

Information: Contact the Curaçao Tourist Board: in New York, 475 Park Avenue South, Suite 2000, New York 10016 or call ☎ 800-270-3350 or 212-683-7660, fax 212-683-9337. In Miami: 330 Biscayne Boulevard, Miami 33132, ☎ 800-445-8266 or 305-374-5811, fax 305-374-6741. In Europe, the bureau may be contacted at Vastland 82-84, 3011 BP Rotterdam, Holland or call ☎ 31-10-414-2639. Once you're on the island, stop by the Visitors Information Booth at the airport (just past customs), for brochures and maps. Website: www.curacao-tourism.com.

Dominican Republic

*F*or lovers on a tight budget, the Dominican Republic or Dominicana (not to be confused with Dominica, a somewhat remote island known for its eco-tourism) is an excellent choice.

The Dominican Republic has long been heralded as one of the least expensive Caribbean destinations, some sources estimating it to be as much as 50 to 70% cheaper than its neighbors. Excepting such resorts as Casa De Campo, where jet-setters come to relax and where Michael Jackson and Lisa Marie Presley wed, the island boasts inexpensive prices and bargain resorts. With the favorable exchange rate, Americans can enjoy a stay on the north shore for under $100 per person, per day, including all meals, tips, and watersports.

Although values abound on this festive island, you needn't worry that you'll be shortchanged in terms of beauty or fun. The Dominican Republic has ancient history, mountain-covered vistas, and a party atmosphere that's as fun as any found throughout the Caribbean.

Geography

Although well known to European travelers, the Dominican Republic's tumultuous neighbor, **Haiti,** may be more familiar to Americans. To be honest, the news accounts of trouble in Haiti almost made us reconsider our trip to the Dominican Republic. But we soon discovered that, even though the two nations share the same island, **Hispaniola,** geography is about all that unites Haiti and the Dominican Republic. The second-largest Caribbean island (only Cuba is larger), Hispaniola is a land of rugged mountains, palm-lined beaches, and two diverse cultures. Haitians speak French; Dominicans, Spanish. The leadership of Haiti has frequently been torn by assassinations and military takeovers, while the citizens of the Dominican Republic enjoy the relative tranquillity of a stable, freely elected government.

Dominican Republic days are carefree, with plenty of time to dance to the throbbing sounds of merengue and to enjoy a glass of *"Dominicana gasolina,"* the nickname for locally produced rum.

Many resorts are found on the Dominican Republic's north side, a region dubbed the **Amber Coast.** The Dominican Republic boasts the fastest growing tourism business in the Caribbean, with over two million visitors a year. Over 60% of the vacationers are European.

The Islands

For visitors, the two primary destinations in Dominican Republic are **Puerto Plata,** on the island's north shore, and the capital city, **Santo Domingo,** on the southern coast.

About 20 minutes from Puerto Plata's La Union international airport lies the resort area of **Playa Dorada.** This horseshoe-shaped complex contains over a dozen resorts, numerous restaurants, a casino, a two-story shopping mall, and a Robert Trent Jones-designed 18-hole golf course, all tucked between the backdrop of the lush mountains and the palm-lined Atlantic beach. Although the sea here is choppier that its Caribbean counterpart on the south shore, a gentle breeze makes it popular with windsurfers, boogie boarders, and families who enjoy playing in the surf. Other guests are just content to lie on the beaches lined with majestic palms.

Santo Domingo is located on the island's southern shore. Here history buffs will find a wealth of Spanish Renaissance architecture to explore. The city was the first permanent European settlement in the New World and has been honored for its cultural landmarks by a United Nations proclamation.

Near Santo Domingo is the nation's most lavish resort: **Casa de Campo,** as well as a host of other first-rate vacation destinations.

Festivals

The vast majority of the population of the Dominican Republic is Roman Catholic, and many of the national festivals are religious in nature. **Carnival** begins the week before Independence Day, February 27. The **Christmas festival** begins in early December and ends on Epiphany Day, January 6. Of a more secular nature, the **Merengue Festival** celebrates the national music of the DR with band performances during the third week of July in Santo Domingo and the second week of October in Puerto Plata.

The **Puerto Plata Cultural Festival** highlights the arts, crafts, and music of the northern region. It is usually held in late January and early February. In addition, many of the towns of the Dominican Republic commemorate their patron saint's day with a large celebration. The dates of these festivals vary from town to town. Being in an area during a celebration can provide added color and fun to your vacation.

> *T IP: One problem, however, is that many businesses close during festivals, and this can be frustrating if you are caught unawares. It's best to check the dates with a local tourist board before you arrive, just to make sure.*

Sweet Dreams

Price Chart

Rates reflect high winter season (expect prices to be as much as 40% lower during the off season) for a standard room for two adults for one night; prices are in US dollars.

$ . . . . under $150
$$ . . . . between $150 and $300
$$$ . . . . between $300 and $450
$$$$ . . . . over $450

Jack Tar Village

PO Box 368, Playa Dorada, Puerto Plata
☎ *809-320-3800; fax 809-320-4161*
Reservations: ☎ *800-858-2258*
www.allegroresorts.com
$

This resort is easy on the pocketbook and still offers couples plenty of activity. The rooms here are separated from the beach by the golf course, but some days you can still hear the waves rolling in on the Atlantic side, which is too rough for snorkeling but nice for a romp in the surf.

Special Features/Activities: beachfront, all-inclusive, casino, golf, tennis, watersports.

Melia Bavaro

Playas de Bavaro, Higuey
☎ *809-221-2311; fax 809-286-5427*
Reservations: ☎ *800-33-MELIA*
$$

Located in Punta Cana on the eastern end of the island, this 57-acre resort offers rooms in two-story bungalows and a two-story hotel for a total of nearly 600 rooms.

Special Features/Activities: beachside, pool, shopping arcade, fine and casual dining, disco.

Casa de Campo

PO Box 140, La Romana
☎ *305-856-5405; fax 305-848-4677*
Reservations: ☎ *800-877-3643*
$$

The nation's most lavish resort is also one of the most activity-oriented in the Caribbean. You name it, you can do it at the 7,000-acre resort. American Airlines offers direct flights into Casa de Campo's own airport, located in La Romana.

Special Features/Activities: golf, tennis, horseback riding, polo, fine and casual dining, pools.

A spectacular setting for newlyweds.
Courtesy of Casa de Campo.

Renaissance Jarangua Hotel and Casino
376 George Washington Ave., Santo Domingo
☎ *809-221-2222; fax 809-686-0528*
Reservations: ☎ *800-331-3542*
www.renaissancehotels.com
$$

Pamper yourself at The Wellness Place, a European-style spa that epitomizes the elegant body holiday that this resort offers. After that, how about a walk through tropical gardens beside beautiful lagoons and cascading waterfalls? Finish off the day with a spin around the disco floor or a lavish show.

Special Features/Activities: spa, tennis, pool, disco, fine and casual dining.

Tables for Two

Price Chart

Restaurant prices are for dinner per person, including a drink, appetizer or salad, and entrée.

$......................	under $15
$$	$15 to $30
$$$	$30 to $45
$$$$	over $45

♥ ## Restaurante Chopin
Melia Bavaro Hotel
Carretera Melia, Higney, Punta Cana
☎ *809-583-3808*
Dress code: elegant
Reservations: required
$$$

Here's a romantic evening for you: take a nature walk through a rain forest to an elegant, open-air restaurant. Following a quiet meal, all the lights go out except for tabletop candles. Suddenly the sound of strings is heard – members of the Symphony Or-

The Islands

chestra of Belgrade. Floating in gondolas and circling the restaurant by waterway, the musicians play classical songs while accompanied by a show of lights beneath the trees. Truly a magical experience.

♥ *Meson de la Cava*
Santo Domingo
☎ *809-533-2818*
Dress code: dressy, jackets required
Reservations: required
$$

Located in a cave (yes, a cave), this romantic setting is the perfect place to enjoy an intimate dinner. Jackets are required in this restaurant, which is open daily. Order up tasty lamb chops or fresh seafood, such as jumbo shrimp or delicious lobster creole.

♥ *Casa del Rio*
Altos de Chavon
☎ *809-632-2319*
Dress code: dressy, long pants and collared shirt required
Reservations: required
$$$

Experience the 16th century of Altos de Chavon at this romantic restaurant. Long pants and collared shirts are required of men. The beautiful view of the Chavon River adds to the elegance of the excellent meal.

Romantic Activities

Island Sights & Museums

Look for amber-encased mosquitoes, termites, ants, ferns, cockroaches, and even a tiny lizard, at the **Amber Museum,** ☎ 809-682-3309, in Puerto Plata. This Caribbean nation is one of only a few sites on the globe where amber is found. The popularity of the book and movie *Jurassic Park*, where fiction gave scientists the ability to use DNA found in amber-encased mosquito blood to spawn dinosaurs, brings visitors flocking to this museum on the north shore of the island.

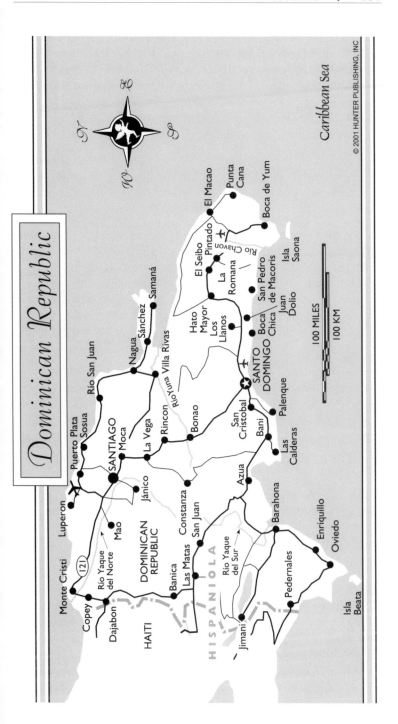

Dominican Republic

© 2001 HUNTER PUBLISHING, INC

Caribbean Sea

100 MILES
100 KM

The Islands

Dating back to the 16th century, the **Fortaleza San Felipe** still stands sentry over the city and the harbor. Built by the Spaniards to protect the city from pirates, in the 20th century it was used as a prison. The doors within the fort are only four feet tall, slowing down would-be attackers (and keeping tourists alert). The fort includes a small museum with a collection of period weapons and cannonballs.

Another fort stands at the top of Puerto Plata's **Pico Isabel de Torres**, one of the highest points in the Dominican Republic. The dome-shaped fortress is topped with a statue of Christ similar to one that overlooks Rio de Janeiro.

Today the fortress is a gift shop for visitors who take the cable-car ride to the summit. The 18-person car travels up the mountain daily except Wednesday. Be warned, however, that lines to board the cars can be long. Although the ride up the mountain is slow, the view from the summit makes it worth the wait. Through a gentle mist, you look down on Puerto Plata, the city named for its "silver port," making it easy to see why Christopher Columbus wrote back to Queen Isabella, "This is the most beautiful land that human eyes have seen."

When we toured the mountain, our guide pointed west in the direction of Haiti and explained why the neighbor that shares one-third of this island has so many difficulties. "In Haiti, they have more people than land." He gestured out over the Dominican mountains, green with vegetation and devoid of any habitation. "We have more land than we have people."

The steep mountainsides are used for growing coffee, and the flatlands along the Amber Coast are rich with sugarcane. It is used in the production of another amber-colored product, this one produced at the **Brugal Rum Factory, ☎** 809-633-2907. Open weekdays, the factory takes visitors through the process of making 9,000 bottles of rum daily, 95% of which stay on the island.

Santo Domingo Sights

Founded in 1496 by Christopher Columbus's brother, **Santo Domingo** has enough Old World history to fill a vacation. The city of over two million residents pulsates with plenty of New World vitality, a mix that keeps many visitors returning year after year. Below is a quick rundown of some of the best sights of Santo Domingo.

El Alcazar: This palace was the home of Christopher Columbus's son, Diego, and it served as the center of the Spanish court. Today it holds period furniture.

Calle Las Damas: The oldest street in the New World, this Santa Domingo street was named for the ladies of the Spanish court.

Museo de las Casas Reales: The Museum of the Royal Houses, 36 Maria Nievas Ricart is filled with 16th-century exhibits, all housed in the former offices of the colony's government.

Fortaleza Ozama: This former prison and fort was the first military station built in the Spanish colonies.

Catedral de Santa Maria: The first cathedral in the Americas, this 1514 church has a Gothic interior and a Spanish renaissance exterior. Until 1992, the mausoleum here held the remains of Christopher Columbus; they were then moved to Faro a Colon, below.

Faro a Colon: Columbus's Lighthouse, built in the shape of a cross, was constructed for the 500th anniversary of the landing of Christopher Columbus. Along with a museum, the building contains what are believed to be Christopher Columbus's remains, which were removed from the Catedral de Santa Maria. Spain disputes that these are actually Columbus's remains.

Amber Museum of Santo Domingo: This well-done museum explains the origin of amber, with examples of amber-encased insects and reptiles. ☎ 809-682-3309.

Beaches

Much of the Dominican Republic's early beach development was along the north shore in Puerto Plata, but today an increasingly popular hot spot is the southeastern coastline.

Just over half an hour's drive from the metropolis of Santo Domingo lies **Boca Chica.** Once a quiet fishing village, today this beachside community is home to major tourist complexes,

The Islands

thanks to its location on the largest reef-protected lagoon in the Caribbean.

What Boca Chica once had, **Juan Dolio** now offers: tranquility. Although it, too, is increasingly popular, at the resorts Juan Dolio travelers still find plenty of peace and quiet under the shade of a tall coconut palm or snorkeling in calm Caribbean waters.

East of Juan Dolio lies a town that may not be well known to travelers, but some of its former residents have become household names. The industrial port city of **San Pedro de Macoris** has produced more baseball players in the major leagues than any other community. Hey, is that Sammy Sosa?

You may not see any stars in the baseball capital, but you very well might make some stellar sightings at the next beach community: **La Romana.** This city is home to **Casa de Campo,** a sprawling resort that attracts a steady clientele of the rich and/or famous. Casa de Campo offers sporting activities ranging from polo to golf to skeet. Nearby is the re-created 16th-century European village of **Altos de Chavon,** where cobblestone streets meander past upscale restaurants and shops filled with artisans plying their crafts.

The easternmost tip of Hispaniola is **Punta Cana** (pronouced Poontah Cah-na), the home of the island's best stretch of white sand beach. This area was undiscovered (until the construction of a Club Med in the '70s), isolated by dense jungle and accessible only by helicopter or boat. Today, however, Punta Cana has definitely been discovered. Here lie many of the Dominican Republic's all-inclusive resorts and facilities that range from championship golf to shopping to fine dining.

Underwater Delights

Offshore from La Romana lies **Isla Catalina,** or Serena Cay, a popular stop with cruise ships as well as guests of Casa de Campo. Known for its white sand beaches, the diving here is some of the island's best.

Diving is also excellent in the village of **Bayahibe,** on the eastern end of the island. The coral reefs, filled with sponges, are popular not only with scuba buffs but also with anglers.

For dive excursions, call **Aqua Dive Las Terrenas** (☎ 809-240-6616); **Golden Arrow Technical Diving** (☎ 809-249-3176); **Neptune Dive Center** (☎ 809-526-1473); or **Rui Watersports** (☎ 809-221-2290, extension 8120).

Shopping

The most unique purchase in the Dominican Republic is **amber,** available at gift shops along the north coast. Amber prices vary from US $3 for small earrings, to US $200 for a mosquito encased in amber, to several hundred dollars for large, chunky necklaces or amber set in gold. The color of the amber affects the price as well. Generally the pale blonde amber is the least expensive.

Spotting True Amber

Amber resembles plastic, so avoid buying from street vendors and make sure to check your item before purchasing. Amber possesses a slight electromagnetic charge, so genuine amber, when rubbed on a piece of cloth, should attract dust particles. Better stores, such as Puerto Plata's **Amber Museum Shop,** (☎ 809-586-2848) have an ultraviolet light for testing. Genuine pieces will always glow under the light. Also, amber will float in saltwater, whereas plastic will sink.

Other popular souvenirs include Brugal rum (about US $4 per liter), Dominican cigars, merengue cassette tapes, and larimar, a blue stone similar to turquoise.

Nightlife

"Do you merengue?"

Heard in a bar it might not be an uncommon line. Or even on the beach. But delivered in a jewelry store by a salesman as an introduction in lieu of "May I help you?", it could only mean one thing: we were in the Dominican Republic.

Merengue (pronounced mare-rhen-gay) is a force of nature on this island nation, both a dance and a music enjoyed in carnivals, fiestas, dance halls, and anywhere there's a gathering.

The music for which the Dominican Republic is best known was first performed by groups of three musicians. These trios, called **pri pris,** produced music with a small drum, an accordion and a güiro (a gourd rhythmically scraped with a stick). Today's merengue is played by all types of musicians and accompanied by the national dance of the same name.

For visitors looking for nightlife, head to **Calle Duarte.** This street is packed with restaurants, clubs, bars and music and is blocked to cars in the evenings. Visitors tend to stay in this area until around 11 pm, but after midnight the pace picks up as many of the locals come in. The party is hopping by 3 am.

Just the Facts

Entry Requirements: US, UK, and Canadian citizens should bring proof of citizenship, either a passport or an official birth certificate with photo ID. Upon departure, vacationers are required to pay a departure tax of US $10 per person.

Getting Around: With 12,000 miles of roads, getting around the Dominican Republic can be achieved many different ways. You can rent a car from a major agency at the airports and in the larger cities. You'll need your driver's license and a major credit card. You'll also need good reflexes to deal with the frequent displays of driving machismo you will encounter. One fortunate thing: driving is (more or less) on the right side. Taxis are a safer bet, but are fairly expensive and are unmetered; you'll need to negotiate a price before you embark. A variety of buses are also available, from luxury lines to those with few creature comforts. The most basic transportation in the DR are the **guaguas,** unregulated taxi-buses which are usually crowded with locals. If you speak Spanish, riding the guaguas can be a good way to get the lowdown on what's happening.

Currency: Dominican Republic peso (US $1 = RD $16.25).

Electricity: 110 volts/60 cycles. Same as US.

Language: Spanish

Information: For information on Dominican Republic attractions, contact the Tourist Information Center in New York at 136 E. 57th St., Suite 803, New York 10022, ☎ 888-374-6361; fax 212-588-1015; in Miami at 2355 Salzedo St., Suite 307, Coral Gables, FL 33134, ☎ 888-358-9594 or 305-444-4592, fax 305-444-4845. In Canada: 35 Church St., Unit 53, Toronto, Ontario MSE IT3, ☎ 888-494-5050 or 416-361-2126, fax 416-361-2130. In the UK: 20 Hand Court, High Holborn, Lomdon WC1, or ☎ 0171-242-7778, fax 0171-405-4202. Websites: www.domrephotels.com.do; www.dr1.com/travel.html. Information from the Dominican Republic Embassy can be found at www.domrep.org.

Jamaica

*F*or us, Jamaica means romance. Maybe it's the mountains covered in lush tropical vegetation. Maybe it's the plush resorts where couples are greeted by an atmosphere that promises romance. Or maybe it's the people, who make visitors feel like they're returning home, a home where hummingbirds dart from bloom to bloom, where waters teeming with colorful marine life lie just steps from your room, where the island's own music makes nights pulsate with a tropical beat.

Jamaica was one of our first Caribbean destinations and a trip back is a homecoming for us. We try to make time for a meal at our favorite jerk joint and stop by our favorite souvenir stand, a bamboo hut painted in Rastafarian colors of gold, green, red and black. And, as we drive the sometimes bumpy roads filled with more-than-sometimes wild drivers, we pass by many of our favorite resorts and restaurants, and relive romantic times we've shared in Jamaica over the last decade.

We have to admit, however, that Jamaica is not for everyone. Many travelers prefer to skip this island because of the issues that inevitably reveal themselves even to the casual tourist.

The Islands

Drugs are a problem, and you will probably be approached by ganja-selling entrepreneurs. Although the resorts patrol their grounds and beaches above the high water line, when you step outside the boundaries of the resort, be prepared. "I have something special for you" is a frequently used line that you can ward off with a friendly but firm "No, thank you."

In general though, we've found that Jamaica has some of the friendliest inhabitants in the Caribbean. Service, even in all-inclusive resorts, is unsurpassable. Taxi drivers are proud to tell you about the island, and we've even had drivers jump out of the car and pick (legal) herbs and plants along the route to describe their uses in the Jamaican household.

Safety in Jamaica

Crime is a serious problem in Jamaica. Use the same precautions you'd exercise at home and then some. Crime is particularly a problem in Kingston, as in any metropolitan area. Around the rest of the island, make sure to use sensible precautions. As a tourist, you are viewed as wealthy in a country where poverty is rampant. We suggest that you consider traveling with licensed taxis (look for red PPV license plates to indicate reputable taxis) or tour companies. If you do experience crime, seek out the Jamaica police. To reach the police, dial 119 anywhere on the island, or call ☎ 0991-9999 for emergency help

---

The People

Jamaica's motto is "Out of Many, One People," and a quick look around the island confirms its multinational history. The predominately African heritage has mixed with that of South America, India, China, and Europe. Along with multi-ethnicity, you'll also see a mixture of city and country life throughout the nation as well. In **Montego Bay,** commerce with the rest of the world takes place in modern office buildings. Out on the roads that wind their way through the countryside, trade takes place from push carts made of discarded automobile parts. Transportation for many residents means walking, often with a load balanced on their heads, which they carry with the grace of ballet dancers.

Along those roads you'll see the diversity of Jamaican life as well. Around one bend lies a palatial home; around another corner a shanty without doors or windows. Towns are frenetic centers of activity, filled with pedestrians, street vendors, colorful fruit markets, and neighbors who take time to visit their friends as they go about their daily duties. Although the roads are rushed and filled with endless honking that is done, not out of anger, but as a warning, a hello, or just for the heck of it, Jamaicans often stop their vehicles to talk to someone in the oncoming lane; others politely wait for the conversation to end.

Diversity

As you wind through the communities in the Jamaican countryside, you'll notice the many churches in every small town. Religion is an important part of Jamaican life. The Church of Jamaica, formerly the Church of England, has the largest following. Methodists, Baptists, Presbyterians, Roman Catholics, Seventh Day Adventists, Christian Scientists, and other groups also have significant memberships. Rastafarianism, a religion centered around the divinity of the late Haile Selassie, emperor of Ethiopia, is also practiced. You'll see many dreadlocked Rastafarians (usually wearing crocheted tams) who are practitioners of this religion, which mandates vegetarianism, a strict code of peace, and, the best-known facet of the religion, the smoking of ganja or marijuana.

Jamaica's diversity comes from its visitors as well, guests from around the globe that make this tropical island home for a short while. Some of those visitors became residents, most notably Errol Flynn, Ian Fleming, and Noel Coward. Flynn came to the island in the 1940s and remained until his death in 1960, but not before he hit upon the idea of putting tourists on bamboo rafts on the Rio Grande. Today, this remains one of the most romantic rides in the Caribbean. Fleming, creator of the James Bond series, wrote from his home named "Goldeneye," located in Oracabessa near Ocho Rios. Today the home is owned by

The Islands

Chris Blackwell, founder of Island Records. At about the same period, Noel Coward arrived on the island, building a home named "Firefly" near Port Maria.

With such a group of stellar residents, it's not surprising that the island has always been a favorite with Hollywood movie producers. Some films produced here include *20,000 Leagues Under the Sea, Dr. No, Live and Let Die, Cocktail,* and, of course, *Cool Runnings,* the story of Jamaica's legendary Olympic bobsled team.

Geography

Because of its size, over 4,000 square miles, Jamaica has a little bit of everything: rivers, mountains, plains, forests, caves, and, of course, a beautiful coastline.

The most mountainous area is the eastern end, home of the Blue Mountains. This is the most rugged, unsettled region of the country, where the island's famous Blue Mountain coffee as well as the world's second-largest butterfly, the *Papilio homerus,* can be found. With peaks that top 7,500 feet above sea level, visitors can find themselves grabbing for a jacket.

The mountains run like a backbone down the island's center from east to west, and along the journey they create a quiltwork of 160 rivers and cascading waterfalls.

Jamaica is also a patchwork of communities. The capital city is **Kingston** on the south shore, a metropolitan area that's visited primarily for business rather than pleasure. The resort communities lie on the north shore. Quiet **Port Antonio,** once a hideaway for Hollywood stars, lies to the east. Heading west, the garden city of **Ocho Rios** is a favorite with couples. **Montego Bay,** or "Mo Bay," is the first taste most visitors have of the island, as it's home to the north shore airport. To the far west, **Negril,** once a hippie haven, is today the preferred vacation spot for anyone to enjoy its laid-back atmosphere and unbeatable sunset views.

Perhaps more than any other Caribbean island except St. Lucia, Jamaica is incredibly lush and fertile. Fruits, orchids, bromeliads, hardwoods, and ferns all thrive in this rich soil and bountiful environment. Sugar remains a major product, and during the summer months don't be surprised to see fires across the island as farmers burn off the stubble of harvested crops. During this time, the air sometimes becomes heavy with smoke and burnt sugar.

Festivals

There are always plenty of reasons to visit Jamaica; a full list of festivals gives couples even more excuses. One of the biggest is February's **Bob Marley Week** with Reggae Sunsplash. The memory of the reggae great is remembered with a week of activities.

One of the most elegant events is the **Sugar Cane Ball,** held in February at Round Hill Hotel in Montego Bay. For over two decades, this formal ball has raised money for local charities.

In April, Ocho Rios and Montego Bay celebrate with **Carnival.** Horse lovers can enjoy the **Red Stripe Horse Show** and **Gymkhana** at Chukka Cove in Ocho Rios, an annual event that brings in top riders from Jamaica, Europe, and the US.

Negril celebrates **Carnival** in May, adding further festivity to this already fun-loving town.

Summer brings plenty of music to the island, starting with the **Ocho Rios Jazz Festival** in June, with a week of international performers from the US, England, France, Holland, Japan, and the Caribbean. Jazz events take place in Ocho Rios as well as Montego Bay, with jazz teas, festivals on the river, barbecues, and more.

The biggest music event is August's **Reggae Sunsplash,** recognized around the globe as the top event for reggae buffs. Now held at Chukka Cove, the two decades-old event features performances by the top names in the world of reggae.

Following Reggae Sunsplash, **Reggae Sumfest** is held in Montego Bay, also featuring top performers.

Jamaican Jargon

Some travel writers claim that after a few days you'll understand the local patois. Forget it. Who would know that a bendung maaket is a sidewalk market, a place where you bend down or "bendung" to shop. Nyameat, an all-purpose word, can mean a person's posterior, a term of endearment, surprise, or even a negative description of someone's character. Use this one with care.

Here are a few other Jamaican patois terms:

a go foreign . . . . to leave Jamaica
batty . . . . bottom
boonoonunus . . . . wonderful, beautiful
duppy . . . . ghost
irie (eye-ree) . . . . all's well, good
mash up, winji . . . . sickly, tired
wagga wagga . . . . bountiful

Sweet Dreams

Price Chart

Rates reflect high winter season (expect prices to be as much as 40% lower during the off season) for a standard room for two adults for one night; prices are in US dollars.

$ . . . . under $150
$$ . . . . between $150 and $300
$$$ . . . . between $300 and $450
$$$$ . . . . over $450

Montego Bay

Breezes Montego Bay
Gloucester Avenue
☎ *876-940-1150; fax 876-940-1160*
Reservations: ☎ *877-GO-SUPER*
www.superclubs.com
$$

Part of the Breezes line, (SuperClubs' budget all-inclusives) this property has plenty of offerings to keep couples busy and, due to its proximity to the airport, it's convenient for those who'll be enjoying only a short Jamaica vacation.

Special Features/Activities: beachfront, all-inclusive, for adults over 16 only, fine and casual dining, watersports, tennis.

Coyaba Beach Resort and Club
North Coast Highway at Mahoe Bay
☎ *876-953-9150; fax 876-953-2244*
Reservations: ☎ *800-237-3237*
www.elegantresorts.com
$$$

This $10 million property has the feel of an intimate inn, but it offers the amenities of a larger resort. Located on a shady stretch of beach, Coyaba is a good option if you're seeking the niceties and luxuries of an exclusive retreat. The hotel offers all-inclusive deals or EP (European Plan or room only). The property features a plantation-style great house, where the main restaurant is located. Amenities include a freshwater pool, hot tub, massage, tennis, watersports and recreation room. Guest rooms are light and airy, decorated in an elegant tropical style with mahogany furniture. You'll be greeted by a basket of banana bread, a sweet introduction to this special property.

Special Features/Activities: pool, spa services, watersports, optional all-inclusive program, tennis, a dive shop, windsurfing.

Half Moon Golf, Tennis and Beach Club
North Coast Highway, 7 miles east of Montego Bay
☎ *876-953-2211; fax 876-953-2731*
Reservations: ☎ *800-237-3237*
www.halfmoon.com.jm
$$$$

Half Moon is considered to be one of Jamaica's most elegant resorts, the place to be pampered. A variety of room configurations is offered, everything from large guest rooms and junior suites to villas that look like something right out of Beverly Hills, complete with sweeping staircases, maids and butlers. The black and white décor, like everything in the resort, is ultra chic.

The Islands

Special Features/Activities: beachfront, 13 tennis courts, 39 swimming pools, croquet, horseback riding, bikes, squash, numerous restaurants, dive shop, kids program, shopping center.

The Imperial Suite.
Courtesy of Half Moon Golf, Tennis and Beach Club.

Holiday Inn SunSpree

PO Box 480, Rose Hall
☎ *876-953-2485; fax 876-953-2840*
Reservations: ☎ *800-HOLIDAY*
www.basshotels.com / holiday-inn
$$

Over a decade ago, we spent our honeymoon at this resort located on the outskirts of Mo Bay. At that time, it was a standard Holiday Inn, albeit one with a private white sand beach, live entertainment every night, and restaurants that introduced us to Caribbean cooking.

But today this hotel has become much more. Following a major recent renovation, the 516-room Holiday Inn SunSpree Resort is now all-inclusive, offering guests a package that includes all meals, drinks, non-motorized watersports, tennis, golf, daily activities, theme parties, shopping excursions, and a Rose Hall Great House tour.

Special Features/Activities: beachfront, all-inclusive, water-sports, fine and casual dining, freshwater pool, historic house tour.

♥ Round Hill Hotel and Villas

PO Box 64, Round Hill Bluff
☎ *876-956-7050; fax 876-956-7505*
Reservations: ☎ *800-972-2159*
www.roundhilljamaica.com
$$$

Located eight miles west of Montego Bay, this elegant resort is "old" Jamaica, a reminder of the time when guests came with their steamer trunks, brought the latest European fashions, and stayed for weeks. Today, this is where the rich and famous come to vacation; Ralph Lauren, Paul McCartney, and the Kennedys have signed the guest register at this exclusive resort. Add your name to this exclusive list.

Special Features/Activities: beachfront, tennis, freshwater pool, watersports.

♥ Sandals Montego Bay

PO Box 100, Kent Avenue, Montego Bay
☎ *876-952-5510; fax 876-952-0816*
Reservations: ☎ *800-SANDALS*
www.sandals.com
$$

The Sandals chain was started in 1981 by Gordon "Butch" Stewart with this resort located next to the city's Donald Sangster International Airport. The location has a potential negative, but Sandals turned the airport traffic to its advantage with its romantically minded guests: every time an airplane flies overhead, guests kiss their partner. With Jamaica's increasing popularity, there's a lot of smooching going on at Sandals. The kissing must be working; Sandals Montego Bay has the highest return guest rate within the chain.

Special Features/Activities: beachfront, all-inclusive, couples-only, casual and fine dining, freshwater pool, watersports.

The Islands

Sandals Royal Caribbean

PO Box 167, North Coast Highway
Mahoe Bay, Montego Bay
☎ *876-953-2231; fax 876-953-2788*
Reservations: ☎ *888-SANDALS*
www.sandals.com
$$

The atmosphere at nearby Sandals Royal Caribbean is slightly less lively than its neighbor, Sandals Montego Bay. What it may lack in liveliness, it more than makes up for in lavishness. Small touches – cool towels on the beach, herbal teas in the gym, aromatic saunas, continental room service – make this resort styled after a Jamaican plantation truly royal.

> *Sandals Royal boasts the only offshore restaurant in Jamaica. Bali Hai serves Indonesian cuisine in an authentic atmosphere. Guests are ferried out to the island (which by day doubles as a nude beach) to enjoy a multicourse meal served family-style. When the two of you arrive at the restaurant, the hostess offers two wraps for you to tie around each other's waist – simultaneously. It's a fun start to a romantic evening of dining by candlelight in a setting that's exotic and elegant.*

The Sandals Royal is one of our favorite properties in the Sandals chain both because of its very friendly staff and its stylish accommodations.

Special Features/Activities: beachfront, all-inclusive, couples-only, casual and fine dining, freshwater pool, watersports.

♥ Tryall Golf, Tennis, and Beach Club

PO Box 1206, North Coast Highway
☎ *876-956-5660; fax 876-956-5673*
Reservations: ☎ *800-742-0498*
www.tryallclub.com
$$$$

This 47-room, 49-villa property is one of the finest in Jamaica with rooms tucked in private villas (with pools) and a traditional greathouse. It is on the site of a former sugar plantation. Don't miss the water wheel (it's right on the road) which is a must for photographers. The 18-hole golf course located here was designed by Ralph Plummer and is considered one of the world's best. The course is home to the LPGA's Jamaica Classic and the Johnnie Walker World Championship.

Special Features/Activities: hillside, golf, pools, tennis, fine and casual dining.

Wyndham Rose Hall

North Coast Highway, 10 miles east of Montego Bay
☎ *876-953-2650; fax 876-953-2617*
Reservations: ☎ *800-996-3426*
www.wyndham.com
$$$

You can enjoy Wyndham Rose Hall on either a room-only basis or as an all-inclusive property. This sprawling resort is just a short drive from the airport, a real boon to those couples who have only three nights on the island. The resort recently underwent a major upgrade, equipping its guest rooms with new furniture, carpeting, 27-inch TVs with movie channels, and more. A golf course is located directly across the street and golfers are also able to use the nearby White Witch golf course at the Ritz-Carlton.

Special Features/Activities: extensive pool complex, watersports, spa services, restaurants, golf, tennis, optional all-inclusive program.

Negril

Beaches Negril

West End Road
☎ *876-957-9270; fax 876-957-9269*
Reservations: ☎ *800-BEACHES*
www.beaches.com
$$$$

Located on Long Bay, this all-inclusive is one of the newest members of the Sandals family. Unlike other Sandals resorts, however, Beaches is for everyone: families, singles and couples. The 225-room property includes five specialty restaurants and plenty of options for fun, ranging from scuba diving to video games at the Sega Center. This $25-million property is the answer to all those couples who enjoyed a vacation at Sandals and then wanted to take the kids back the next time. Beaches brings the all-inclusive fun couples-only resorts are famous for to everyone.

Special Features/Activities: beachfront, pool, watersports, restaurants.

♥ *The Caves*
West End Road
☎ *800-OUTPOST*
www.islandoutpost.com
$$$$

At this tranquil property, guests fall asleep to the sound of waves echoing through the namesake for this inn, sea caves formed from ancient volcanic rock and the pounding surf. In the daytime, vacationers leave one of the handcrafted cottages and snorkel among grottoes and caves or sun on the decks among the cliffs.

> *A special treat at the Caves is a massage in the sea cave, during which you can listen to the undulating waves. The resort offers Aveda services, from massage to an invigorating sea salt glow using salts from the Dead Sea.*

Breakfast and lunch are served beneath a thatched palapa and dinner is available by arrangement. The Caves also has a saltwater plunge pool and cliffside hot tub. Rooms are decorated with hand-carved furniture and center around a bed draped in mosquito netting. All rooms have CD/cassette players, TV/VCR, phone, and outdoor bamboo-enclosed shower.

Special Features/Activities: cliffside, restaurant, pool, spa.

♥ *Couples Negril*
Norman Manley Boulevard
Reservations: ☎ *800-268-7537*
www.couples.com
$$$$

This is the newest resort in Negril, a couples-only property that exudes a relaxed Caribbean atmosphere. Everything is included, from top-shelf liquors to watersports to transfers, as well as some off-property tours. Be sure to ask about the package deal, which combines a stay at Couples Ocho Rios with Couples Negril.

Special Features/Activities: beachfront, all-inclusive, restaurants, watersports.

Grand Lido Negril

PO Box 88, Norman Manley Boulevard
☎ *876-957-5010-4; fax 876-957-5517*
Reservations: ☎ *877-GO-SUPER*
www.superclubs.com
$$$

This resort, a study in elegance and style, is aimed at those looking for pampering and the highest quality service. From the marble entrance to the elegant columns, this resort is a step above a typical beachfront hotel. Standard offerings include 24-hour room service, private room valets, and direct dial phones.

Daily lessons are offered in snorkeling, scuba diving, tennis, and water skiing. For something less strenuous, there's the white sand beach (plus a nude beach) for lazy sunbathing or satellite TV back in the room. For the ultimate in pampering, guests can indulge with a complimentary manicure or pedicure.

Grand Lido faces the clear blue waters of Bloody Bay (named during the days when whalers cleaned their catch here), home of the MV *Zein*. This majestic 147-foot motorized yacht was once owned by Aristotle Onassis, who gave the yacht to Princess Grace as a wedding present. Today, guests enjoy cruises and even specially arranged parties and weddings aboard the honeymoon yacht.

Special Features/Activities: beachfront, all-inclusive, adults only, casual and fine dining, freshwater pool and hot tub, complete watersports facilities, nude beach.

The Islands

Hedonism II

PO Box 25, Westmoreland
☎ *876-957-5200; fax 876-957-5289*
Reservations: ☎ *877-GO-SUPER*
www.superclubs.com
$$

More than any other resort in the Caribbean, everyone asks us about Hedonism II. Maybe it's the name. Maybe it's the wild reputation for late-night revelry in the nude hot tub. Maybe it's the stories (not unfounded) of wild swingers' clubs that convene at the resort every year for annual conventions.

Whatever the reason, folks are curious about this Negril all-inclusive. We were as well. We checked in. Things looked pretty normal. Nice grounds. Nice room.

Then the maid knocked on the door and delivered white sheets. But these weren't for the bed. They were for us to wear to dinner that night.

> *Be warned: "No sheet, no eat" is the motto of the weekly toga party at this resort, known for its adults-only atmosphere.*

Hedonism II attracts fun-loving couples and singles over 18 who come to the westernmost point of Jamaica for a vacation of sun, sand, and something more. Guests come to leave their inhibitions behind, seeking pleasure in the form of festivities like Toga Night, buffets to tempt the most devoted calorie counters, bars that remain open until 5 am, and nonstop adult fun.

Hedonism's credo is that "A vacation should be whatever you want it to be," and for some that means a break from the cares, or even the clothes, of the everyday world.

Although some form of dress is required in the dining room (no need to worry about packing a dinner jacket for this resort), many guests wear only suntan oil and shades on the beach. The wide, white sand beach has room for everyone though, whether prude or nude. Half is "formal," with swimsuits required. The rest of the beach is reserved for those seeking the total tan. The nude beach also has its own hot tub, bar and grill cabanas, volleyball and shuffleboard courts, and its own swimming pool.

With its emphasis on unlimited pleasures, you might expect guests at Hedonism to be primarily college-aged. However, the average age here is 42. Over one-third of the guests are returnees, coming back year after year to partake of the food, fun and fantasy.

Nightly shows are organized by the resort's entertainment crew. Guests and staff strut their stuff during talent night, which might include an amateur strip-tease, flying through the air during the circus show, or bending over backwards for the limbo contest.

It's in these after-dark hours when the hedonists really get busy. Following the night's beach party, reggae dance, pajama party, or the ever-popular Toga Night, guests head to a disco that flashes with a $500,000 lighting system, or to the nude hot tub. Others hang out at the bars, open until just before the Caribbean sun peeks over the horizon at 5 am. (If you're staying at another Negril resort and want to see Hedonism II for yourself, you can buy an evening pass.)

Even members of the party-till-you-drop crowd eventually head back to their rooms, which at Hedonism are comfortable but not luxurious. Twin- and king-size beds are available. Rooms do not have balconies or patios, although some rooms face the beach. In keeping with the adult atmosphere, there is one special feature in the rooms: mirrored ceilings above every bed.

Special Features/Activities: beachfront, all-inclusive, adults only, freshwater pools, hot tubs, complete watersports facilities, nude beach.

♥ *Negril Cabins Resort*
PO Box 118, Norman Manley Boulevard
☎ *876-957-5350; fax 876-957-5381*
Reservations: ☎ *800-382-3444*
www.negrilcabins.com
$

Negril is bordered on the east by the Great Morass, a swampland rich with peat, a substance that was considered as a possible energy source in the 1970s when scientists studied the feasibility of mining this resource. Environmental concerns about the possibility of damaging Negril's famous Seven Mile Beach put a stop to the mining plans.

During the study of the Morass, researchers lived in cabins in Negril. Today, Negril Cabins utilizes those original structures plus several new buildings and operates as a resort for those who want to combine the luxuries of a hotel with the natural experience of camping. Visitors enjoy Swiss Family Robinson-style accommodations in cabins perched on stilts. Lush grounds are filled with indigenous Jamaican flora and fauna and dotted with colorful hummingbirds. Negril Cabins offers tours to the Royal Palms Reserve, located directly behind the property.

> *Inexpensive wedding packages are available at Negril Cabins Resort, which include license, minister or justice of the peace, a best man and maid of honor if needed, a Jamaican wedding cake, flowers, champagne, and dinner.*

Special Features/Activities: across the street from beach, fine and casual dining, freshwater pool.

♥ *Rockhouse*
West End Road
☎ *876-957-4373; fax 876-957-0557*
www.rockhousehotel.com
$$$

Just steps from busy West End Road, though once through the gates you'll feel that you are tucked away from the world. The restaurant and bar are perched high on Negril's bluffs and look directly out to sea and an unbeatable sunset. Rooms are constructed from wood, thatch and stone, like something out of *Gilligan's Island*. The natural theme of this resort is carried out in the open-air showers. This inn has studio rooms and a spectacular cliff-top pool. "We can give more individual service because we are not a 300-room hotel," explains the managing director of the 28-room resort. "What is special about this property is that it's situated on a pristine cove."

Special Features/Activities: cliffside, pool, restaurant.

♥ *Sandals Negril*

PO Box 12, Norman Manley Boulevard
☎ 876-957-5216; fax 876-957-5338
Reservations: ☎ 800-SANDALS
www.sandals.com
$$

On the southern side of Hedonism II lies Sandals, a couples-only resort that's especially popular with honeymooners because it is couples-only. Don't look for a nude beach here, but instead an atmosphere focused on couples in love. Within the Sandals chain, this location is also popular with sports-conscious guests because of its extensive watersports program.

Special Features/Activities: beachfront, all-inclusive, couples-only, fine and casual dining, watersports, freshwater pool.

Swept Away

PO Box 77, Norman Manley Boulevard
☎ 876-957-4061; fax 876-957-4060
Reservations: ☎ 800-545-7937
www.sweptaway.com
$$$

Swept Away, located on Negril's famous Seven Mile Beach, focuses on quiet relaxation for couples that are fitness and diet conscious. Sure, there are the requisite beach bars and buffets, but Swept Away also boasts a beachside veggie bar with pita sandwiches, grilled chicken, and pasta salads. It is known as one of the top sports destinations in the Caribbean. Courts for tennis, racquetball, squash, basketball, plus an Olympic-size pool, a fully equipped gym, and aerobics classes keep visitors busy.

But all work and no play does not a vacationer make, so Swept Away also emphasizes romance. The 20-acre property offers plenty of room for private walks through acres of tropical gardens where hummingbirds dart from hibiscus to bird-of-paradise blooms.

Special Features/Activities: beachfront, all-inclusive, couples-only, fine and casual dining, watersports, freshwater pool.

The Islands

Ocho Rios

Couples Ocho Rios

PO Box 30, St. Mary, North Coast Highway
☎ *876-975-4271; fax 876-975-4439*
Reservations: ☎ *800-COUPLES*
www.couples.com
$$$

Formerly part of the SuperClubs chain, this elegant all-inclusive has something for every couple. You can start the day with continental breakfast in bed or order from the 24-hour room service. Then head off to explore the sports offerings: scuba diving, water-skiing, windsurfing, canoeing, squash, racquetball, or horseback riding. The resort has professional class tennis courts (which host, appropriately enough, the Couples Cup, a professional doubles tennis tournament every year), not to mention plenty of more leisurely pursuits: daily trips to Dunn's River Falls, shuttles into Ocho Rios for duty-free shopping, glass-bottom boat reef excursions, and sunset catamaran cruises, all part of the all-inclusive package.

> *For those looking for a total tan, Couples has a small island to enjoy the tropical sun au naturel. You just catch the transfer right off the beach and head out for a day of sunning and swimming (in the sea or the pool) on the private island, which also has a full bar.*

Complimentary weddings are also part of the package and include the license, marriage official, flowers, two-tiered cake, sparkling wine, musical accompaniment, and use of either of two wedding gazebos.

Special Features/Activities: beachfront, all-inclusive, couples-only, freshwater pools, private island, horseback riding, watersports, tennis.

♥ Enchanted Garden

Eden Bower Road
☎ *876-974-1400; fax 876-974-5823*
Reservations: ☎ *800-554-2008*
$$$

This romantic resort is best known for its tropical gardens and waterfalls. It's set on the hillside, with the beach just a short shuttle ride away. There are 113 rooms and five restaurants.

Special Features/Activities: mountainside, restaurants, all-inclusive, tennis, fitness center, yoga, Tai Chi classes, bird feeding, non-motorized watersports.

♥ Grand Lido Sans Souci
PO Box 103, Ocho Rios
☎ 876-974-2353; fax 876-974-2544
Reservations: ☎ 877-GO-SUPER
www.superclubs.com
$$$

Like Grand Lido in Negril, this property is SuperClubs' top-of-the line all-inclusive. The two of you will be pampered from the moment you arrive with gourmet meals, 24-hour room service, a nightclub and plenty of activity. Located on a beautiful swath of beach, the resort also has mineral springs that fill the swimming pool and hot tub.

> According to legend, those springs were shared by an English admiral and a Spanish maiden, and today lovers who dip in their waters will feel the power of their forbidden love. Sounds like it's worth checking out.

Elegant and sophisticated, this resort is for those ready to feel special.

Special Features/Activities: beachfront, all-inclusive, adults only, casual and fine dining, swimming pool with natural mineral water, nude beach, spa, golf, tennis, watersports.

Jamaica Inn
PO Box 1
☎ 876-974-2514; fax 876-974-2449
Reservations: ☎ 800-837-4608
www.jamaicainn.com
$$$$

Enjoy an old-money atmosphere at this elegant inn that recalls the sophisticated days of Caribbean travel. This is the kind of

The Islands

place where jackets come out in the evening hours and afternoon fun might include a round of croquet or high tea.

Special Features/Activities: beachfront, fine dining, pool.

Renaissance Jamaica Grande Resort
Main Street
☎ *876-974-2201; fax 876-974-5378*
Reservations: ☎ *800-HOTELS1*
www.renaissancehotel.com
$$-$$$

This sprawling hotel has the largest meeting space in Ocho Rios and hosts many meetings and conventions. Many convention-eers bring along spouses and children, who find plenty of activity. But there are plenty of reasons for couples to stay at Jamaica Grande. We enjoyed a beautiful seaside room here.

Downtown is just a short walk away. A protected beach offers calm, quiet waters for an afternoon swim. The swim-up bar in the pool sits beneath a 26-foot replica of Dunn's River Falls.

The resort features two towers of rooms, but our choice would be the cabana rooms, located on the beach. Lower floor rooms step right out onto the sand.

Special Features/Activities: beachfront, pool, numerous restaurants, watersports, downtown location.

♥ Sandals Dunn's River
PO Box 2, St. Ann, North Coast Highway
☎ *876-972-1610; fax 876-972-1611*
Reservations: ☎ *800-SANDALS*
www.sandals.com
$$

Sandals Dunn's River is the largest of the Jamaica hotels, a high-rise by island standards with 256 rooms. Built in Italian Renaissance style, the resort has lavish public areas, including two swim-up bars, a replica of Dunn's River Falls, four restaurants, a disco and the Forum, used for cabaret-style shows.

Special Features/Activities: beachfront, all-inclusive, couples-only, casual and fine dining, watersports, freshwater pool with waterfall.

♥ *Sandals Ocho Rios*
PO Box 771, Main Street, St. Ann
☎ *876-974-5691; fax 876-974-5700*
Reservations: ☎ *800-SANDALS*
www.sandals.com
$$

Just down the road from Sandals Dunn's River, Sandals Ocho Rios is one of the most romantic resorts in the chain, located on lavishly planted grounds that bloom with bird of paradise and buzz with the sound of hummingbirds. Sandals' founder Butch Stewart grew up on these grounds; the building used for the piano bar was once his grandparents' home.

Special Features/Activities: beachfront, all-inclusive, couples-only, casual and fine dining, watersports, freshwater pool.

Outlying Ocho Rios Areas

Breezes at Runaway Bay
PO Box 58, St. Mary, Ocho Rios
☎ *876-973-2436; fax 876-973-2352*
Reservations: ☎ *877-GO-SUPER*
www.superclubs.com
$$

Formerly known as Jamaica-Jamaica, this resort is especially well suited to sports-minded couples. Just across the road from the resort, golfers can enjoy golf school or a round on the beautiful 18-hole course, which includes spectacular sea views.

Special Features/Activities: beachfront, all-inclusive, over 16 only, fine and casual dining, watersports, golf.

♥ *Grand Lido Braco Village Resort*
West of Runaway Bay on North Coast Highway
☎ *76-954-0000; fax 876-954-0020*
Reservations: ☎ *877-GO-SUPER*
www.superclubs.com
$$$$

New to the SuperClubs chain, this resort was built with the purpose of re-creating a Jamaican village, and you'll find every-

one from a peanut man offering fresh roasted goodies to a jerk cook to a woodcarver. The resort is built around a town square with cafés, art stores and a friendly feel. It's no substitute for getting out and experiencing a real Jamaican village, but for first-timers it can be educational and fun. There's also a full array of all-inclusive diversions: tennis, soccer, golf, beaches and watersports.

Special Features/Activities: beachfront, pools, restaurants, all-inclusive, adults only, nude beach, watersports, tennis, golf.

Hedonism III
Runaway Bay
☎ *876-973-4100; fax 876-973-5402*
Reservations: ☎ *877-GO-SUPER*
www.superclubs.com
$$-$$$

This all-inclusive resort is the sister to Negril's Hedonism II, although it has its own distinct atmosphere. Here the emphasis is on activity, whether that comes in the form of the circus workshop, scuba diving, sailing or more hedonistic pursuits. Rooms at this newly constructed resort are luxurious, with two-person whirlpools (with a mirrored ceiling, of course). You'll also find swim-up rooms (the first in Jamaica), a nude beach, nude pool, waterslide, and more.

Special Features/Activities: four restaurants, five bars, two grills, two hot tubs, three pools, dive shop, dance club.

Port Antonio

Goblin Hill Villas at San San
Drapers
☎ *876-925-8108; fax 876-925-6248*
Reservations: ☎ *800-472-1148*
$$$

Goblin Hill overlooks San San Bay, Port Antonio's beautiful harbor, and offers its guests peace and quiet. The 28 villas include the services of a housekeeper/cook who will prepare any of your favorite dishes. The villas are a short walk away from the water.

Special Features/Activities: overlooks water, gardens, pool, tennis.

Hotel Mocking Bird Hill
Point Ann
☎ *876-993-7267; fax 876-993-7133*
www.hotelmockingbirdhill.com
$$-$$$

This 10-room hotel is often cited for its eco-friendly policies, solar energy use, locally made furniture, and natural landscaping. Even the restaurant, the excellent Mille Fleurs, features local produce.

> *This property is very popular with eco-tourists and offers many tours that explore the natural attractions of the Port Antonio area.*

Special Features/Activities: restaurant, hiking, gardens.

Trident Villas and Hotel
PO Box 119
☎ *876-993-2602; fax 876-993-2590*
Reservations: ☎ *800-742-4276*
www.tridentjamaica.com
$$$

With only 26 rooms, this intimate hotel makes visitors feel like royalty, from afternoon tea to white-glove service. Each of the rooms is decorated with antiques.

Special Features/Activities: cliffside, casual and fine dining, freshwater pool, tennis, private beach.

Tables for Two

Jamaican cuisine is among the most flavorful in the Caribbean. Spicy dishes trace their origin back to the earliest days of the island when the Arawak Indians first barbecued meats. Distinctive seasonings were developed by Africans who came to the island as slaves in the days of Spanish rule. In the 17th century, English influences developed the Jamaican pattie, a turnover filled with spicy meat that's a favorite lunch snack with locals.

A century later, Chinese and East Indian influences made their way to Jamaica, when indentured laborers who replaced slaves after emancipation also brought their own culinary talents. Today, curried dishes grace nearly every Jamaican menu, using local meats such as goat, chicken, and seafood.

For breakfast, the national dish is **ackee and saltfish**. Ackee is a small fruit that is harvested only when it bursts and reveals its black seeds; before that time the fruit is poisonous. When ackee is cooked, it resembles and tastes much like scrambled eggs.

But the best single Jamaican dish, at least for us, is **jerk**. Meat – pork, chicken, or fish – is marinated with a fiery mixture of spices that includes Scotch bonnet, a pepper that makes a jalapeño seem like a marshmallow, pimento or allspice, nutmeg, scallion, and thyme. It's all served up with even more hot sauce (use with caution!), rice and peas, and a wonderful bread called **festival,** similar to hush puppies. Wash it all down with a cold Red Stripe beer. Ya, mon!

Price Chart

Restaurant prices are for dinner per person, including a drink, appetizer or salad, and entrée.

$. . . . . under $15
$$ . . . . $15 to $30
$$$ . . . . $30 to $45
$$$$ . . . . over $45

Montego Bay

♥ *Ambrosia*
Wyndham Rose Hall , North Coast Highway
☎ *876-953-2605*
Dress code: dressy
Reservations: required
$$$$

Located at the golf club across the street from Wyndham Rose
Hall, this elegant eatery features Mediterranean cuisine served
in a beautiful garden setting. Closed Wednesdays.

> *Set off with tiny white lights, Ambrosia's dining area
> is a good spot for a romantic dinner out.*

♥ Belfield 1794
Barnett Estate, Granville Main Rd.
☎ *876-952-2382*
Dress code: dressy
Reservations: required
$$$$

This elegant restaurant, located on the 3,000-acre Barnett Estate near Montego Bay on Granville Main Road, is operated by
Elegant Resorts International. The open-air restaurant features a view of the city and a menu that combines a taste of Jamaica and the Caribbean. Selections include spicy ackee
tomato salsa on smoked marlin, plantation salad, jerk pork Belfield, steamed fish Port Royal, as well as a sweet potato pudding.

> *After your meal at Belfield 1794, enjoy a leisurely
> stroll over to the greathouse. The restored historic site
> is open to visitors; guided tours are available before or
> after dinner.*

Richmond Hill Inn
Union Street
☎ *876-952-3859*
Dress code: casually elegant
Reservations: suggested
$$-$$$

The view from this restaurant alone makes the trip to Richmond Hill Inn worthwhile. The open-air restaurant serves up a
variety of continental and Jamaican fare, all enjoyed with a
beautiful view of the city lights and the bay.

The Islands

Sakura Japanese Restaurant
North Coast Highway, Half Moon Village
☎ *876-953-9686*
Dress code: dressy or casually elegant
Reservations: required
$$$$

This restaurant features hibachi grill-top cooking at your table. With his flying knives, the chef will prepare a delicious meal of seafood, steak or chicken. The food is as good as the spectacular show.

Negril

Cosmo's Seafood Restaurant and Bar
Norman Manley Boulevard
☎ *876-957-4330*
Dress code: casual
Reservations: optional
$$$

Cosmo's is a long-time favorite with Negril travelers looking for good seafood. The super-casual restaurant is located right on the beach, and folks wander in and out on their way to the sand and sea.

Rick's Café
West End Road
☎ *876-957-0380*
$$

Rick's, known as Negril's top sunset bar, is also a popular restaurant. Burgers, filet mignon, kingfish, broiled lobster, jerk chicken, coco bread pizza and blackened chicken breast are served in the open-air dining room. It's not the best restaurant in Negril and definitely not the place to go for a quiet, romantic dinner (the daredevils jumping off the cliffs take care of that), but it is always a fun hangout and a terrific spot to watch the sunset.

Rockhouse Restaurant and Bar
West End Road, Rockhouse
☎ *876-957-4373*
Dress code: casual
Reservations: optional
$$

Breakfast, lunch and dinner are served at this open-air eatery. It's just steps from busy West End Road but, once through the gates at Rockhouse and seated beneath the restaurant's thatched roof, you are tucked away from the world. The restaurant and bar are perched high on Negril's bluffs and look directly out to sea and an unbeatable sunset. Jamaican cuisine with European influences is the specialty here.

Ocho Rios

Jamaica Inn
North Coast Highway, two miles east of Ocho Rios
☎ *876-974-2514; fax 876-974-2449*
Dress code: dressy; jacket and tie required, except in summer
Reservations: required
$$$$

Chef Wilbert Matheson serves up varied fare in this al fresco restaurant. No children under age 14 are permitted to dine here, as the restaurant strives for an elegant atmosphere. Some of the most tempting entreés are grilled beef tenderloin topped with chicken liver compote, poached yellowtail tuna with steamed mussels and tomato concasse, and pork loin with a pineapple and honey glaze.

Plantation Inn
Main Street
☎ *876-974-5601*
Dress code: dressy
Reservations: required
$$$$

This elegant restaurant has been a favorite with Jamaica vacationers for over four decades. Guests can start their day with breakfast served on their ocean-view balcony, complete with

The Islands

starched linens and silver. Or they can opt to eat in the main dining room with local specialties such as ackee and codfish, liver and bananas, pan-fried fish, or eggs, pancakes and freshly-baked breads. This inn is open to the public for meals.

♥ *The Ruins*
DaCosta Drive
☎ *876-974-2442*
Dress code: casually elegant
Reservations: suggested
$$-$$$

The menu here is diverse: Oriental specialties such as lotus lily lobster and Far Eastern chicken, Jamaican specials, and even vegetarian dishes are available.

The site of the restaurant has an interesting history. In 1831, Englishman Robert Rutherford built a sugar factory near these falls, using their energy to grind the cane. Allegedly, he married a local girl named Rose Dale and they moved into a great house near the falls. Later, while Rutherford was in England on business, Rose fell in love with one of the plantation's overseers. When her husband returned home, he learned of his wife's indiscretions and began seeing Annie Palmer, better known as the White Witch of Rose Hall (see page 234) in Montego Bay. One night, after finding his wife with her lover, Rutherford took them to a cave between the falls, chained them to the wall, and sealed the cave with a boulder. Later Rutherford married Annie Palmer and the plantation became, literally, ruins.

The Ruins is perched right beside a waterfall. Tables sit at the base of a 40-foot cascade, a wonderfully romantic site for lunch or dinner.

Port Antonio

♥ *Mille Fleurs*
Hotel Mocking Bird Hill
☎ *876-993-7267 or 993-7134*
Dress code: dressy
Reservations: required
$$$-$$$$

Sit on the terrace surrounded by tropical vegetation and enjoy the sunset (manager Shireen Aga recommends that guests arrive by 6 pm to enjoy cocktails and a sunset view). The restaurant offers an à la carte menu that changes daily. Lunch is served from noon to 2 pm; dinner starts at 7 pm, with the last order taken at 9:30. Some of the interesting entrées served here include chicken in June plum sauce; grilled fish with spicy mango-shrimp sauce; and spiced fish with tamarind and coconut sauce.

Mille Fleurs overlooks Port Antonio and the Caribbean Sea, and is a romantic favorite.

● *Trident Restaurant*
Trident Villas and Hotel, Point Ann
☎ *876-993-2602*
Dress code: dressy; jackets required
Reservations: required
$$$$

If you're ready for an extra-special night out, Trident is the place to go. Dinners here are enjoyed by candlelight and served on fine china and crystal.

Continental and Jamaican entrées are prepared by European-trained chefs at one of Jamaica's most elegant restaurants. Can't afford the dinner here? Do like we did: come for lunch. The view is beautiful, you'll have a chance to see the resident peacock, and you'll experience the property at far lower prices.

Romantic Activities

With its lush tropical setting, anything can be a romantic activity in Jamaica: walking from your room to the restaurant; listening to the pip of tiny tree frogs hidden in the dense foliage at night; or sitting beneath a tall cotton tree and thinking of the centuries that the magnificent tree has witnessed.

The Islands

Golf

Golf lovers have courses to challenge even the most dedicated. The best-known course, and the home of the PGA World Championship, is the **Tryall Golf Club** (☎ 876-956-5660) in Montego Bay. Other top courses include **Half Moon Golf Course** (☎ 876-953-2211) and **Ironshore Golf and Country Club** (☎ 876-953-2800) in Montego Bay; **Runaway Bay Golf Club** (☎ 876-973-4820); and **Negril Hills Golf Club** (☎ 876-957-4638), just southeast of downtown Negril.

Underwater Delights

If golf's not your game, how about diving? The Negril area is especially popular with excellent visibility. **Montego Bay** and **Runaway Bay,** near Ocho Rios, also offer top diving.

For diving in Montego Bay, call:

> **Fun Divers.** ☎ 876-953-2650
>
> **Poseidon Divers.** ☎ 876-952-3624
>
> **North Coast Marine Sports.** ☎ 876-953-2211

In Ocho Rios, call:

> **Couples Ocho Rios.** ☎ 876-975-4271
>
> **Fantasea.** ☎ 876-974-2552
>
> **Garfield's Dive Station.** ☎ 876-974-5794
>
> **Jamaqua Dive Centre.** ☎ 876-973-4845
>
> **Resort Divers.** ☎ 876-974-5338
>
> **Reef Divers.** ☎ 876-973-4400

In Negril, call:

> **Blue Whale Divers.** ☎ 876-957-4438
>
> **Hedonism II.** ☎ 876-957-4200
>
> **Marine Life Ventures.** ☎ 876-957-4834
>
> **Negril Scuba Centre.** ☎ 876-957-4425

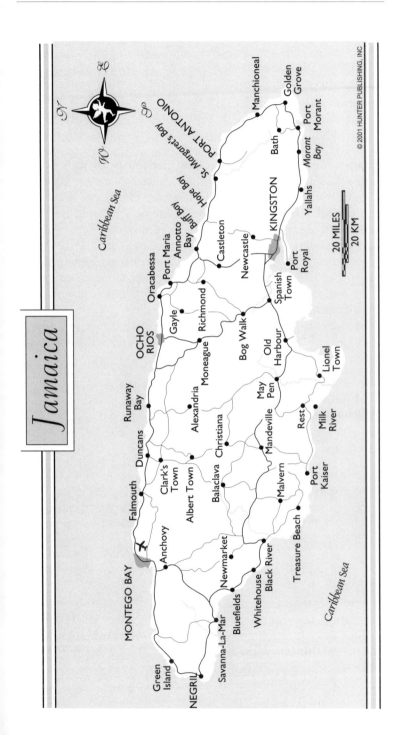

Jamaica

The Islands

MONTEGO BAY

NEGRIL

OCHO RIOS

PORT ANTONIO

KINGSTON

Caribbean Sea

Caribbean Sea

© 2001 HUNTER PUBLISHING, INC

20 MILES
20 KM

St. Margaret's Bay
Hope Bay
Buff Bay
Annotto Bay

Manchioneal
Golden Grove
Port Morant
Morant Bay
Bath
Yallahs
Port Royal
Newcastle
Castleton
Spanish Town
Port Maria
Oracabessa
Gayle
Richmond
Bog Walk
Old Harbour
Lionel Town
Moneague
Alexandria
May Pen
Rest
Milk River
Runaway Bay
Christiana
Mandeville
Duncans
Clark's Town
Albert Town
Balaclava
Malvern
Port Kaiser
Falmouth
Anchovy
Newmarket
Treasure Beach
Black River
Whitehouse
Bluefields
Savanna-La-Mar
Green Island

> *Warning: In every resort area, be prepared for numerous offers by **higglers**, Jamaica's word for peddlers. Also be ready for offers of "something special." Ganja or marijuana is widespread, but purchase or use of the drug is strictly illegal.*

Ocho Rios Sights

In Ocho Rios, the most popular attraction is **Dunn's River Falls.** This spectacular waterfall is actually a series of falls that cascade from the mountains to the sea. Here, you don't just view the falls, but you climb up the cascading water. Led by a sure-footed Jamaican guide (who wears everyone's cameras slung around his neck), groups work their way up the falls hand in hand like a human daisy chain. You'll be assigned a guide who will escort the entire group; tips are accepted. Be prepared to get wet and have fun, but don't expect a quiet, private getaway. This is Jamaica for the masses and, no matter what day of the week, the masses do come. At the end of the climb, you'll be deposited into a hectic market for an opportunity to buy crafts, carvings, and the ubiquitous T-shirt.

West of Ocho Rios in the town of Oracabessa, 007 fans can visit the **James Bond Beach.** Located near Ian Fleming's home, Goldeneye, the beach has plenty of options for a day of activity: waverunners, helicopter tours, and horseback rides, as well as a beach bar and grill.

If you're serious about horseback riding, check out the **Chukka Cove Equestrian Centre** (☎ 876-972-2506) between Runaway Bay and Ocho Rios. Well known for its world-class polo matches, the center also offers guided horseback trips along the beach and in the mountains.

Montego Bay Sights

Several greathouses, which once oversaw huge sugar plantations, are today notable visitor attractions. **Rose Hall** is one of the best-known and is an easy afternoon visit for Montego Bay guests. This was once the home of the notorious Annie Palmer, better known as the White Witch. According to legend, Annie murdered several of her husbands and her slave lovers.

You can pick up a copy of the novel *The White Witch of Rose Hall*, in bookstores around the island.

Eco-tourists will also find plenty of nature-related attractions that lie off the beaten path. Bird lovers should make a stop at the **Rocklands Bird Sanctuary** (☎ 876-952-2009), in the village of Anchovy. This is the home of octogenarian Lisa Salmon, Jamaica's best-known amateur ornithologist. Her home is a veritable bird sanctuary surrounded by grassquits, saffron finches and, most notable, hummingbirds. Through the years, Salmon and her guides have hand-fed the birds, even the tiny hummers. Visitors can come by during the afternoons, have a seat on the patio, and hand-feed the regular guests of this bird diner. You can even hold a bottle of sugar water and have the fast-as-lightning hummingbirds feed just inches from your face. This is truly a once-in-a-lifetime experience that any nature lover should plan to enjoy. Visitors are invited between 3:30 and 5 pm.

Negril Sights

Negril visitors don't have to venture all the way to Ocho Rios to enjoy waterfalls. Western Jamaica has a much quieter alternative in **Y.S. Falls** (☎ 876-997-6055, admission charged). These spectacular waterfalls cascade in steps through the tropical forest. As spectacular (and far less crowded) as Dunn's River Falls, Y.S. is a Jamaican attraction that has remained untouched by hassling vendors and long lines. At the top, swimmers enjoy clear waters under a canopy of fern. The falls have been open to the public since the late '80s, but the property has existed as a farm since 1684.

> *Some say the falls' unusual name (the shortest place name in Jamaica) came from the Gaelic word wyess, meaning winding or twisting. Others believe the name was formed from the initials of the farm's original two owners: John Yates and Lt. Col. Richard Scott.*

Nearby in the community of Black River, enjoy the **Black River Safari Cruise,** ☎ 876-965-2514, a popular day-trip for Negril vacationers looking for a little respite from sun and sand. This 1½-hour tour takes travelers up the Black River (at 44 miles, the longest river in Jamaica). The waters are home to

The Islands

snook and tarpon, some reaching as large as 200 pounds. You may see spear fishermen with a snorkel, mask and speargun, swimming in the dark water stained by peat deposits. The fishermen's canoes are hand-hewn and burned out using a generations-old technique. Among the catch are tiny brine shrimp, sold by women in the St. Elizabeth parish along the roadside. Highly salted and spiced, these are a popular snack with locals and visitors.

> *Crocodiles are the biggest attraction on the Black River. Once hunted, the crocodiles are now protected. These reptiles can live as long as 100 years, so long that some have become known by local residents. One 15-foot-long specimen named Lester is seen nightly.*

You'll also find plenty of opportunities to get out on the water aboard sunset cruises, most with an open bar. During the day, catamaran trips take visitors out to small offshore cays. For cruises, call **Calico Sailing Cruises,** ☎ 876-954-2565.

For a look at the countryside around Negril the way it used to be, consider at day at **Belvedere Estate,** one of the first sugarcane plantations on the island. Located an hour from town, the estate is set up as a living museum with costumed guides to show you the ruins of the 1800s great house, the sugar factory, and the boiler where the juice of the cane is made into brown sugar. In the craft village, watch a weaver make coconut palms into baskets, talk to an herbalist about Jamaica's bountiful herbs, visit a canoe maker, and have a taste of island bread at the bakery. A traditional Jamaican lunch is included with the tour. For reservations, call ☎ 876-952-6001 or 957-4170.

Port Antonio Sights

The top activity in quiet Port Antonio is a romantic raft ride aboard a bamboo float powered by a pole-maneuvering captain. If at all possible, take the two- to three-hour excursion down the Rio Grande; it's an experience the two of you won't forget. Call **Rio Grande Rafting,** ☎ 876-993-5778, for reservations.

Nearby, **Boston Beach** is the place to go on the island for jerk, slow cooked in pits.

Cool off with a dip in the **Blue Lagoon** (remember the Brooke Shields movie of the same name?). The beautiful swimming hole that's been termed "bottomless" because of its uncanny blue hue is actually a lagoon about 180 feet deep.

Shopping

Our favorite Jamaica purchases are wood carvings, Some are freestanding; others are bas relief pieces featuring local animal life, faces, fish, and just about everything else you can imagine. The finest pieces are carved from *lignum vitae*, or "wood of life," a pale hardwood that is so dense it won't float, sold by many vendors as well as in shops.

You'll find traditional shopping centers with the finest items: jewelry, china, crystal, collectible figurines, watches, and more. Prices are firm, just like at home. In **Montego Bay,** the top shopping centers are **City Centre,** a block-long collection of duty-free shops; **Holiday Village Shopping Centre,** near Holiday Inn SunSpree; and the luxurious **Half Moon Shopping Village,** a compendium of fine stores where you'll find shops selling designer wear, fine jewelry, perfumes, resort wear, local crafts, and more.

In **Negril,** the **Hi-Lo Shopping Center** offers a good selection of souvenirs, liquor, music, and sportwear stores. The Hi-Lo grocery itself is an excellent shopping stop; pop in to purchase spices, hot sauces, liquor, and Blue Mountain coffee at prices far lower than you'll see in the hotel gift shops.

Ocho Rios is home to the **Taj Mahal Shopping Centre,** a complex of fine duty-free shops and other stores that sell souvenir items, liquor, and Blue Mountain coffee.

Jamaican Blue Mountain coffee is considered one of the finest coffees in the world. Gift shops at the resorts and the airport sell the coffee in small burlap gift bags for about US $1 per ounce (less than half the price found in American coffee shops). You can find the coffee even cheaper at local markets.

Jamaica's rums and liqueurs are also popular souvenirs. **Appleton** and **Myers's Rum, Tia Maria** coffee liqueur, and **Red Stripe** beer are sold throughout the island. Each visitor

The Islands

can return to the US with one liter without paying duty charges.

Nightlife

For most vacationers, nightlife is found in the resorts, most which feature nightly shows ranging from reggae performers to SuperClubs' Elvis impersonator (don't laugh – he's good!) to "island night," featuring fire eaters, limbo dancers, and contortionists.

Those looking for something else will find plenty, though. In Negril, evenings start about an hour before sunset at **Rick's,** ☎ 876-957-0380, the most popular sunset spot on the island. Located on the cliffs of the town's West End, this open-air restaurant and bar is a favorite with American visitors. The action starts with daredevil cliff divers who leap from the rocky crags into the aquamarine depths below, to the cheers of onlookers.

> *As the sun begins to set, the attention turns to the west and couples look for the green flash, a natural phenomenon that only occurs when the sun sets on a cloudless evening. Under the right conditions, you can see a momentary green sizzle on the horizon. Science explains this as the refraction of sunlight through the thick lens of the Earth's atmosphere. Island lore links it to romance: couples who witness the flash are guaranteed true love.*

In **Negril,** probably the most festive of the resort areas, you can boogie down until the wee hours with a night pass at **Hedonism II** (call ☎ 876-957-4200 to reserve this popular, but pricey, night pass). A half-million dollar disco pulsates until 5 am with laser effects, flashing lights, and all kinds of music.

In **Montego Bay,** a popular night excursion is **An Evening on the Great River,** ☎ 876-952-5047, held every Sunday and Thursday. Beginning with pick up at your hotel, the evening includes a boat ride up the torch-lit river, an open bar, Jamaican dinner, reggae band, and a native floor show with limbo dancers.

Mo Bay is also the home of **Lollypop,** ☎ 876-953-5413, an open-air bar on Sandy Bay. This popular spot has reggae shows and also a "Jamaica night" weekly with a local cuisine buffet.

Just the Facts

Entry Requirements: Visitors from the US, UK, or Canada need their passport or proof of citizenship: either a certified birth certificate or voter registration card and a photo ID.

Getting Around: Taxis are the easiest mode of travel and can be obtained at any resort. Look for red PPV license plates; these indicate legitimate taxis. Agree on the price with the driver before you depart.

Rental cars are pricey, and are available from most major rental companies. You must be 25 years of age to rent a car and also show a valid driver's license and a major credit card. The speed limit is 30 mph in town and 50 mph on the highways, but be warned: Jamaica has some wild drivers! We've often seen two cars passing an auto at the same time. On top of that, you'll be driving on the left side of the road and dealing with round-abouts at every intersection.

Language: English

Currency: Jamaican dollar, fluctuates with the US dollar.

Electricity: 110 volts

Information: For more information on Jamaica, contact the Jamaican Tourist Board at 866 Second Avenue, 10th Floor, New York, NY 10017, call ☎ 800-233-4582. Miami: 1320 S. Dixie Highway, Suite 1101, Coral Gables, FL 33146, ☎ 305-665-0557, fax 305-666-7239. Chicago: 500 N. Michigan Ave., Suite 1030, Chicago 60611, ☎ 312-527-1296, fax 312-527-1472. Los Angeles: 3440 Wilshire Boulevard, Suite 805, Los Angeles 90010, ☎ 213-384-1123, fax 213-384-1180. Canada: 1 Eglinton Ave. East, Suite 616, Toronto, Ontario M4P 3A1, ☎ 416-482-7850, fax 416-482-1730.Website: www.jamaicatravel.com.

The Islands

Puerto Rico

Ready for a fiesta? Then set your sights on Puerto Rico. In the capital city of **San Juan,** you'll find a pulsating atmosphere that can't be topped anywhere in the Caribbean. Casinos ring with the clink of slots; showgirls kick up their heels in lavish revues; couples jump out on the dance floor and shake to the sounds of salsa and merengue.

Beyond the boundaries of San Juan, the sounds change to the slap of waves on the honey-colored shore or the peep of the tiny *coqui* (co-kee), a frog that's a national symbol of Puerto Rico. (It's said that the coqui can survive only on the island, so to be as Puerto Rican as a coqui is a declaration of national pride.)

Puerto Rico is an easy destination to like. It's simple to reach – just 2½ hours from Miami and under four hours from New York; there's a wide variety of attractions no matter what your interest; it's still in the United States, while at the same time offering all the intrigue of a foreign destination.

Geography

Your first introduction to Puerto Rico will probably be arrival in San Juan. This high-rise city hugs the coastline like a Caribbean version of Miami Beach (but with casinos) and offers all the amenities you'd expect in a metropolitan area this size. It's so large that it's divided into several districts. Tourists typically visit **Condado, Isla Verde,** and **Old San Juan,** the historical heart of the city. Here you'll find buildings so old and quaint they look more like a movie set than a modern downtown district.

Mountains form a rugged ridge from east to west. These mountains, the **Cordillera Central** and the **Sierra de Luquillo,** loom at about 3,000 feet above sea level and ease into rolling hills before reaching the coastal plains. The rainiest area is in the northeastern mountains in **El Yunque** rain forest, an area rich with tropical flora ranging from breadfruit to mahogany trees to orchids. On the opposite end of this large island, the southwestern side, you'll see cacti and succulents, because the area receives only a fraction of the rain forest's total precipitation.

Rincón, on the island's northwestern end, is the surfing capital of the Caribbean. From January through April, those surfers are joined by migratory humpback whales, so even if you're not ready to hang 10, the two of you can head out from Rincón on a whale-watching excursion.

Off Puerto Rico's shores, the islands of **Mona, Culebra,** and **Vieques** offer quiet getaways for those willing to take an extra hop.

Festivals

If you're looking for a party, you're in luck: Puerto Rico enjoys fiestas throughout the year. In February, the **Coffee Harvest Festival** celebrates the end of the coffee harvest in the mountain town of Maricao, the capital of the coffee-growing region.

Classical music is the focus of the **Casals Festival** in late June and early July. Honoring the late cellist and composer Pablo Casals, this event features a month of romantic music.

If you're more interested in art, make plans to attend the **Barranquitas Artisans' Fair** in mid-July, the oldest crafts fair in Puerto Rico. Shoppers will find everything from carvings to pottery to musical instruments for sale, plus plenty of local food and folk music to enjoy.

In late July, the town of Loiza, on the northeast end of the island, celebrates its African heritage with the **Loiza Carnival.** Look for parades, colorful floats, pulsating music, folk masks, and bomba (an Afro-Caribbean dance rhythm) dancers at this lively festival.

Folkloric and classical music, ballet, modern dance, and musical theater are featured during the **Inter-American Festival of the Arts,** held in late September in San Juan. In early November, the **Festival of Puerto Rican Music** highlights classical and folk music. A special contest at this festival features the cuatro, a 10-stringed instrument shaped like a small guitar.

The Islands

Christmas shoppers find over 100 artists and craftsmen selling their work at the **Bacardi Artisans' Fair,** held on the grounds of the Bacardi rum plant in Cataño in early December. Along with plenty of shopping opportunities, the fair also includes a troubadour contest, rides, and plenty of old-fashioned Puerto Rican fun.

Contact the **Puerto Rico Tourism Company,** ☎ 800-223-6350, for details on these events.

Sweet Dreams

Price Chart

Rates reflect high winter season (expect prices to be as much as 40% lower during the off season) for a standard room for two adults for one night; prices are in US dollars.

$ . . . . under $150
$$ . . . . between $150 and $300
$$$ . . . . between $300 and $450
$$$$ . . . . over $450

Doral Resort at Palmas del Mar
170 Candelero Drive, Humacao
☎ 787-852-6000; fax 787-852-6395
Reservations: ☎ 800-PALMAS-3
www.palmasdelmar.com
$$-$$$

For couples looking to get away from the glitz of San Juan, the Doral Resort at Palmas del Mar (formerly Wyndham Palmas del Mar) is a good choice. Located 45 minutes from the capital city, the resort is tucked on the Caribbean side of the island near the town of Humacao. Actually a compendium of resorts that range from standard hotel rooms to a bed and breakfast inn to luxury condominiums, Palmas is a city in itself, with a staff of over 500 employees.

Although 3½ miles of groomed beach (plus another six miles of nearly deserted beach) tempt vacationers to soak up sun and sometimes rolling surf, the sports facilities offer plenty of opportunities to stay busy. The Palmas del Mar Golf Club features a championship course designed by Gary Player, with holes offering views of El Yunque rain forest, the sea, and the nearby island of Vieques. The largest tennis center in the Caribbean has classes for players of every level, and nine restaurants make sure that, with all that activity, no one stays hungry for long.

Special Features/Activities: beachfront, casino, casual and fine dining, golf, watersports, tennis.

Hyatt Regency Cerromar Beach Resort & Casino
Highway 693, Dorado
☎ *787-796-1234; fax 787-796-4647*
Reservations: ☎ *800-233-1234*
www.hyatt.com
$$$

The Hyatt Cerromar is for couples looking to combine the glitz of San Juan with the peacefulness of the Puerto Rico countryside. Located 22 miles from the city, this high-rise resort has just about everything lovers could want, from luxurious massages to floating in what the hotel calls the world's longest swimming pool.

The hotel works in close conjunction with its sister property, the nearby Hyatt Dorado. The two resorts share 1,000 acres west of San Juan, and guests enjoy reciprocal privileges. Connected by a free shuttle system, guest cards are honored at both resorts.

For the more adventurous, watersports are available on Cerromar's strip of beach.

Special Features/Activities: beachfront, golf, tennis, in-line skating, biking, freshwater pool and hot tub, complete watersports center, windsurfing center, casino, casual and fine dining.

The Islands

> *At the Windsurfing School and Watersports Center,*
> *☎ 787-796-1227, Puerto Rico's only certified windsurf-*
> *ing school, lessons are offered by Lisa Penfield, the two-*
> *time women's windsurfing champion and former*
> *member of the US Olympic team. Guests learn in the*
> *reef-protected calm waters of nearby Hyatt Dorado.*

♥ ## Hyatt Dorado Beach Resort & Country Club
Highway 693, Dorado
☎ 787-796-1234; fax 787-796-2022
Reservations: ☎ 800-233-1234
www.hyatt.com
$$$

Located on a former grapefruit and coconut plantation, the
Hyatt Dorado Beach is our favorite type of Caribbean property:
a low-rise hotel with easy access to the beach. Apparently this
style appeals to others as well; the Hyatt Dorado Beach boasts
the highest repeat visitor rate of any properties in the popular
chain.

The atmosphere is elegantly casual. The guest rooms are deco-
rated in a West Indian style, with furniture inspired by Carib-
bean antiques.

Lazing at the pool with a view of the ocean.
© Tere Martinez

T he most romantic accommodations are the 17 casita rooms that include a marble shower beneath a clear skylight and a private lawn.

You'll find that the public areas are some distance from your guest room, however, and from the golf club shop and tennis center. A complimentary shuttle transports guests between the areas every half-hour, and bellmen pick up guests in golf carts any time on request. Two beaches include both wave action and calm pools created by a ring of boulders just offshore.

Special Features/Activities: beachfront, casual and fine dining, freshwater pools and hot tub, tennis, golf, complete watersports facilities, windsurfing, casino.

Wyndham El Conquistador Resort & Country Club

PO Box 270000, 1000 El Conquistador Avenue, Las Croabas
☎ *787-863-1000; fax 787-863-6500*
Reservations: ☎ *800-468-5228*
www.wyndham.com
$$$

This is one of the grandest resorts in the region, perched atop a 300-foot cliff. With 918 guest rooms, it's not the place for those looking for privacy, but you'll find just about everything else at this $250 million resort.

Choose from an 18-hole championship golf course, a private marina with rental boats and charters for deep-sea fishing, scuba facilities, six swimming pools, seven tennis courts, a nightclub, casino, fitness center, salon, and luxurious shops. Not to mention a 100-acre private island, Palomino, where guests can be whisked on complimentary ferries.

R omantic features: On secluded Palomino, couples can enjoy snorkeling, nature trails, and siestas in hammocks stretched between tall palms. The hotel is also home to the exclusive Golden Door Spa at Las Casitas Village. El Conquistador also offers two wedding packages, including one that features a ceremony in Palomino Island's 50-seat wedding chapel.

The Islands

Special Features/Activities: near beach, spa, fine and casual dining, golf, tennis, private island, casino, watersports, dive shop.

♥ Wyndham El San Juan Hotel & Casino
PO Box 9022872, 6063 Isla Verde Road, San Juan
☎ 787-791-1000; fax 787-253-0178
Reservations: ☎ 800-468-2818
www.wyndham.com
$$$

Located just minutes from the airport, this hotel could symbolize the elegance of San Juan. A lobby paneled in rich woods greets visitors and steps away, the most elegant casino in the Caribbean offers games of chance managed by croupiers in black tie. A new cigar bar recently opened off the casino. The pool area is beautifully landscaped with tropical gardens, the perfect place to relax after a morning of touring or shopping in San Juan.

Special Features/Activities: beachfront, casual and fine dining, casino, freshwater pool, cigar bar, rooftop country and western restaurant.

Tables for Two

Don't leave Puerto Rico without a taste of the island's distinct cuisine, a blend of Spanish, African, and Taino Indian elements in dishes that will have you ordering more. Start with an appetizer of **tostones, fried plantains,** or **empanadillas,** little meat turnovers. Other Puerto Rico dishes include **asopao,** a rice stew made with chicken or other meat, and **mofongo, mashed** plantains mixed with fried pork rinds and seasoned with garlic. Save room for **flan,** a wonderful custard or, our favorite, **tembleque,** a custard made with coconut milk and sprinkled with cinnamon.

You won't go thirsty during a Puerto Rico stay; the island offers some of the Caribbean's best rums, Medalla beer, and stout Puerto Rican coffee.

Price Chart

Restaurant prices are for dinner per person, including a drink, appetizer or salad, and entrée.

$...........................	under $15
$$	$15 to $30
$$$	$30 to $45
$$$$........................	over $45

♥ *La Mallorquina*
207 San Justo St., Old San Juan
☎ *787-722-3261*
Dress code: casually elegant
Reservations: not needed
$$$

Since 1848, this casual eatery has offered fine Puerto Rican cuisine: paella, fried rice with shrimp, chicken asopao, and even Puerto Rican-style beef tenderloin.

The Parrot Club
363 Fortaleza St., Old San Juan
☎ *787-725-7370*
Dress code: casually elegant
Reservations: suggested
$$-$$$

This fun restaurant has a tropical courtyard and a definite Caribbean feel. The menu features a wide array of Latino dishes with a twist, from ceviche to blackened tuna.

♥ *Su Casa*
Hyatt Dorado Beach Resort, Dorado
☎ *787-884-0047*
Dress code: casually elegant
Reservations: required during peak season
$$$

Dine in an authentic hacienda on which the Hyatt Dorado sits. You can dine on a balcony or in a romantic courtyard, sur-

The Islands

rounded by the Spanish Colonial style of this 1900 home. The restaurant, which features Puerto Rican and Spanish dishes, is open for dinner only during peak season.

The Ranch

El San Juan Hotel
☎ *787-791-1000*
Dress code: casual
Reservations: suggested
$$-$$$

Cowboys and great food are the themes of this unique restaurant found atop the El San Juan Hotel. Diners can have a delicious meal while they watch replays of old rodeos on the TV screens, listen to country music on the loudspeaker, and enjoy the waitstaff's line dances. Entreés include baby back ribs and "branding irons" (grilled scallop and shrimp kabobs).

Romantic Activities

Island Sights & Museums

The attractions of Puerto Rico are as vast as the island itself, ranging from eco-tourism jaunts to historic sites that date back to the days of Spanish explorers. Undoubtedly, the most popular stop on the island is **Old San Juan.** Dotted with museums and historic sites and rich with the atmosphere of Spanish explorers and conquistadors, this region is a must for every visitor. You can take a self-guided walk among the historic streets, strolling hand in hand where lovers have walked for centuries. The city's best shopping is also found in this area.

The most recognized site in Old San Juan is **Fuerte San Felipe del Morro,** better known as *El Morro*. This fort, one of the most photographed spots in the Caribbean, contains a museum and is administered by the National Park Service, ☎ 787-729-6777. The Spanish constructed this formidable structure in 1539 to protect the entrance into San Juan Harbor, a point from which the Spanish monitored their shipping between the Caribbean and Europe. *El Morro* means promontory, or headland, in Spanish.

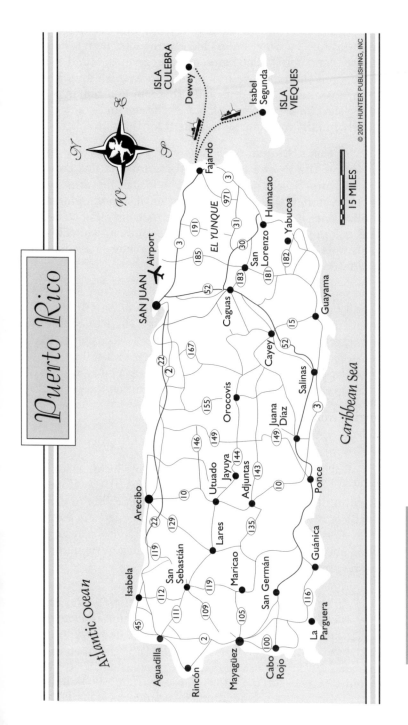

Puerto Rico

Atlantic Ocean

Caribbean Sea

15 MILES

© 2001 HUNTER PUBLISHING, INC

The Islands

The park is open daily from 9 am to 5 pm; there is no admission charge. Start by watching a video on the site, then take a self-guided tour. You'll find maps at the entrances, and exhibits throughout the park are posted in both English and Spanish. Even if you're not a history buff, this site is a romantic place where the two of you can look out on the sea and enjoy a gentle trade wind. Bring along your camera for this scenic stop.

Nearby, **Casa Blanca,** ☎ 787-724-4102, contains two separate museums: the **Ponce De Leon Museum** and the **Taino Indian Ethno-Historic Museum.** The former features exhibits on 16th- and 17th-century life and on its most famous residents: Ponce de Leon and his family. (Actually, Ponce de Leon died before the home was completed.) Built in the 1520s, the home was the city's first fortress. It is now open for tours Wednesday through Sunday.

If the two of you are history lovers, then make time for a trip to the city of **Ponce.** Ninety minutes south of San Juan, Ponce boasts more than 500 restored buildings. The **Ponce Art Museum,** ☎ 787-848-0505, features the most extensive collection in the Caribbean, with over 1,000 paintings and 400 sculptures. Ponce is also home to **Hacienda Buena Vista,** ☎ 787-722-5882, a restored 19th-century coffee plantation today open as a museum.

Natural Attractions

Not all of San Juan's attractions are man-made; for a look at the natural beauty of the island, make a stop at the **Botanical Garden of the University of Puerto Rico.** This 75-acre garden blooms with 30,000 orchids as well as heliconias and water lilies. For a peaceful lunch away from the city crowds, bring along a picnic and enjoy it in grounds shaded by cinnamon and nutmeg trees.

> *The garden is a popular site for wedding photos and even for ceremonies themselves, many which take place in a small chapel on the grounds. For more information, call ☎ 787-250-0000, ext. 6580.*

If your interests run more toward eco-tourism, you're in luck in Puerto Rico as well. One of our favorite excursions is a snorkeling trip out to **Monkey Island.** More fun than a barrel of monkeys, this island of curious primates is located off the southeast coast of Puerto Rico. It's a sanctuary for hundreds of monkeys, and access to the island is prohibited. Visitors cannot actually step on land, but you can snorkel around the fringes of the island while excited primates hoot and holler at you. We found the snorkeling here excellent, full of colorful fans and bright corals. **Coral Head Divers** at Palmas Del Mar, ☎ 787-850-7208, offers scuba and snorkel trips to Monkey Island.

Another natural attraction is **El Yunque National Forest,** the only tropical rain forest administered by the US National Forest Service. Forty-five minutes east of San Juan (close to El Conquistador resort), the rain forest boasts 240 species of trees and flowers, including 20 varieties of orchids and 50 types of ferns. Walking trails carve through the dense forest, and guided tours are available through **Rent-A-Ranger,** ☎ 787-888-1880.

If you're interested in a quiet walk beneath Puerto Rico, the island also offers one of the finest cave systems in the world. The **Rio Camuy Cave Park,** ☎ 787-898-3100, located 2½ hours west of San Juan, was carved by large underground rivers. Today the park includes a new visitors center with reception area and cafeteria, and a theater with AV presentation. Visitors reach cave level by trolley, then follow walkways on a 45-minute guided tour.

Golf

Puerto Rico has earned a reputation as the "Scotland of the Caribbean" because of its many golf courses. Over a dozen courses, including those at **Hyatt Dorado Beach, Hyatt Regency Cerromar Beach, Wyndham El Conquistador Resort and Country Club, Doral Resort at Palmas del Mar,** offer golf enthusiasts a variety of golf experiences in a tropical setting.

Shopping

Shopping is a major activity for Puerto Rico visitors. Duty-free shopping is found at the **Luis Muñoz Marín International Airport** and at factory outlet shops in **Old San Juan.**

The Islands

If you're looking for gold and jewelry or factory outlets, check out the shops on **Calle Christo** and **Calle Fortaleza** in Old San Juan. Island products include **cuatros** (small handmade guitars), **mundillo** (bobbin lace), **santos** (hand-carved religious figures), **rum,** and **cigars.** To find these local items, try **Plazaleta del Puerto** on Calle Marina, the **National Center for Popular Arts** at 253 Cristo Street, or **Puerto Rican Arts and Crafts** at 204 Calle Fortaleza.

Nightlife

The action doesn't stop when the sun goes down in Puerto Rico. In true Latin fashion, the city puts on its best clothes and gets ready to party during the cooler hours, starting with a late dinner. Evenings are then followed with dancing in the many discos in San Juan or in the luxurious casino hotels.

Casino gambling is found at many Puerto Rico hotels. Most casinos open at noon and remain open until the early hours of the morning. Most have dress codes that require semi-formal attire; leave the shorts, tank tops, and flip-flops in the room for your night at the tables. This is your chance to dress up and party; with San Juan's lively atmosphere the rule of thumb is the tighter, the shinier, the better.

> *You may be surprised to learn that alcohol cannot, by law, be served in Puerto Rico's casinos. You will find bars in each hotel, but no drinks are served on the casino floor.*

One of the most sophisticated casinos in San Juan, and, indeed in the Caribbean, is found at **El San Juan Hotel.** With a tuxedoed staff and an elegant European air, it's a favorite for couples looking for a fine casino. ☎ 787-791-1000.

The Wyndham El Conquistador offers a large casino with a view of the sea (yes – windows in a casino!). The entire casino is well-lit and bright, with pale paneling, beautiful views, and an airy atmosphere. ☎ 787-863-1000.

The casino at **Hyatt Cerromar** sports a recent expansion with a bright carnival theme, nearly 300 slots, and plenty of table games to test your luck and skill. ☎ 787-796-1234.

Just the Facts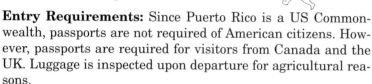

Entry Requirements: Since Puerto Rico is a US Commonwealth, passports are not required of American citizens. However, passports are required for visitors from Canada and the UK. Luggage is inspected upon departure for agricultural reasons.

Getting Around: You'll find that you have many of the same options in Puerto Rico as you do in the US. Rental cars from the major agencies are available. Driving is on the right and signage is bilingual. The Old San Juan area is especially congested, with old, narrow streets.

Taxis are a good choice, especially within San Juan. A new taxi program sets specified rates within certain zones. These taxis are white and bear the words "Taxi Turisticos" and a drawing of El Morro. These are an excellent choice for first-time visitors. The drivers have received special training to serve the tourist zones. A drive from the airport to the Isla Verde area costs about $8; a trip from the airport to Old San Juan runs about $16.

Language: Spanish and English are both official languages.

Currency: US dollar.

Electricity: Same as US; Europeans need an adapter.

Information: In the US, contact the Puerto Rico Tourism Company at 3575 Cahuenga Boulevard, Suite 405, Los Angeles, California 90068; ☎ 800-223-6350 or 213-874-5991; or at 901 Ponce de Leon Boulevard, Suite 101, Coral Gables, Florida 33134; ☎ 800-223-6350 or 305-445-9112; fax 305-445-9450. In Canada, contact Puerto Rico Tourism Company, 41-43 Colbourne Street, Suite 301, Toronto M5E 1E3; ☎ 800-223-6350 or 416-368-2680. European headquarters for the Puerto Rico Tourism Company are at Calle Serrano 1, 2 Izda. 28001 Madrid, Spain; ☎ 341-431-2128; fax 341-577-5260. Website: www.prtourism.com.

The Islands

St. Barts

W hether the two of you call it St. Barts, St. Barth, or St. Barthélemy, you'll find this charming island to be trés chic. At just nine square miles, this isle packs a lot of punch in the world of the glitterati, perhaps more than any other Caribbean destination. Especially during the peak winter months, don't be surprised to see celebrities wandering the streets of Gustavia, enjoying a glass of fine French wine in an open-air restaurant, or puttering around the island in a little vehicle called a Mini-Moke.

Without a doubt, St. Barts attracts high-end travelers, and its prices reflect this crowd. Prices are some of the highest in the Caribbean in terms of accommodations, dining, and transportation. A look at the merchandise of the little shops in the capital city of Gustavia will also confirm this island's typical price tags.

But St. Barts does have a somewhat different package to offer. Much more so than French St. Martin, this island is rich with the spirit of French élan. While you'll find that most shopkeepers, taxi drivers, and restaurateurs speak English and the American dollar is welcomed most places, this is definitely an outpost of France. Enjoy a taste of Europe with a hearty dash of Caribbean sunshine.

St. Bart visitors fall into two categories: day-trippers and overnighters. Day-trippers arrive, by prop plane or by boat from St. Martin to enjoy a morning and afternoon of shopping, touring, and lunch at one of the many French eateries. Overnighters are typically well-heeled, eager for the exclusive getaway that this island can provide.

St. Barts is shaped somewhat like a boomerang, with the two points facing northward. The capital city of **Gustavia** is located on the southwestern side of the island and boasts one of the prettiest harbors in the Caribbean. The U-shaped harbor is dotted with yachts whose white sails yield a stark contrast to the green hills punctuated by traditional red roofs around the town.

Northwest of Gustavia lies the community of **Colombier,** home of many older women, who can be seen wearing traditional clothing such as the white bonnet. In the traditional village of **Corossol,** many of the island's fishermen can be seen on the beach.

North of Gustavia, you can travel across the island to the community of **Saint Jean,** site of the island's first hotel. Today this region is home to many of the island's watersports on the **Baie de St.-Jean**. East of St. Jean lies the community of **Lorient,** a small village located on the beautiful **Anse de Lorient.** Continuing east, **Marigot** has many of the island's gourmet restaurants. This region is also the location of some of the island's most beautiful bays and beaches: **Anse de Marigot, Grand Cul de Sac, and Petit Cul de Sac,** to name a few.

South of here lies **Grand Fond,** a favorite stop for scuba divers. This village, with just 200 residents, has traditional limestone homes.

Festivals

St. Barts has a full calendar of festivals. On January 5, **Three Kings Day,** or *Galette des Rois*, is celebrated with Epiphany cake. Also in January, the **St. Barts Music Festival** offers two weeks of music ranging from jazz to chamber music to opera, with concerts in Gustavia and Lorient. **Carnival** is scheduled for February, with Mardi Gras costumed parades and partying in Gustavia; and **Ash Wednesday burning of Vaval** (King Carnival) at Shell Beach. Most businesses are closed during these festivities.

In April, the **Festival Gastronomique of St. Barts** includes presentations of regional wine and cooking from France at select island hotels and restaurants.

For information on any St. Barts festivals, call ☎ 877-956-1234.

The Islands

Sweet Dreams

Price Chart

Rates reflect high winter season (expect prices to be as much as 40% lower during the off season) for a standard room for two adults for one night; prices are in US dollars.

$ . . . . under $150
$$ . . . . between $150 and $300
$$$ . . . . between $300 and $450
$$$$ . . . . over $450

♥ Hotel Carl Gustaf
rue des Normands, BP700, Gustavia
☎ *590-278283; fax 590-278237*
Reservations: ☎ *800-9-GUSTAF*
www.carlgustaf.com
$$$$

Overlooking Gustavia, this hotel offers 14 suites, each with a hot tub plunge pool and private sun deck. The hotel is just a short walk from the beach and the views by day or night are incredible. Each suite includes a stereo system, fax machine, cable TV with English and French-language programming, kitchen facilities, air conditioning, and ceiling fan. The hotel is located 500 feet from a white sand beach and a 48-foot yacht is available for island-hopping, snorkeling trips, or deep-sea fishing.

Special Features/Activities: fine dining, botanic gardens, marina, horseback riding, snorkeling, racquetball, squash, windurfing, tennis, waterskiing, yacht charters.

Sofitel Christopher Coralia
Pointe Milou
☎ *590-276363; fax 590-279292*
Reservations: ☎ *800-221-4542*
$$$

This 40-room hotel (all with ocean views) is located on Pointe Milou in the northeastern part of St. Barts, about a 10-minute drive from the airport and 15 minutes from Gustavia. All rooms have ceiling fans, private terrace, and hair dryers. The hotel restaurant serves French cuisine and offers a prix fixe gourmet dinner plan. Facilities include a swimming pool, and the hotel staff can arrange scuba diving, snorkeling, deep-sea fishing, horseback riding, and other activities.

Special Features/Activities: fine dining, pool.

♥ *Hotel Guanahani*
PO Box 609, Anse De Grand Cul de Sac
☎ 590-276660; fax 590-277070
Reservations: ☎ 800-223-6800
$$$-$$$$

Trés chic, this full-service resort consists of 75 West Indian style cottages, each brightly colored and overlooking the sea. *Guanahani* is the Arawak name for San Salvador, the first island discovered by Christopher Columbus.

The hotel, set on a 16-acre peninsula on the northeastern side of the island, offers two tennis courts lit for night play (a tennis pro is also on hand if you want to improve your game), two freshwater pools and a heated hot tub. It's hard for pools to compete with Guanahani's two beaches, however. Here guests can go snorkeling, sail a Hobie Cat, windsurf, or go deep-sea fishing. One beach is located on a quiet lagoon and the other at the edge of a coconut grove facing the ocean. Complimentary continental breakfast is included as well as round-trip airport transfers, service and tax charges.

Special Features/Activities: beach, gourmet restaurant, watersports, tennis, two main pools, two bars.

Tables for Two

Dining is as much an adventure on St. Barts as watersports or hiking. The island has earned a reputation as the "French cuisine capital of the Caribbean." Expect these meals to set you back at least US $50 per person in most cases, and sometimes much more.

The Islands

T IP: Stop by the Tourist Office in Gustavia for restaurant brochures and a copy of Ti Gourmet, *a free guide that includes several bonus coupons.*

Price Chart

Restaurant prices are for dinner per person, including a drink, appetizer or salad, and entrée.

$............................ under $15
$$ .... $15 to $30
$$$ .... $30 to $45
$$$$....................... over $45

Cheeseburger in Paradise

rue de France, Gustavia
☎ *590-27-86-87*
Dress code: casual
Reservations: not needed
$-$$

Named for St. Barts regular Jimmy Buffett, this casual eatery is located in a garden right in the heart of Gustavia. A favorite with yachties, it's a fun place to grab a brew and a burger and watch the parade of activity in town.

Carl Gustaf

rue des Normands, Gustavia
☎ *590-27-82-83*
Dress code: casually elegant
Reservations: suggested
$$$

Fine food served in a beautiful atmosphere brings diners to the Carl Gustaf for a memorable meal. Typical dishes include Caribbean lobster tail and green papaya salad, Oriental prawn risotto, or breast of duck served in its own juices. If you can't spare the kind of change required for a meal here, drop by the piano bar for a drink and a spectacular sunset.

♥ ### François Plantation

Colombier
☎ *590-27-78-82*
Dress code: casually elegant
Reservations: recommended
$$$

Located in Colombier, this terraced restaurant features lobster gazpacho, cold or hot foie gras, Jamaican roasted tournedos of ostrich in Cajun spices, jumbo shrimp sautéed with citronella and ginger, and more. Save room for one of the desserts: crème brûlée flavored with candied ginger and lime or banana and coconut tarte Tatin. An extensive wine list is also available. Open for dinner only.

♥ ### Hotel Le Toiny's Restaurant Le Gaiac

Anse le Toiny
☎ *590-27-88-88*
Dress code: casually elegant
Reservations: recommended
$$$

This restaurant, located in the main house of Hotel Le Toiny, is named for the rare gaiac trees found on the property. Gourmet dishes include cold caviar soup with anise and beetroot, medallions of lobster with a passion fruit vinaigrette and candied sweet peppers. Stop by on a Sunday afternoon for a poolside buffet luncheon.

La Paradisio

rue du Roi Oscar II, Gustavia
☎ *590-27-80-78*
Dress code: casually elegant
Reservations: suggested
$$-$$$

With indoor and outdoor dining in a garden terrace, this restaurant also offers a good list of French wines and dishes such as creole squid on a bed of macaroni, mahi mahi, filet mignon, or pink salmon over French lentils.

The Islands

♥ *La Sapotillier*
rue du Centenaire, Gustavia
☎ *590-27-60-28*
Dress code: casually elegant
Reservations: optional
$$$

Dine beneath an old sapodilla tree or inside in the dining room at this downtown restaurant. Dishes include pan-fried dover sole, cocotte of fishes with anise flavoring, or filet of duck. Save room for the créme brûlée. Open for dinner only.

Restaurant le Bistrot des Arts
rue Jeanne d'Arc (far side of harbor), Gustavia
☎ *590-87-55-20*
Dress code: casual
Reservations: optional
$$-$$$

Decorated with artwork, this bistro offers up pizzas prepared in the brick oven, including a creole pizza with pineapple, spicy West Indian sausage, and crab. Parisian onion soup, Caribbean fish soup, and other specialties are served as well. This restaurant also boasts a good view of the harbor.

Romantic Activities

Start your visit with a look around **Gustavia.** Day-trippers enter this harbor town at the waterfront, an easy walking distance to its fine shops and sidewalk cafés. Filled with a delicious French atmosphere, this small town can sometimes be bustling, with streams of traffic. The town is built in a U-shape, following the harbor. On one side lies the tourist office, duty-free shops and several cafés; on the other side, you'll find many good restaurants and the **Musée de St. Barthélemy, ☎** 590-27-89-07. Exhibits explain the island's history through old photos, paintings, and documents.

Beyond Gustavis, visit the small communities of **Colombier** and **Corossol.** These two small towns of 300 residents each (located northwest of Gustavia) are home to a population of older women who wear the traditional dress of the French provincial regions of Brittany, Normandy and Poitou. Long-sleeved

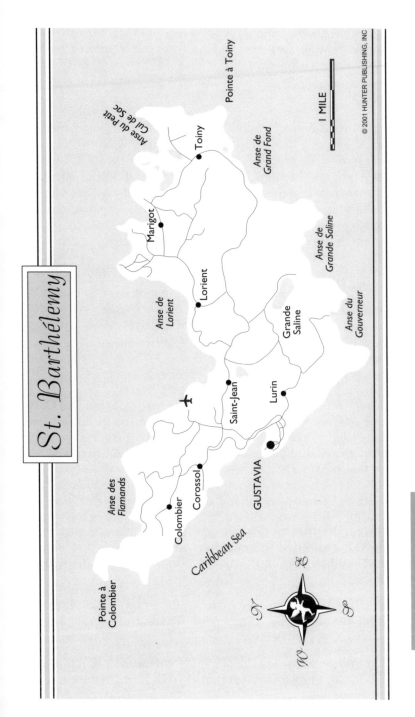

St. Barthélemy

Pointe à Colombier

Anse des Flamands

Colombier
Corossol

Caribbean Sea

GUSTAVIA

Saint-Jean

Lurin

Anse de Lorient

Lorient

Grande Saline

Anse de Grande Saline

Anse du Gouverneur

Marigot

Anse du Petit Cul de Sac

Toiny

Anse de Grand Fond

Pointe à Toiny

I MILE

© 2001 HUNTER PUBLISHING, INC

N
E
S
W

The Islands

dresses and sunbonnets (called calèches or quichonettes) are commonly seen. Many produce straw hats and baskets for the tourist market. Requests for photos are rarely granted, so do respect their wishes.

Beaches

St. Barts is home to 14 beaches. All have white sand and most are very quiet. Topless bathing is *de rigueur* here, although total nudity is prohibited. Several of the beaches, such as **Marigot** and **Lorient,** both on the north side of the island, are very private and quiet. **Shell Beach** is one of our favorites and readily accessible. Within walking distance of Gustavia, this beach is covered with the small shells, which lend the site its name. Nearly every shell is identical in shape and size.

> *While on the island, you can pick up a good deal of free information about what's happening.* St. Barth Magazine, *available at the tourism office, includes good information.* Ti Gourmet *offers tips on dining and coupons. Website: www.st-barths.com.*

Shopping

When you're through sunbathing, take a stroll back into Gustavia for a little shopping. You'll find the usual duty-free shops, but also some small, charming boutiques featuring one-of-a-kind clothing, small paintings, and unique souvenirs.

Just the Facts

Entry Requirements: For visitors who plan to stay in St. Barts for under three weeks, all that is needed is a valid passport or other proof of citizenshop. There are no vaccinations required.

Getting Around: To rent a car on St. Barts, you must present a valid driver's license from home. There are several places to rent cars on the island.

Language: French is the official language of St. Barts and locals speak a type of French that's an old Norman dialect. However, most people, including shopkeepers and restaurant staff, speak English.

Currency: The French franc (FF) is legal tender, but US dollars are widely accepted. The exchange rate is roughly FF $7.1 to the $US 1.

Electricity: Voltage is 220 AC, 60 cycles. American-made appliances require a transformer, as well as French plug converters.

Information: Before your trip, contact "France on Call" for brochures and questions, ☎ 877-956-1234, or write the French Government Tourist Office nearest you. Addresses can be found in the *Appendix*, page 385.

While on the island, stop by the visitors center in Gustavia. The Office du Tourisme is locate on the Quai Général de Gaulle just steps from the harbor. The office is open 8:30 am to 6 pm, Monday through Friday, and 8:30 to noon on Saturdays during peak season; and has somewhat shorter hours during summer months. Brochures and maps in both French and English are available and helpful assistance about any tourist needs. You can also write the local office at Office du Tourisme, Quai General de Gaulle, Gustavia, 97133 St. Barthelemy, French West Indies, ☎ 590-27-87-27, fax 590-27-74-47, or e-mail odtstbarth@ europost.org.

St. Kitts & Nevis

I magine a country inn where rooms brim with antiques and are cooled by a gentle breeze off a wide porch. You ease into a wicker chair, sip an icy drink, and enjoy a view unbroken by roads, electrical lines, or even fellow travelers.

This is St. Kitts, an island that offers bed-and-breakfast luxury you might look for in a New England getaway. Here, however, palms replace pines and color comes from azure seas, beaches in shades of both black and white, and verdant forests that engulf the island.

The Islands

St. Kitts and Nevis, its partner in this two-island nation, boast one of the Caribbean's largest concentrations of plantation homes. The islands were once dotted with sugar plantations and greathouses, but today these stately manses have been transformed into elegant bed-and-breakfast inns especially popular with European vacationers and Americans looking to experience a slice of the Caribbean "the way it used to be." Don't look for reggae lessons, limbo contests or mixology classes at these properties; instead, expect a sophisticated atmosphere similar to a fine country inn, where the emphasis lies in pointing the way for independent travelers to make their own discoveries.

Just two miles away from St. Kitts lies the tiny island of **Nevis** (pronounced NEE-vis). Columbus first named this island because of the ever-present cloud that circles Mount Nevis, giving it almost a snow-capped look. Today the cloud still lingers over the mountain peak. Home to only 9,000 residents, this country cousin has a charming atmosphere all its own, plus a good share of plantation houses where guests can enjoy a look back at Caribbean history.

St. Kitts and Nevis are both mountainous by Caribbean standards and rich with undeveloped regions. Both islands are home to small rain forests, although visitors will find plenty of tropical foliage wherever they venture.

Geography

Shaped like a guitar, St. Kitts is the more developed of the two. Most of its 35,000 residents live in the town of **Basseterre** (pronounced bos-tear) on the south shore (just where the guitar handle meets the body).

South of Basseterre, the island slims, the land becomes drier, and the population scattered. This is the **South Peninsula,** an area that until a few years ago was only accessible by boat. Today a modern highway makes this region available to motorists. Here, you'll find some of the island's most beautiful remote beaches and roadside overlooks, with views of both sides of the island and the Caribbean Sea to the south and the Atlantic Ocean to the north. Several hotel chains have purchased property in this area, but it remains, at least for today, remote and isolated.

A̸nimal lovers: the South Peninsula is your best chance for spotting vervet monkeys. Look in the underbrush and not in the trees, however. These monkeys don't have a prehensile tail, so they are usually seen on the ground.

The north end of St. Kitts is the lushest, due to soil that owes much of its fertility to a volcano named **Mount Liamuiga,** a Carib word that means "fertile island." The remote reaches of Mount Liamuiga are home to St. Kitts' rain forest.

For all the tropical splendor of St. Kitts, Nevis is even more verdant. Tall coconut palms cover hills carpeted in tropical undergrowth. Eco-tourism is also a major draw on Nevis. Mount Nevis offers many hikes of varying difficulty levels. History buffs find numerous sites of interest in the capital city of **Charlestown.** Like its sister island, Nevis is home to many vervet monkeys, a reminder of the French occupation of the island centuries ago. When the British took over the island from the French, they didn't mind transporting their enemies back home but they weren't about to take along their favorite pets: monkeys. Small vervet monkeys had been imported from Africa by the French. The British turned the monkeys loose on the island, where they prospered. Today it's estimated that the monkeys of St. Kitts and Nevis outnumber humans two to one. If you get up early or go out after sunset, you'll stand a chance of spotting one of the primates.

N̸evis recognizes the value of its environmental resources and has declared that, by law, no building may be taller than a palm tree.

Festivals

The calendar of St. Kitts and Nevis is dotted with special events through the year. During most holidays and festivals, Nevis comes to life with **horse racing**. Race days are scheduled during most special events and draw crowds in one of the Caribbean's most unique events. Horse racing is sponsored by the Nevis Jockey Club and held at the Indian Castle Race Track. For information, call ☎ 869-469-3477.

The Islands

Of special interest to lovers is the **Nelson/Nesbit Wedding Anniversary Tea,** held at the Hermitage Plantation Inn. This afternoon tea commemorates the union of Admiral Nelson and Fanny Nesbit. For information, call ☎ 869-469-3477.

In August, the **Caribbean Festival of the Arts** in Nevis features the history, folklore, and culture of the islands. Over 30 countries participate in this showcasing of culinary arts, literary skills, performing arts, film, and more. ☎ 869-465-1999.

 *Sweet Dreams*

Price Chart

Rates reflect high winter season (expect prices to be as much as 40% lower during the off season) for a standard room for two adults for one night; prices in US dollars.

$ . . . . under $150
$$ . . . . between $150 and $300
$$$ . . . . between $300 and $450
$$$$ . . . . over $450

St. Kitts

Fort Thomas Hotel
PO Box 407, Fortlands, Basseterre
☎ 869-465-2695; fax 869-465-7518
Reservations: ☎ 800-851-7818
$

If you want to stay in the heart of town, here's the place to be. Located within walking distance of restaurants and shops, this hotel is also a good choice for the budget-conscious. Along with recently refurbished guest rooms, it offers one of the island's largest swimming pools, a shuttle to the beach, and a good restaurant.

Special Features/Activities: downtown, freshwater pool, casual and fine dining.

♥ *Golden Lemon Inn and Villas*
Dieppe Bay
☎ *869-465-7260; fax 869-465-4019*
Reservations: ☎ *800-633-7411*
www.goldenlemon.com
$$

Fine dining and elegant accommodations lead travelers to the Golden Lemon, located on a black volcanic sand beach in the shadow of the island's volcano. Owned and managed by former *House and Garden* decorating editor Arthur Leaman, this 17th-century greathouse and the 15 contemporary seaside villas are filled with West Indian antiques. For the ultimate in luxury, two suites offer plunge pools literally a step from the living room door. The hotel is located about 15 minutes from Basseterre, and most guests rent cars during their stay.

Special Features/Activities: beachfront, freshwater pool, fine dining.

Horizons Villa Resort
PO Box 1143, Fort Tyson
Frigate Bay, Basseterre
☎ *869-465-0584; fax 869-465-0785*
Reservations: ☎ *800-830-9069*
$$

You'll feel like the two of you are at home during a stay in one of these lovely villas. Perched up on a hillside with a path down to a crescent-shaped beach, the villas are comfortable, cozy, and maintained by a friendly staff.

Special Features/Activities: hillside, small beach, pool.

Jack Tar Village St. Kitts Beach Resort and Casino
PO Box 406, Frigate Bay, Basseterre
☎ *800-999-9182, 869-465-8651; fax 869-465-1031*
www.jacktar.com
$

This all-inclusive resort, renovated in 1995 after Hurricane Luis, is recommended for couples looking for activity. Home of the country's only casino, the resort offers plenty of organized fun and evening entertainment, as well as a modest golf course.

The Islands

All activities, along with food and drink, are included in the price. Although it is not located on the beach, it's just a short walk to the sand and surf.

> *Jack Tar is recommended for couples on a budget; it's one of the best-priced accommodations on the islands.*

Special Features/Activities: across street from beach, all-inclusive, casino, watersports, golf, tennis.

The low-rise units at the resort are nestled in a valley.
Courtesy of Jack Tar Village Beach Resort and Casino.

♥ *Ottley's Plantation Inn*
PO Box 345, Basseterre
☎ *800-772-3039, 869-465-7234; fax 869-465-4760*
www.ottleys.com
$$$

Legend has it that this 18th-century greathouse is haunted, but that doesn't stop vacationers from coming here looking for peace and quiet. Guest rooms in the greathouse and in nearby cottages are nestled on 35 acres of tropical grounds. Along with golf and tennis, guests can explore a small rain forest on the grounds and search for vervet monkeys. Visitors have access to a nearby black sand beach.

Special Features/Activities: mountainside, fine dining, freshwater pool.

Rawlins Plantation

PO Box 340, Mount Pleasant
☎ *800-346-5358, 869-465-6221; fax 869-465-4954*
www.rawlinsplantation.com
$$

As far back as 1690 a plantation now named Rawlins began producing sugar. Nearly 300 years later, the greathouse, burned in an early fire, was reconstructed and opened as an inn. Today Rawlins is in the hands of Cordon Bleu-trained chef Claire Rawson and her husband, Paul.

Along with dining, the chief activity around here is pure relaxation. With no phones or televisions in the 10 guest rooms, the emphasis is on leisure.

> *The most romantic of the hideaway rooms is the honeymoon suite, housed in a 300-year-old sugar mill. Guests climb a winding stair from the downstairs living room to the upstairs bedroom perch, its walls made of volcanic stone.*

Special Features/Activities: mountainside, freshwater pool, restaurant.

Nevis

Four Seasons Nevis

PO Box 565, Pinneys Beach, Charlestown
☎ *869-469-1111; fax 869-469-1112*
Reservations: ☎ *800-332-3442 US; 800-268-6282 Canada*
www.fourseasons.com
$$$$

When word went out that the Four Seasons was coming to Nevis, doomsayers predicted the end of the quaint atmosphere for which Nevis is known. However, during the hotel's construc-

The Islands

tion, Hurricane Hugo hit the island and the Four Seasons' bosses stopped building and put crews to work cleaning up the island. Today, even the island inns sing the praises of this corporate giant.

One of the Caribbean's most lavish hotels, the Four Seasons Nevis sprawls across grounds dotted with coconut palms and other carefully tended flora. Guests can enjoy the Robert Trent Jones II-designed golf course, scuba diving, windsurfing, order from around-the-clock room service, watch movies on their VCRs or cable TV, hit the 10 tennis courts, lounge in two outdoor hot tubs, or just sun around the pool, cooled by Evian sprayed on guests by mindful pool attendants.

Special Features/Activities: beachfront, casual and fine dining, freshwater pool, golf, tennis, watersports.

♥ *Montpelier Plantation Inn*
PO Box 474, Montpelier Estate
☎ *869-469-3462; fax 869-469-2932*
Reservations: ☎ *800-223-9832*
www.montpeliernevis.com
$$

You may have heard of Montpelier because of one of its most famous guests: Princess Diana. When Diana and her children visited Nevis, they opted for this hotel's seclusion. Both royalty and honeymooners are offered peace and quiet in this very British hotel located on the slopes of Mount Nevis.

Princess Diana focused the eyes of the world on Montpelier, but it was hardly the property's first brush with royalty. On March 11, 1787, Admiral Horatio Nelson married Fanny Nisbet in front of a royal audience right on these grounds.

Today the plantation includes a 16-room inn that exudes a dignified British air appreciated by travelers who come to the Caribbean for tranquility. The inn provides shuttle service to the beaches. Evenings here are spent at the open-air restaurant that features classical cuisine with many local ingredients.

Special Features/Activities: mountainside, freshwater pool, fine dining.

Nisbet Plantation Beach Club

St. James Parish, Main Road, Newcastle
Reservations: ☎ *800-742-6008*
☎ *869-469-9325; fax 869-469-9864.*
www.nisbetplantation.com
$$$

Nelson's bride, Fanny Nisbet, was a resident of Nevis, and lived on the beachfront plantation that today bears her name. This 38-room inn boasts a striking vista: a quarter-mile palm-lined walk from the greathouse to Nisbet Beach. Lemon-tinted bungalows are scattered throughout the property. Couples can enjoy tennis, swimming, or that oh-so-British sport, croquet.

Special Features/Activities: beachfront, casual and fine dining, freshwater pool, tennis, watersports.

Golden Rock Plantation Inn

PO Box 493, Main Road, Gingerland
☎ *869-469-3346; fax 869-469-2113*
Reservations: ☎ *800-223-9815*
www.golden-rock.com
$$

Eco-tourists come here because of the diligent efforts of its owner, Pam Barry. A fifth-generation Nevisian, Barry emphasizes local culture, history, and nature studies, offering her self-guided nature trails to both guests and non-guests alike.

> *The most romantic room at this historic plantation inn is the two-story sugar windmill.*

Special Features/Activities: mountainside, restaurant, nature walks, pool.

Hermitage Inn

PO Box 49, Main Road, Charlestown
☎ *800-742-4276, 869-469-3477; fax 869-469-2481*
www.hermitagenevis.com
$$$

When magazines look for a classical Caribbean setting for fashion shoots, they often select the Hermitage Inn. This plantation inn is built around a 245-year-old greathouse. Sprinkled around grounds bursting with tropical blooms are restored plantation cottages that serve as guest rooms for those looking for the ultimate in privacy.

Guests have access to a swimming pool and tennis courts, as well as romantic pursuits such as carriage rides and horseback riding. Rates here include breakfast and a four-course dinner nightly.

Special Features/Activities: mountainside, fine dining, freshwater pool, tennis, horseback riding.

Hurricane Cove Bungalows
Main Road, Oualie Beach
☎ 869-469-9462; fax 869-469-9462
www.hurricanecove.com
$

If you're pinching pennies, don't despair, because the enchantment of Nevis can still be enjoyed on a budget. For instance, the moderately-priced Hurricane Cove Bungalows feature some of the most splendid views on the island. Each of the 10 hill-hugging cottages was constructed in Scandinavia, broken down and reassembled on a slope overlooking St. Kitts in the distance. Today they're all open-air and furnished with Caribbean artwork. One-, two-, and three-bedroom bungalows with kitchens are available, and guests can walk down to the beach. For our money, this is one of the island's best buys.

Special Features/Activities: mountainside.

 Tables for Two

A meal in St. Kitts and Nevis means traditional Caribbean fare such as snapper, grouper, salt fish or even flying fish accompanied by side dishes such as breadfruit, pumpkin, yams, and the obligatory rice and (pigeon) peas. Everything will be flavorful and often spicy.

Wash down dinner with the local beer, **Carib,** or the island's own liqueur: **Cane Spirit Rothschild** or CSR. Made from cane, this clear liqueur was developed by Baron Rothschild and is manufactured in Basseterre.

Price Chart

Restaurant prices are for dinner per person, including a drink, appetizer or salad, and entrée.

$............................ under $15
$$ .... $15 to $30
$$$ .... $30 to $45
$$$$ .... over $45

St. Kitts

Rawlins Plantation
PO Box 340 Mount Pleasant
☎ 869-465-6221
Dress code: casually elegant
Reservations: suggested
$$

Guests and non-guests stop by Rawlins Plantation for the daily West Indian lunch buffet which features local favorites such as saffron rice, curried chicken, and flying fish fritters, followed by soursop sorbet. The dishes are prepared using fresh seafood and complemented with herbs and vegetables from the plantation's garden.

Royal Palm Restaurant
Ottley's Plantation Inn
PO Box 345, Basseterre
☎ 869-465-7234
Dress code: casually elegant or dressy
Reservations: recommended
$$

This is often cited as one of the island's top restaurants, the prix fixe menu features dishes such as tomato dill bisque, pan-seared red snapper, and roast herb-infused tenderloin of prime beef.

The Islands

Fisherman's Wharf

Fortlands, Basseterre
☎ *869-465-2754*
Dress code: casual
Reservations: suggested
$-$$

Relax in the informal seaside atmosphere at this open-air restaurant featuring local dishes. The restaurant itself is located on a wharf and offers romantic views of Basseterre at night.

Nevis

♥ Montpelier Plantation

Pond Hill on Main Road
☎ *869-469-3462*
Dress code: dressy
Reservations: required
$$$

Evenings begin with a cocktail hour enjoyed in the great room as guests discuss their day, while amiable owners James and Celia Gaskell take orders for dinner. Eventually, guests make their way to the veranda for an open-air dinner served with elegance and style. Some typical dishes include fillet of mahi mahi with a Swiss cheese crust, breast of duck in soya and ginger, tenderloin of veal, and grilled lobster with creole hollandaise. Although many resorts make the claim, Montpelier is a place that truly defines casual elegance and offers a taste of the Caribbean the way it used to be.

♥ Mount Nevis Hotel and Beach Club

Mount Nevis, Newcastle
☎ *869-469-9373*
Dress code: casually elegant
Reservations: suggested
$$-$$$

This hillside hotel is well known for its reasonably priced contemporary accommodations, spectacular views and, most of all, gourmet dining. The Mount Nevis Restaurant, overlooking the aquamarine waters of the Caribbean and St. Kitts, is highly regarded in gastronomic circles.

Look for specialties such as lobster wontons with ginger-soy dipping sauce, grilled snapper with mango and tomatillo salsa, and island spiced crème brûlée.

♥ Nisbet Plantation
Main Road, Newcastle
☎ *869-469-1111*
Dress code: dressy
Reservations: suggested
$$$

The focal point of the resort is the Great House, dating back to the earliest days of the sugar plantation, which opened in 1778. This two-story building, with a wide, screened veranda across the back, is a fine restaurant. Start your evening with a drink at the Great House bar, then step out on the veranda for a memorable meal accompanied by fine wine.

Oualie Beach Hotel
Main Road
☎ *869-469-9735*
Dress code: casual or casually elegant
Reservations: optional
$$

This restaurant features the creations of Chef Patrick Fobert, who combines French recipes with a Caribbean flair. Diners select from chicken mousse filled with creole conch, roasted rack of lamb in Jamaican jerk crust, tamarind rum-basted wahoo loin, and more.

Romantic Activities

Island Sights & Museums

Couples should budget at least half a day for an island tour, which can be booked through any hotel. (Another alternative for those wishing more privacy is to hire a taxi driver by the hour.) On St. Kitts, an island tour includes a stop at **Brimstone**

The Islands

Hill National Park, ☎ 869-466-5021, for a self-guided tour of this impressive fortress located on the island's west side. Visit **Romney Manor** for a look at **Caribelle Batik.** Nevis island tours include a stop in the capital city of **Charlestown.** Here you can see the ruins of the **Bath Hotel**, ☎ 869-465-1680, built in 1778 for wealthy Nevisians to bask in 108° waters (modest facilities are still open for visitors to "take the waters"); and the **Alexander Hamilton House,** the birthplace of the American patriot.

Beaches

Most activities on these islands center around the sea. Couples will find many romantic beaches on both islands. On St. Kitts, don't miss the quiet beaches along the **Southeast Peninsula.** On Nevis, check out **Pinney's Beach,** one of the island's best with waters protected by reefs, and **Oualie Beach,** the most active beach on Nevis, with many watersports operators.

Underwater Delights

Scuba divers will find a variety of trips, including reef and wreck dives. On St. Kitts, call **Kenneth's Dive Center**, ☎ 869-465-2670; **Pro-Divers,** ☎ 869-465-3223; or **St. Kitts Scuba,** ☎ 869-465-1189. On Nevis, call **SCUBA Safaris**, ☎ 869-469-8518.

St. Kitts is fairly new to the diving world and offers divers a world of pristine sites without crowds. The most common dive sites are found on the western side of the island in the calmer Caribbean waters. Here visibility runs as much as 100 feet. Some top dive spots include the following.

- ♥ **Black Coral Reef.** This dive site is located 40-70 feet below the surface and is best known for its protected black coral.

- ♥ **Bloody Bay Reef.** Located at 60-80 feet, this dive site is noted for its healthy undersea life, from anemones to sea fans. A popular fishing site as well, an occasional shark is seen here, the result of chumming. Divers will find several caves in this area.

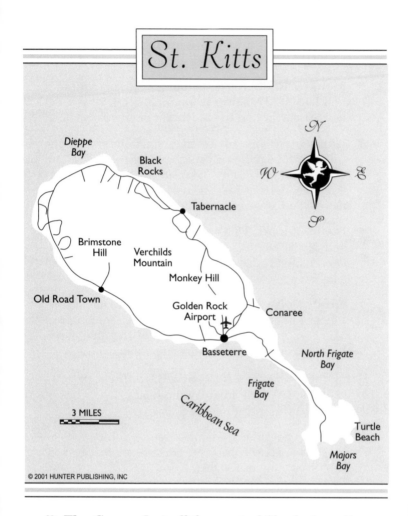

St. Kitts

Dieppe
Bay

Black
Rocks

Tabernacle

Brimstone
Hill

Verchilds
Mountain

Monkey Hill

Old Road Town

Golden Rock
Airport

Conaree

Basseterre

North Frigate
Bay

Frigate
Bay

Caribbean Sea

3 MILES

Turtle
Beach

Majors
Bay

© 2001 HUNTER PUBLISHING, INC

♥ **The Caves.** Just off the coast of Charlestown lies this undersea adventure, a series of coral grottos that invite exploration. Marine life is plentiful along this shallow 40-foot dive and divers usually spot plenty of squirrel fish, lobster, sponges, and an array of corals.

♥ **Coconut Tree Reef.** A variety of dive experiences, from beginner to advanced, are available on this reef. It starts at 40 feet below the surface before plunging to over 200 feet deep. Beautiful corals and bountiful marine life found here.

The Islands

- ♥ **Grid Iron.** Found in the channel between St. Kitts and Nevis, this dive follows an undersea shelf. Look for angelfish as well as rich aquatic life on this dive.

- ♥ **Monkey Reef.** You'll see nurse sharks, stingrays, and lobster. This dive is approximately 50 feet below the surface off the southeast peninsula.

- ♥ **Nags Head.** This advanced dive is found where the calm Caribbean Sea meets the more rugged waters of the Atlantic Ocean. The result is a strong current and rich marine life, including rays, turtles, and more. This dive averages about 80 feet.

- ♥ **Booby Island.** This site is located in the St. Kitts and Nevis channel "The Narrows" and is for advanced divers because of the current. Jacks and snapper are common here.

- ♥ **Sandy Point Bay.** Over 50 anchors and marine artifacts have been spotted at this site nicknamed "Anchors Away." On other parts of the dive, large basket sponges, jacks, and snappers may be seen.

On Nevis, the scuba operator is **SCUBA Safaris** (☎ 869-469-9518, fax 469-9619), located at Oualie Beach. Nevis has many dive sites of its own, including the following.

- ♥ **Monkey Shoals.** Two miles west of the Four Seasons Resort Nevis, this reef starts at 40 feet and offers dives of up to 100 feet. Angelfish, turtles, nurse sharks, corals, sea fans, and sea whips noted here.

- ♥ **Booby Shoals.** This site, located off the coast of St. Kitts, is between Cow 'n Calf Rocks and Booby Island. Divers find an abundance of marine life here, including stingray, nurse sharks, and lobster. This shallow site is up to 30 feet in depth and can be used by both certified and resort course divers.

- ♥ **The Devil's Caves.** Located on the south tip of Nevis, this 40-foot dive has a series of coral grottos and underwater lava tubes. Lobsters, needlefish, turtles, and squirrelfish are seen at this site used by both certified and resort course divers.

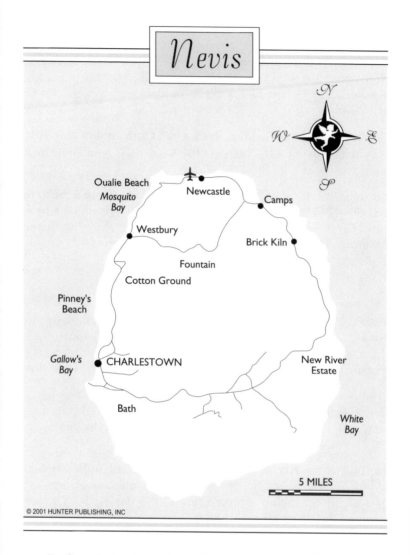

Nevis

♥ **Coral Garden.** Two miles west of Pinney's Beach, this reef has schools of Atlantic spadefish and large sea fans. With a maximum depth of 70 feet, it's a favorite with both resort course and certified divers.

♥ **Champagne Garden.** Located just minutes from Pinney's Beach, this site is named for the bubbles created by an underwater sulfur vent. Many tropical fish are drawn to this site because of its warm waters.

The Islands

Other Activities

For those who want to stay above water level, the ***Spirit of St. Kitts,*** ☎ 869-469-9373, catamaran offers day sails to Nevis and the ***Spirit of Mount Nevis*** takes couples on sunset cruises every Tuesday.

Golf is available at **Golden Rock Golf Club,** ☎ 869-465-8103; **Royal St. Kitts Golf Course,** ☎ 869-465-8339; and **Four Seasons Nevis,** ☎ 869-469-1111.

Eco-tourists can visit St. Kitts' rain forest with **Greg's Safaris,** (☎ 869-465-4121) on a half-day hike. For a very rugged adventure, Greg takes visitors on a Volcano Safari, climbing Mount Liamuiga to the crater rim to view the cloud forest.

Nightlife

The best advice for couples looking for nightlife on St. Kitts and Nevis is to make their own. Nights are often spent looking up at the moon or watching the sea on both quiet islands. Some restaurants feature local musicians and occasionally the local steel pan band.

On St. Kitts, the **Jack Tar Village,** ☎ 869-465-1031, has a casino and disco for guests and non-guests alike. The casino includes both slots and gaming tables.

For music, the **Kittitian Monkey Bar** on Frigate Bay Beach, ☎ 869-465-8935, on the Southeast Peninsula, sometimes has live music featuring island sounds. Similarly, the **Cotton House Club and Disco,** ☎ 869-465-8031, located 10 minutes from Basseterre, offers music and is open both Friday and Saturday nights. The club requires proper attire.

On Nevis, **Club Trenim,** ☎ 869-465-9173, located on Government Road in Charlestown, features disco dancing in an informal setting. **Golden Rock Estate,** ☎ 869-469-3346, presents the music of David Freeman's Honey Bee String Band on Saturday nights.

Just the Facts

Entry Requirements: Passports are required for citizens of the UK and for all other visitors, except those from the US and Canada, who may present a voter's registration card, naturalization papers, or a certified birth certificate (not a copy) instead. All visitors must possess a valid return ticket.

Getting Around: Rental cars are available on both islands, but be advised that driving is on the left side of the road. A visitor's license is available from the Police Traffic Department for EC $30. Excellent taxi and mini-bus service is available on St. Kitts and Nevis.

Many couples take a day-trip to the other island aboard the passenger ferry *The Caribe Queen*. The 45-minute crossing costs about US $8 round-trip. Air St. Kitts Nevis (☎ 869-465-8571 on St. Kitts; 869-469-9241 on Nevis) whisks visitors from island to island in less than 10 minutes.

Language: English

Currency: Eastern Caribbean dollar. US $1 = EC $2.70

Electricity: 230 volts/60 cycles; US appliances need coverters.

Information: For a free tourist guide to St. Kitts and Nevis, call the Tourist Office at ☎ 800-582-6208, 212- 535-1234; fax 212-734-6511, or write 414 East 75th St., New York, NY 10021. In Canada: 365 Bay Street, Suite 806, Toronto, Ontario M5H 2V1, ☎ 416-368-6707; fax 416-368-3934; and in the UK: 10 Kensington Court, London W8 5DL, ☎ 0171-376-0881; fax 0171-937-6742. Website: www.stkitts-nevis.com.

St. Lucia

*W*e first heard St. Lucia before we saw it. Flying in from the States near the midnight hour, we stepped off the prop plane and instantly received a warm welcome from the humid night winds. Just yards away, we could hear the sound of the Carib-

The Islands

bean lapping against the shoreline, right off the Vigie Airport runway.

The next morning we learned what St. Lucia was really about. Jagged peaks clothed in velvety tropical plants. Honey-colored beaches shaded by towering palms. And everywhere, colorful blooms and greenery that promised romantic walks in a true Garden of Eden.

The two of you really will feel like Adam and Eve in this wonderland, a place where every hill, valley, and roadside is a veritable garden. Orange, lime, lemon, mango (over 100 varieties, we learned), breadfruit, plum, and coffee trees cover the landscape. Pineapples sprout alongside the highway. Spices such as vanilla, nutmeg, and cinnamon grow in thick profusion.

Most evident are the bananas. Not just banana trees, but banana plantations. Miles of bananas that stretch to the horizon. Along with its reputation as a drive-through grocery market, St. Lucia is also abloom with color. Tall flame flowers. Orchids. Hibiscus. Shrimp plants.

Romance comes easily in such a fertile environment. You'll find plenty of excuses to kiss in the shade of a tall coconut palm, in the spray of a mountainside waterfall, or in a hillside lookout with a view of the mountains rearing from the sea.

Travelers in the mood for love – whether that means an exchange of vows, a honeymoon, or a romantic getaway – will find plenty of options on St. Lucia. This fertile environment, overflowing with tropical birds, fragrant blooms, and spectacular scenery, is just what many travelers picture when they imagine a romantic island retreat.

Geography

The **Pitons** are rugged mountains that climb from the sea on the island's southwest coast. **Gros Piton,** the shorter but stouter of the two, and **Petit Piton,** are among the Caribbean's most recognizable landmarks. Couples who enjoy nature will have plenty of diversion in this part of St. Lucia, starting with the rain forest. You will need a guide to enter the restricted rain forest region, and can sign up for a tour to walk through the dense foliage, swim in a tropical waterfall, and learn more about the plants that make up this fragile ecosystem.

This area is also home to a unique **Sulphur Spring volcano**, often called the "drive-through volcano." Couples can walk to the edge of the volcano which last erupted two centuries ago. Near the volcano, the **Diamond Waterfalls and Gardens** are perfect for honeymooners. A flower-lined trail winds to Diamond Waterfalls, a cascade that leaves a spray of "diamond" twinkles suspended in the air. Here, steamy mineral baths built among ruins of the first baths commissioned by French King Louis XIV for use by his troops can still be enjoyed by today's travelers.

On the northern end of the island, the capital city of **Castries** is located near some of the island's top attractions: excellent beaches, the **St. Lucia Golf and Country Club,** the Friday night **Jump Up** in the small fishing community of Gros Islet, and **Pigeon Point National Landmark.** This site, formerly an island, now connected to the mainland by a causeway, is one of St. Lucia's most popular wedding locations.

Festivals

During the month of February preparations for **Carnival** are underway, which include costume making, "King and Queen" competitions and bands getting ready for the big bash. Carnival is an exciting time on St. Lucia and is celebrated throughout the island.

With June comes the **Fisherman's Feast,** which begins with a church service and the blessing of boats and boat sheds which have been decorated.

After the service comes a whole day of feasting and festivities for those who with to participate. The **St. Lucia Squash Open,** which brings some of the world's best squash players for competition, is also held during this month.

For a unique Caribbean festival, visitors should come to St. Lucia during October. **International Creole Day** is celebrated on the island with traditional foods and folklore to observe the common culture of creole-speaking people around the world.

The Islands

Sweet Dreams

Price Chart

Rates reflect high winter season (expect prices to be as much as 40% lower during the off season) for a standard room for two adults for one night; prices in US dollars.

$ . . . . under $150
$$ . . . . between $150 and $300
$$$ . . . . between $300 and $450
$$$$ . . . . over $450

♥ *Anse Chastanet*
PO Box 7000, Soufrière
☎ *800-223-1108, 758-459-7000; fax 758-459-7700*
www.ansechastanet.com
$$$

A stay at Anse Chastanet is an experience to remember. Tucked between one of St. Lucia's finest beaches, Anse Chastanet, and the Pitons, this hillside resort blends with nature. Walls give way to scenic vistas and guests enjoy rooms where luxury means views uninterrupted by hindrances such as windows.

> *Many accommodations in this 48-room resort have only two or three exterior walls, with bedrooms flowing directly onto terraces and out to the breathtaking scene beyond. Tiny birds make chattering roommates, and just beyond the balcony railing, flitting hummingbirds work the tropical blooms like oversized bees.*

Anse Chastanet (pronounced on-chas-tan-ay) is perched right on the hillside. Steep steps wind from beach to the main reception and dining area and lead up to the hilltop bungalows above. Not the place for visitors with any walking problems – and leave the high heels at home for this destination. Casual is the order of the day, although in the evening men traditionally wear slacks or Bermuda-length shorts.

We enjoyed room 7F, a unique room. Like others in the #7 block, this accommodation has an unbeatable view of Petit Piton and Gros Piton. From our king-size bed, we looked across our immense room (even the smallest room measures 900 square feet), straight at the Caribbean's most recognizable mountains. The two-person shower even has a view.

Anse Chastanet also does weddings wherever the couple chooses: on the beach, in the Treehouse restaurant, or even on the patio of their guest room. And, to soothe muscles that might be tired from walking that steep hill, the resort offers a special massage course for couples.

Special Features/Activities: beachfront, fine and casual dining, watersports; dive shop.

♥ *Hyatt Regency St. Lucia*
Castries, Pigeon Island Causeway
Reservations: ☎ *800-55-HYATT*
www.hyatt.com
$$$

The 300-room property offers lagoon rooms with swim-up verandas, a spa, golf, tennis, and even a private helipad.

This hotel offers a Honeymoon Romance Package that includes room, bottle of champagne, honeymoon breakfast for two, candlelight dinner with a bottle of wine, couple's massage, and more.

Special Features/Activities: pool, restaurants, swim lagoon, outdoor hot tub, spa treatments.

♥ *Ladera Resort*
PO Box 225, Soufrière
☎ *758- 459-7323; fax 758- 459-5156*
Reservations: ☎ *800-738-4752*
www.ladera-stlucia.com
$$$

This intimate hillside resort, tucked above the sea between the Pitons, features villas and suites, with private pools. This unique property offers six villas and 18 suites. Rooms are decorated with 19th-century French furniture and local artwork.

The Islands

> *Every room here opens on one side to reveal the mountain view; all the units include a pool or a plunge pool to be enjoyed in complete privacy.*

Special Features/Activities: mountainside, excellent restaurant, freshwater pool, shuttle service to Soufrière and beaches.

LeSport

PO Box 437, Cariblue Beach, Castries
☎ *758- 450-8551; fax 758-450-0368.*
Reservations ☎ *800-544-2883*
www.lesport.com.lc
$$$$

LeSport differs from other all-inclusives; this recently renovated resort doesn't emphasize a vacation with a week-long blowout of buffets, beach bumming, and boozing. Instead, this Moorish-style resort promotes the "body holiday," a chance to pamper your body with spa treatments, physical activity, and fine food. You'll have an initial consultation, then a program of treatments will be designed specially for you, ranging from a salt loofah rub to a Swedish massage to work out kinks after a round of tennis, a lesson in fencing, or a class at the golf school on the nine-hole course.

Special Features/Activities: beachfront, all-inclusive, spa, golf school, fine dining.

Rendezvous

PO Box 190, Malabar Beach, Castries
☎ *758-452-4211; fax 758-452-7419*
Reservations: ☎ *800-544-2883*
www.rendezvous.com.lc
$$$

Rendezvous is comfortable and a good choice for those on a budget. You'll get the full array of all-inclusive offerings: meals and liquor, nightly shows, plus a weekly excursion to Pigeon Point. Rooms here include ocean view accommodations with pink marble baths, island style furniture, and private porches. Approximately 70% of the resort's clientele is British, so you'll notice a distinct international atmosphere.

This resort recently added SolangeMa, patois for release, relief and relaxation. These open-air gazebos offer a variety of massages including a couple's honeymoon massage, aromatherapy, foot massage, salt loofah rub, and more.

Special Features/Activities: beachfront, all-inclusive, couples-only, fine and casual dining, watersports, scuba diving, tennis.

Royal St. Lucian
Reduit Beach
☎ *758-452-9999; fax 758-452-9639*
Reservations: ☎ *800-255-5859*
www.rexcaribbean.com
$$$-$$$$

This luxurious resort offers a special eight-day/seven-night honeymoon package that pampers newlyweds with deluxe suite accommodations, a candlelit dinner on the beach with wine, car rental for one day, a romantic sunset cruise, two spa treatments each, and more.

Special Features/Activities: beachside, pool, spa, restaurants.

♥ Sandals Halycon St. Lucia
PO Box GM 910, Choc Bay, Castries
☎ *758-453-0222; fax 758-451-8435*
Reservations: ☎ *800-SANDALS*
www.sandals.com
$$

This Castries-area resort is one of our favorite Sandals properties. Rooms are nestled in one- and two-story buildings, most outlined in trailing vines and blooming tropical plants.

> *Beautiful grounds offer couples plenty of romantic, shady nooks for time together.*

Sandals Halycon has the highest percentage of European guests within the popular chain, so the mood here is somewhat more reserved than at some Sandals hotels. You'll still find basketball in the pool and volleyball at the beach, plus plenty of other activity thanks to those enthusiastic "Playmakers," but couples who want to do nothing at all will feel right at home here as well. Halcyon guests are also a more adventurous group than at many properties; most book several off-property excursions during their stay. The tour desk can set up jeep tours to the rain forest, bus tours to the volcano, and catamaran excursions that trace St. Lucia's beautiful western shore. There are two specialty restaurants; our favorite is The Pier. Built on a pier perched over the sea, this open-air eatery serves seafood in an elegant atmosphere. Every room here is identical; the only difference in category and price comes from the room view.

Special Features/Activities: beachfront, all-inclusive, couples-only, fine and casual dining, pools, whirlpools, watersports.

♥ *Sandals St. Lucia*

PO Box 399, Castries, 10 minutes feom Vigie Int'l. Airport
☎ *758- 452-3081; fax 758- 452-1012*
Reservations: ☎ *800-SANDALS*
www.sandals.com
$$

The largest of the two Sandals properties on St. Lucia, this hotel is a veritable honeycomb of activity. Full-time "Playmakers" make sure that no one is left out of the fun and games. From the bars and billiards room in its elegant lobby, to the tennis, golf, and watersports on the 155-acre resort, guests have plenty of fun to choose from. Of course, if you and your partner want to be alone, that's all right, too. You can hang out by the freeform pools, daysail in a Sunfish, or dine by candlelight.

Even more than most Sandals locations, this resort does things in a big way. The pool, which Sandals says is the largest in the Caribbean, includes a waterfall, bridges, and, of course, a swim-up bar, where the two of you can order frozen and frothy concoctions.

Four restaurants keep guests well fed. Our favorite is La Toc, a French restaurant with a wine and sparkling wine list and white glove service. Although the restaurant is enclosed (not our choice in the Caribbean), the service is friendly and the atmosphere makes couples feel that they are enjoying a meal to celebrate a special occasion, even if that event is just another night on vacation where the focus is on the two of you.

Special Features/Activities: beachfront, all-inclusive, couples-only, fine and casual dining, freshwater pools, watersports, golf.

Tables for Two

Creole food is popular in restaurants across St. Lucia. Spices liven up beef, chicken, pork, and lamb dishes, served up with favorites such as rice and peas, **dasheen** (a root vegetable similar to a potato), and **plantains.** Enjoy it with a taste of local spirits such as **La Belle Creole, Bounty Rum,** and **Piton** beer.

Price Chart

Restaurant prices are for dinner per person, including a drink, appetizer or salad, and entrée.

$. . . . . under $15
$$ . . . . $15 to $30
$$$ . . . . $30 to $45
$$$$ . . . . over $45

Jimmie's
Vigie Cove, Castries
☎ *758-452-5142*
Dress code: casual
Reservations: optional
$$-$$$

Tucked right beside Vigie Cove, this open-air hillside restaurant offers saltfish, black pudding, souse, green fig, and plenty of other local favorites. If you're a little less daring, you can fall back on seafood dishes such as conch (reputed to be an aphrodisiac), scampi, sautéed scallops, or a T-bone steak.

The Great House
Cap Drive, Gros Islet
☎ *758-450-0450*
Dress code: casually elegant
Reservations: suggested
$$$$

On Friday nights, save time before the Jump Up (see *Nightlife,* page 296) for a run by this elegant plantation-style restaurant,

The Islands

located at Cap Estate. Enjoy a candlelight dinner of lime-grilled dorado, rack of lamb with mint sauce, jerk pork, or a local favorite, curried chicken and mango with rice. Finish off with truly sinful desserts: coconut cheesecake with tropical fruit toppings, passion fruit mousse, or soursop ice cream in filo pastry.

♥ *Auberge Seraphine*
Vielle Ville Bay, Castries
☎ *758-453-2073*
Dress code: casually elegant
Reservations: suggested
$$-$$$

This seafood restaurant, with a sprinkling of French and Caribbean dishes, serves both lunch and dinner. Start with grilled calamari or Gros Islet-style fish cakes served with tamarind sauce, then try the breadfruit vichyssoise or Caribbean fish chowder. Entrées range from curried shrimp with coconuts to Caribbean lobster.

Bang
Soufrière
☎ *758-459-7864*
Dress code: casual
Reservations: suggested
$-$$

What a location! Tucked between the magnificent mountains, this waterfront restaurant specializes in jerk barbecue. This restaurant also has a rum shop. Perfect for a memento of your trip.

The Treehouse
Anse Chastanet, Soufrière
☎ *758-459-7000*
Dress code: casually elegant
Reservations: suggested
$$$

Like its name suggests, this restaurant sits perched, tree level, on a steep hillside. Happily, the view is matched by the food. We started with coconut-crusted local crab backs, then moved on to a creamy celery and bacon soup. Entrées include pork medallions with a light mustard sauce, vegetarian roti on curried lentils, grilled dorado, St. Lucian beef pepperpot, and other dishes using local products. The wine list here is excellent as well.

The Still
Soufrière
☎ *758-459-7224*
Dress code: casual
Reservations: not needed
$

This is one of our favorite St. Lucian diners, a delightful local eatery that dishes out tasty local cuisine. Family-owned, the service is friendly, and if you see something that you don't recognize, just ask. We dined on Creole chicken served with mango salad, rice, beans, and yam pie. Don't expect anything fancy here, but it's the place to come for lunch or dinner for a true taste of Creole cooking at a very reasonable price.

Les Pitons.
Courtesy of the Jalousie Hilton Resort & Spa.

The Islands

Romantic Activities

Island Sights

The toughest part of your St. Lucia vacation is trying to decide what to do. The choices are all so tempting that you can easily spend several days touring the island – and still have plenty of sights to justify a return visit.

On the northern reaches of the island lies **Pigeon Island,** a 35-minute drive from Castries. No longer a true island but connected to the main island by causeway, Pigeon Island has a long history as everything from a pirate hideout to a military fort. The ruins of the fort can still be seen at **Pigeon Island National Park,** a popular day-trip for north shore vacationers, and the site of many of St. Lucia's festivals. North of Pigeon Island lies **Gros Islet,** known throughout the Caribbean for its Friday night Jump Up (see *Nightlife*, page 296).

Most couples stay on the northeast section of the island near **Castries,** the island's largest city with a population of 60,000. This capital city was destroyed by fire several times, but some colonial period wooden structures still remain. You'll see several of them as you head south on **Government House Road.** This twisting, climbing slice of road is slow going but offers you a great view. Save time for a stop across from the **Governor's House** for a panoramic look at the city. From atop **Morne Fortune** (Hill of Good Luck), you'll have a postcard view over Castries Harbour, Vigie Peninsula and Pigeon Island.

Continuing south, the road soon drops into a veritable forest: the first of several banana plantations. Driving past this display of the island's number one crop, you'll see blue plastic bags hanging from many trees. These cover the bananas to shield the crop from insects and bruising by the banana leaves. The banana plant yields only one crop during its lifetime, a process that takes nine months to bear fruit.

Marigot Harbour, located just off the main road, on Bridge Street, is the next stop. This magical harbor, often considered to be the most beautiful in the Caribbean, is dotted with yachts from around the globe. If you don't have your own, don't worry. **The Moorings,** a company headquartered in the British Virgin

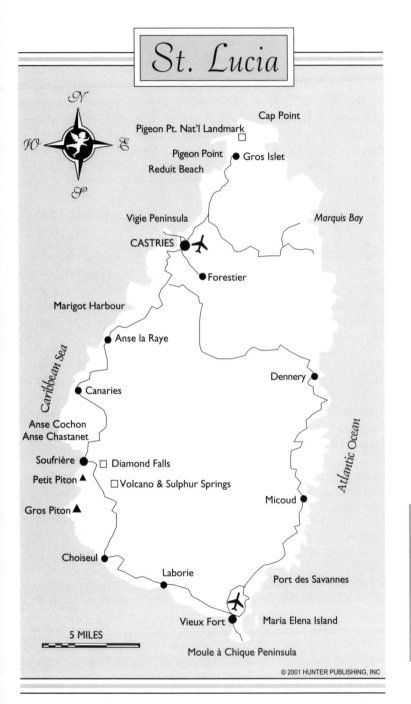

St. Lucia

Cap Point

Pigeon Pt. Nat'l Landmark

Pigeon Point
Reduit Beach

Gros Islet

Vigie Peninsula

Marquis Bay

CASTRIES

Forestier

Marigot Harbour

Anse la Raye

Dennery

Canaries

Caribbean Sea

Anse Cochon
Anse Chastanet

Soufrière

Diamond Falls

Petit Piton ▲

Volcano & Sulphur Springs

Gros Piton ▲

Micoud

Atlantic Ocean

Choiseul

Laborie

Port des Savannes

5 MILES

Vieux Fort

Maria Elena Island

Moule à Chique Peninsula

© 2001 HUNTER PUBLISHING, INC

The Islands

Islands, can rent you a yacht, with or without a crew, to enjoy a sailing vacation of your own, ☎ 758-452-4256. Landlubbers will enjoy the scenic harbor as well, and may recognize it from the movie *Dr. Doolittle*.

South of Marigot, the road passes through many small communities and fishing villages. Make time for a walk around **Anse La Raye** (Beach of the Ray), a traditional St. Lucian fishing village. Enjoy a walk along the waterfront to view the handcrafted fishing canoes painted in bright primary colors and the various fishing nets and traps used in these waters. In town, stroll past traditional Caribbean homes with lawns outlined in conch shells, past the large Roman Catholic church, and make a stop in the authentic Creole bakery for a treat.

The **Soufrière** region is the heartland of the island's many attractions. There's no denying that the most scenic part of the island is this south-central area. Starting with the rain forest and continuing down to the **Pitons,** this spectacular region is the breadbasket of the island. Every tropical fruit and vegetable thrives here, and it is sparsely populated.

For many visitors, the most fascinating area is the **rain forest.** You'll need a guide to enter the restricted region, so sign up for a guided tour with one of the island's tour operators. Call the St. Lucia Tourist Board at ☎ 758-452-4094, for more information. Hiking tours are available with guides from the **Forestry Department,** ☎ 758-450-2231. You'll walk through the dense foliage, swim in a tropical waterfall, and learn more about the plants that make up this fragile ecosystem. And, if you're lucky, you may have the opportunity to see the rare St. Lucian parrot.

This area is also home to a unique **Sulphur Spring volcano,** often called the "drive-through volcano." Actually, visitors cannot drive or walk through the volcano anymore (a few years ago a Rasta guide fell through a weak part of the crust; fortunately he received only severe burns). Groups walk only to the edge of the volcano which last erupted two centuries ago. With the smell of sulphur heavy in the air, you'll see jets of bubbling water black with ash and gases released from deep in the earth's core.

T IP: *Leave your silver jewelry back at the hotel for this trip. The gases can cause silver to tarnish.*

Near the volcano, the **Diamond Waterfalls and Gardens** bloom with tropical splendor. A self-guided walk through the garden leads the two of you past well-marked trees and flowers, and finally to the Diamond Waterfalls, a cascade that leaves a spray of "diamond" twinkles in the air. If you stop by on a Sunday, you can also enjoy a soak in the mineral baths. Originally funded by French King Louis XVI, these baths date back to 1784, when the king had the baths constructed for use by his troops.

Tour companies also offer a wide array of guided full- and half-day tours of the island. Visit the rain forest in open-air jeep (book early for this one since space is limited); take a bus tour to the volcano, the botanical gardens, and the waterfalls; or enjoy a combination tour with a drive down the coast and a catamaran ride back. **Sunlink Tours** offers a good selection of tours and we found the guides very knowledgeable about everything from island vegetation to history, ☎ 758-452-8232.

Underwater Delights

Another major attraction of St. Lucia is its scuba diving. **Anse Chastanet** is considered to be the top dive spot on the island and one of the best in the Caribbean. The reason? Extraordinary fish life, coral formations, and sponge growth right off shore. Divers and snorkelers can enjoy spectacular underwater exploration just yards from the beach. Call ☎ 758-459-7000.

Night divers have the chance to see Anse Chastanet's unidentified sea creature, known only as "The Thing." Frequently spotted on night dives, this shy creature, a 15-foot-long worm-like being with hundreds of legs, has never been identified.

Beaches

St. Lucia's beaches run from golden brown to a salt-and-pepper mixture of sand and volcanic elements. Some of the most popular beaches are **Anse Chastanet, Anse Cochon,** and **Reduit Beach.**

Sunbathers, take note: topless and nude sunbathing are prohibited throughout St. Lucia.

The Islands

Shopping

Castries, the island's largest town, is also its top shopping area. Here, you'll have a choice between malls and markets for everything from fine jewels to handmade crafts that capture the island spirit.

Gablewoods Mall, located near Sandals Halcyon, offers many gift shops such as **Island Cotton.**

Pointe Seraphine is the island's duty-free port. Here you'll find well-known chains such as **Little Switzerland, Colombian Emeralds** and **Benetton.**

> *TIP: Remember to bring your passport and return airline tickets to take advantage of the duty-free shopping. Items can be taken with you at point of purchase.*

Pointe Seraphine is open weekdays, and on Saturdays, until 1 pm only. Like most shops in St. Lucia, the mall is closed on Sundays.

Outside of Castries, make a stop at **Caribelle Batik** for handmade batik shirts, wraps, and scarves. In Choiseul, stop by the **Choiseul Arts and Crafts Center.** This town is known as the crafts center of the island, and you'll find straw, wood, and clay handcrafts, all manufactured locally.

Another local item that's a good reminder of your vacation is perfume. **Caribbean Perfumes,** located in Castries, captures the scents of the islands with perfumes for both men and women. Caribbean Perfumes are sold at shops across the island, including most resort gift stores.

Nightlife

The hottest show on the island is Friday night's **Jump Up** in the town of **Gros Islet,** on the northwest end of the island. Street-side music blares and residents and locals alike jam to the sounds of reggae, soca, and calypso. This is a chance to enjoy a true Caribbean celebration. Dance to local music, eat genuine St. Lucian food, and enjoy the island spirit.

One of the best places for nightlife is **The Lime** (☎ 758-462-0761). This restaurant and bar features music and dancing on Wednesday nights.

Just the Facts

Entry Requirements: US, Canadian, and UK citizens need either a passport or birth certificate and a return or onward ticket.

Getting Around: Taxis are the most common means of transportation for vacationers, but be advised that a journey from the north end of the island to the Piton region is an expensive one: about US $50 one way. Rental cars are available from the airports and the major hotel. You'll need to obtain a local license from the immigration desk at either airport, police station, or from the larger rental dealers. You will also need to present your driver's license from home.

Taxis can also be rented by the hour for a private tour. Work out the price with the driver before you leave, but estimate about US $20 per hour.

Language: English

Currency: Eastern Caribbean dollar: US $1 = EC $2.70

Electricity: 220 volts/50 cycles

Information: Contact the St. Lucia Tourist Board in the US at 820 Second Ave., 9th Floor, New York, NY 10017; ☎ 800-4ST-LUCIA or 212-867-2950; fax 212-867-2795. In Canada, 8 King St., Suite 700, Toronto, Ontario M5C 1B5, ☎ 416-362-4242; fax 416-362-7832. In the UK, 421A Finchley Road, London NW3 6HJ, ☎ 207-431-3675; fax 207-431-7920. Website: www.stlucia.org.

The Islands

St. Martin - Sint Maarten

*F*ine French food. Topless French beaches. Dutch architecture. Casinos that ring with baccarat and roulette.

This is St. Martin, the island that calls itself "a little bit European and a lot Caribbean." Located 150 miles southeast of Puerto Rico, this 37-square-mile island is comprised of **Dutch Sint Maarten** and **French St. Martin,** and is the smallest land mass on the globe shared by two nations.

Passing between the French and Dutch sides is the simplest border crossing you'll ever make. No passports. No customs. No immigration. Just a simple sign marking the demarcation between two nations.

Although the border is almost superficial, there are distinctions between the two countries. Mention "St. Martin" and many visitors will immediately think of the topless bathing that's de rigueur on the Gallic beaches. And on one 1½-mile stretch, *au naturel* is the order of the day. **Orient Beach** or Baie Orientale is the home of **Club Orient,** a naturist resort. The public beach is an equal mixture of nudists and cruise ship gawkers, sprinkled with folks who just want to enjoy gentle surf and powdery sand the color of toasted coconut.

The most cosmopolitan area of the island is found on its Dutch acres. Most visitors arrive in Simpson Bay's **Princess Juliana International Airport.** Don't let the modest size of the terminal fool you. This is one of the Caribbean's busiest airports, with direct service from New York, Newark, Miami, Baltimore, and San Juan, not to mention Paris and Amsterdam. Regional air service to many small islands also goes through this hub.

Simpson Bay, on the Dutch side, hops with vacationers who come to enjoy pristine beaches. The island's best snorkeling is at **Mullet Bay.** In nearby **Philipsburg,** it's shopping that draws visitors. Duty-free stores line the busy streets, and pedestrians can spend an entire day browsing in this commercial center.

> *Cameras, electronic goods, perfumes, and fine jewelry are especially good buys.*

Festivals

The biggest event on each side of the island is **Carnival.** On the Dutch side, Carnival occurs after Easter and continues until April 30, the birthday of Queen Beatrix of the Netherlands. The festival includes traditional Caribbean jump ups, parades and gatherings filled with island dishes, and music. The Grand Carnival Parade is the festival's biggest event, a colorful scene with elaborate costumes and a contagious spirit of fun.

And for early risers (or real night owls) there's the J'Ouvert (jou-vay) Morning Jump Up Parade. This festivity starts at four in the morning and continues until sunrise. Carnival's end is marked with the burning of King Momo, a straw figure who "rules" Carnival. When King Momo is burned, legend says that the island is left pure.

On the French side, Carnival is scheduled just before Shrove Tuesday, ending on Ash Wednesday.

Sweet Dreams

Price Chart

Rates reflect high winter season (expect prices to be as much as 40% lower during the off season) for a standard room for two adults for one night; prices in US dollars.

$ . . . . under $150
$$ . . . . between $150 and $300
$$$ . . . . between $300 and $450
$$$$ . . . . over $450

French St. Martin

Club Orient Resort
Baie Orientale
Reservations: ☎ *800-742-4276*
www.cluborient.com
$

Located on the nude end of Orient Beach, Club Orient Resort is a naturist, or nudist resort known throughout the world. Everything – from watersports to dinner – is available for guests to enjoy *sans* clothes. Just a look at the signs at the beach bar ("No tan lines, no problem") confirms the philosophy of this resort.

Cabins here are modest, camp-like structures with baths and fully equipped kitchens. Guests can stock up with supplies at a small store located on property or take their meals at Pappagallo's restaurant right on the beach. The restaurant is clothing-optional (although the waitstaff is clothed).

Special Features/Activities: beachfront, restaurant, watersports, nude beach.

When Visiting a Nude Beach

Don't take photos. Cameras are actually prohibited at Orient Beach, and security will come have a little talk with you if you start snapping. Feel free to join in or not. Clothed, topless, and nude vacationers all frequent the nude beach. Stretch out your towel or (at Orient Beach) rent a chaise lounge. Don't assume this is some sort of love-in. Sexual activity is one adventure that's a definite no-no. In fact, families are commonly seen on Orient Beach, both nude and clothed.

Esmeralda Resort, Orient Beach

PO Box 5141, Baie Orientale
☎ *590-87-3636; fax 590-87-3518*
Reservations: ☎ *800-742-4276, 800-622-7836*
$$

From the action-packed waters off Orient Beach, the green roofs of Esmeralda Resort are easy to spot. Fifteen villas, accommodating 54 guest rooms, are sprinkled across the low hills that rise up from Baie Orientale. Each villa includes its own swimming pool; accommodations offer air conditioning, satellite TV, telephones, fully equipped kitchenettes, and private terraces.

Special Features/Activities: beachfront, nearby restaurants, snorkeling, windsurfing, tennis, watersports.

Le Meridien L'Habitation and Le Domaine

BP 581, Anse Marcel
☎ *590-87-6700; fax 597-87-3038*
Reservations: ☎ *800-543-4300*
$$$

These two adjoining resorts, L'Habitation and Le Domain, are located on the island's northeast coast, tucked into Marcel Cove. Surrounded by a 150-acre nature preserve, the resort is landscaped with bougainvillea, hibiscus, and oleander. Guest rooms, with bright Caribbean colors, include 251 rooms at L'Habitation with garden or marina views, and 145 rooms and suites at the newer wing, Le Domaine. Facilities include swimming pools, private white sand beach, shuttle service to casinos, Philipsburg, and Marigot. Watersports activities include deep-sea fishing, motorboating, sailing, catamaran, power, and glass-bottom boating; scuba diving; waterskiing; canoeing; Jet Skiing; kayaking, and more. Horseback riding, racquetball, squash, and tennis are also available, as well as a fitness center.

Special Features/Activities: beachfront, swimming pools, restaurants, watesports, tennis, marina.

The Islands

Dutch Sint Maarten

Holland House Beach Hotel
PO Box 393, 43 Front Street, Philipsburg
☎ *599-542-2572; fax 599-542-24673*
Reservations: ☎ *800-223-9815*
www.hhbh.com
$

This charming European-style hotel has 54-rooms and is ideal for serious shoppers. Especially popular with Dutch travelers in town on business. The junior suite is an excellent value, with two rooms, a kitchen, living room and a large balcony.

Special Features/Activities: beachfront, convenient to downtown shopping, restaurant.

♥ Maho Beach Hotel and Casino
Maho Bay
☎ *599-55-2115; fax 599-55-3604*
Reservations: ☎ *800-223-0757*
www.ssholidays.com
$$

This 600-room hotel, set on a beautiful beach with calm waters, is perfect for beginning swimmers and snorkelers.

Special Features/Activities: beachfront, casino, fine and casual dining, watersports, close to nightlife.

 Tables for Two

Price Chart

Prices are for dinner per person, including an appetizer or salad, entrée, and drink.

$............................ under $15
$$ .... $15 to $30
$$$ .... $30 to $45
$$$$......................... over $45

Cheri's Café
Maho Bay
☎ *599-54-5336*
Dress code: casual
Reservations: optional
$-$$

This lively nightspot is also open for lunch and dinner (until midnight) and features American favorites such as burgers and sandwiches as well as pasta specials, seafood, and grilled steaks and chicken. Bring your dancing shoes to this fun-loving place.

► Rancho Argentinean Grill
Palapa Center, Simpson Bay
☎ *599-52-2495*
Dress code: casually elegant
Reservations: suggested
$$-$$$

Housed in a thatched-roof building, this large restaurant serves up Argentinean delights. Start with sangria or wine and some *empanadas* or *chorizos criollos* (Argentinean grilled sausage) and continue with the house specialty: steak. Sirloin, tenderloin, rib eye and T-bone cuts are served with side orders such as *cebollas fritas* (fried onions), *maiz choclo* (grilled corn on the cob), *arroz criollo* (seasoned rice), or p*lantos fritos* (fried plantains).

Holland House
35 Front Street, Philipsburg
☎ *599-52-2572*
Dress code: casually elegant
Reservations: optional
$$

Dine on veal Wiener schnitzel, beef brochette, duck or Dutch pea soup at this waterfront restaurant located at the Holland House Beach Hotel. We especially enjoyed the appetizers: miniature chicken parmigiana and spicy skewers of pork satay.

The Islands

♥ *Chesterfields Restaurant*
Bobby's Marina, Philipsburg
☎ *599-52-3484*
Dress code: casually elegant
Reservations: optional
$-$$

Enjoy a yacht club atmosphere in this waterside eatery, which offers many excellent seafood dishes. Both indoor and outdoor seating is available.

Lynette's
Simpson Bay
☎ *599-52-2865*
Dress code: casually elegant
Reservations: suggested
$$

The King Beau Beau Show, a calypso revue, enlivens this restaurant every Tuesday and Friday night. Any evening, however, you can find island favorites on the menu: Creole dishes, lobster, steak, fish and more.

♥ *Saratoga*
Simpson Bay Yacht Club
☎ *599-544-2421*
Dress code: casually elegant
Reservations: suggested
$$$

Located right at the yacht club, this elegant restaurant features an ever-changing menu that highlights local ingredients. Start with wild mushroom bisque or fish soup with rouille and Gruyère cheese, then select a main course: grilled mahi-mahi, sautéed red snapper, or grilled duck breast.

♥ *Le Bec Fin*
119 Front Street, Philipsburg
☎ *599-52-25725*
Dress code: casual
Reservations: not needed
$$

This seaside restaurant has a casual downstairs eatery for breakfast and lunch, and an upstairs section for an elegant dinner. Grilled lobster flambé, marinated duck breast, soufflés, and more tempt evening visitors. The lunch crowd enjoys quiche, burgers, fish sandwiches, and Neptune salads with sea scallops, smoked salmon, and marinated fish.

L'Escargot

84 Front Street, Philipsburg
☎ *599-52-2483*
Dress code: casually elegant
Reservations: optional
$$-$$$

Located right on busy Front Street, this French eatery features, you guessed it, escargot. Try the snails in garlic butter, in cherry tomatoes, baked in mushroom caps, or cooked up in an omelet. Seafood includes yellowtail filet, snapper in red wine sauce and shallots, and lobster. The specialty dish is Le Canard de L'Escargot, a crisp duck in pineapple and banana sauce. It was a *Gourmet* magazine award winner. Open Monday through Friday for lunch and dinner; dinner only on weekends.

Wajang Doll

137 Front Street, Philipsburg
☎ *599-52-2687*
Dress code: casually elegant
Reservations: suggested
$$

Rijstaffel ("rice table") is the order of the day at this wonderful eatery that serves up delicious Indonesian dishes satisfying even the pickiest of eaters. Choose from a 14- or 19-dish spread. Rijstaffel, an Indonesian feast, creates an evening of entertainment. Come with a big appetite.

The meal begins with an appetizer of egg rolls followed by main courses such as *sateh ajam* (skewered chicken covered with a spicy peanut-flavored sauce), *kerrie djawa* (beef curry), *daging ketjap* (beef braised in soy and ginger sauce), and *telor* (egg in spiced coconut sauce).

The Islands

Passanggrahan

Philipsburg
☎ *599-52-3588*
Dress code: casually elegant
Reservations: suggested
$$

This guest house serves a spicy menu: jumbo prawns Marco Polo (red and green bell peppers in cream sauce flamed with Pernod), Pla Pow (grilled whole snapper with Thai seasoning) and Thai chicken curry.

Jean Dupont

Marina Port la Royale
☎ *599-87-71-13*
Dress code: casually elegant
Reservations: not needed
$$

This lovely restaurant is the perfect place for lunch or dinner. A great view of the Marina Port La Royale accompanies a menu with diverse selections from filet mignon to hamburgers.

California

Blvd. de Grand Case
☎ *599-87-55-57*
Dress code: casual
Reservations: not needed
$$

This popular restaurant entertains locals as well as tourists with its great food and good location. Diners choose between pizzas, grilled salmon and other delicious entrées while watching the St. Martin sunset over Grand Case Bay. California's casual atmosphere is the perfect way to end a day on the island.

Surf Club South

Cul de Sac
☎ *599-29-50-40*
Dress code: casual
Reservations: not needed
$-$$

If you're looking for a Caribbean beach bar like the ones in the movies, you'll find it here. A visit to this beach bar/restaurant is an experience in itself. Diners can order from the menu of casual entreés and snacks and enjoy the swimming pool and memorabilia from New Jersey (oddly enough). Live music six nights a week.

Romantic Activities

Boat Racing

Let's get this straight. We're not boaters. But we would name this boat race as one of the most exciting activities in the Caribbean. Our boat: the *Stars and Stripes* (yes, the same one that brought Dennis Conner to glory). Our mission: to win the America's Cup.

Well, maybe not *the* America's Cup. Actually, this race is the 12-Metre Challenge, ☎ 599-54-2075, for both first-time sailors and salty skippers alike, held three times daily, six days a week from the Philipsburg marina. We learned that this was no pleasure cruise – we were there to work. For the better part of an hour we practiced our jobs, tacking and jibing, kicking up a

Looking down on a sailboat at the Heineken Regatta.

The Islands

salty spray and often leaning so far into the wind that half the crew enjoyed a cool Caribbean bath.

With the wind whipping as hard as 20 knots and swells churning up at six feet, we were quickly doused as we turned into position. "Red flag up! Start!" The race was on. We were now on course, racing upwind and zigzagging through the eye of the wind by tacking as fast as the crew could shout orders.

For 45 minutes, we edged two Canadian vessels for the lead. Finally, on the last stretch, *Stars and Stripes* pulled ahead. With one last "Primary grinders, go!" instruction, we were leading. And suddenly, there was one last shout. "Blue flag up!" Blue for *Stars and Stripes*. We had won. Dennis would have been proud.

There's plenty of action on St. Martin's shores as well. Beaches such as **Cupecoy, Mullet Bay, Maho,** and **Dawn Beach** on the Dutch side attract sunlovers. On the French side, beaches are all topless and include **Baie Rouge** and **Orient Beach,** best known for its clothing-optional stretch. Orient Beach is lined with restaurants, beach bars, and souvenir stands, but on the nude beach photography is prohibited (although tour bus loads of gawkers come by daily). Chairs and umbrellas rent for about US $5 each.

Shopping

In **Philipsburg,** shops line **Front Street,** the narrow boulevard nearest the waterfront. In these duty-free stores, electronic goods, leather, jewelry, and liquor (especially guavaberry liqueur) are especially good buys.

> *T IP: For the best prices, shop when the cruise ships are not in port. Bargaining is much more difficult during busy days.*

No duties are charged in or out of port, so savings run about 25-50% on consumer goods. Shop carefully, though, and research prices on specific goods before you leave home. Some items are not such bargains.

On the French side, the best shopping is in the capital city of **Marigot.** A crafts market close to the cruise terminal offers

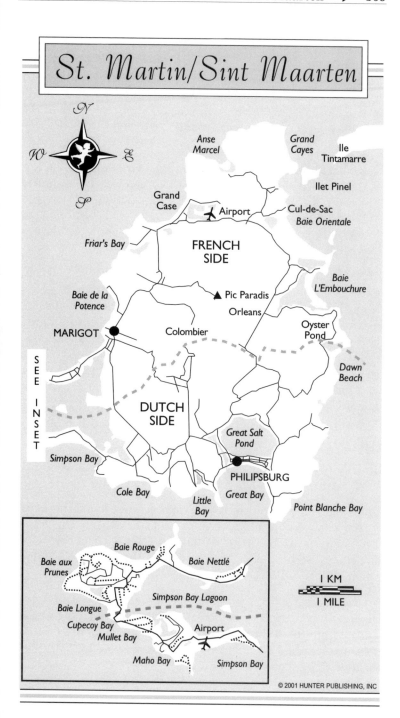

St. Martin/Sint Maarten

Anse Marcel
Grand Cayes
Ile Tintamarre
Ilet Pinel
Grand Case
Airport
Cul-de-Sac
Baie Orientale
Friar's Bay
FRENCH SIDE
Baie de la Potence
Pic Paradis
Baie L'Embouchure
MARIGOT
Colombier
Orleans
Oyster Pond
Dawn Beach
SEE INSET
DUTCH SIDE
Great Salt Pond
Simpson Bay
PHILIPSBURG
Cole Bay
Little Bay
Great Bay
Point Blanche Bay

Baie Rouge
Baie aux Prunes
Baie Nettlé
Simpson Bay Lagoon
Baie Longue
Cupecoy Bay
Mullet Bay
Airport
Maho Bay
Simpson Bay

1 KM
1 MILE

The Islands

© 2001 HUNTER PUBLISHING, INC

jewelry, T-shirts, souvenir items, carvings, and paintings (we were especially taken with the Haitian artwork available here). Marigot also is home to boutique shops, open 9 am to 12:30 pm and from 3 to 7 pm, which offer liqueurs, cognacs, cigars, crystal, china, jewelry, and perfumes, many from France.

Shopping for duty-free goods.

Nightlife

Casino gambling is a prime activity on the Dutch side of the island. Here's your chance to enjoy slots and table games; the atmosphere is fun and relaxed at all the casinos. One of the biggest is located at **Maho Beach Hotel, ☎** 599-55-2115.

Cheri's Café, located near Maho Bay Hotel, is one of the island's hottest night spots with live music nightly.

Much nightlife on French St. Martin revolves around the beach bars after a long day of watersports and sunworship. On Orient Bay, favorites are **Kontiki** (☎ 599-87-43-27), with its South Pacific theme and thatched roof, and **Waikiki** (☎ 599-87-43-19), which offers a wide variety of tropical drinks.

If you're looking for live music, check out **Peace and Love Disco** at La Savanne resort (☎ 599-87-58-34), which showcases many local bands. Bring your dance shoes to **Zenith Club-L'Atmo** (Marina Port la Royale, Marigot, ☎ 599-87-98-41), a favorite with locals as well as French travelers.

Just the Facts

Entry Requirements: US citizens need a current passport, an expired one less than five years old, or other proof of citizenship (a birth certificate with raised seal or a notarized copy, or a voter registration card along with driver's license) and a return or onward ticket. Immigration is in the airport only; there is no border check between the French and Dutch sides. Canadian citizens need to present a valid passport as well as a return or onward ticket.

Getting Around: Taxis are the common mode of transportation, albeit an expensive one. A ride from the Philipsburg courthouse taxi stand to Mullet Bay runs US $12, across the island from Mullet to Dawn Beach runs $26.

Language: French/Dutch, but English widely spoken.

Currency: Dutch side: Netherland Antilles Florin (NAF), US $1 = NAF $1.79. French side: French franc, US $1 = FF$6.9.

Electricity: Dutch side: 110 volts, 50 cyles, same as the US. French side: 220 volts, 60 cycles; Americans needs converters.

Information: In the US, the Sint Maarten Tourist Office is located at 675 Third Ave., Suite 1806, New York 10017, ☎ 800-ST MAARTEN (800-786-2278) or 212-953-2084, fax 212-953-2145. For information on French St. Martin, contact the French West Indies Tourist Board at 444 Madison Avenue, New York 10022, ☎ 212-757-1125, ext. 227 or 877-956-1234, fax 212-838-3486. In Canada: French Government Tourist Office, 30 St. Patrick St., Suite 700, Toronto, Ontario, ☎ 416-593-6427. Website: www.st-martin.org (French side); www.st-maarten.com (Dutch side).

Trinidad & Tobago

Trinidad and Tobago share membership in the same independent republic. They share the Trinidad-Tobago currency, the TT dollar. And they both enjoy the same idyllic climate, located south of the hurricane zone and rarely disturbed by the storms that can ravage other Caribbean islands in the summer and fall months.

But that's where the similarities between these two islands end. Like city and country cousins, Trinidad and Tobago both have a unique personality and distinct attractions.

Geography

Trinidad is by far the largest, both in terms of population and size. This anvil-shaped island bustles with activity in **Port of Spain,** the capital city that's also a capital in the world of Caribbean commerce. Here, you'll hear accents from residents who have relocated from around the world to work in this modern metropolis. The Indian influence is stronger here than anywhere else in the Caribbean, and is seen in the faces of islanders, the architecture, the food, and the religion, where nearly one quarter of all residents are Hindu.

Port of Spain lies on the northwest coast, an area bordered by a mountain range to the north and a dense, wildlife-filled swamp to the south. On the south shore lies Trinidad's oil industry, a business that brought the island prosperity in the 1970s. At over 1,800 square miles, the island is too large to be fully seen in one vacation, It tempts return visitors with promises of new discoveries.

In contrast, **Tobago** covers just over 100 square miles, and the only bustling occurs in the city of **Scarborough.** Life here moves to a Caribbean beat, with a leisurely pace enjoyed by visitors primarily from Europe, especially Germany, as well as Trinidadians on holiday. Goats graze in every field; coconut palm-lined beaches offer quiet getaways; luxury resorts pamper guests with everything from dining to spa experiences.

Both islands are especially popular with nature lovers. Trinidad is a favorite among the world's birders, who come to seek out species such as **toucans, hummingbirds, scarlet ibis,** and rare noctural **oilbirds.** In Tobago, divers seek out giant manta rays near the village of **Speyside.**

> *Among honeymooners, Tobago is the definite favorite. Its quiet pace is one that Trinidadians say is "for the newly wed and the nearly dead."*

Festivals

Arriving into **Port of Spain** just past midnight, we worried that we'd oversleep and miss the start of the **J'Ouvert,** or the Mud Parade, at 4 am. Were we silly.

Like a monster heartbeat, the sound of the throbbing speakers shook our hotel room – and our own bodies. The room pulsated to the beat of speakers on flatbed trucks on the street 10 stories below our room, winding through Port of Spain. The Mud Parade was beginning. The city was ready to party.

Long before dawn, we followed the masses and headed out to the streets. Heeding the warnings by those who had experienced the Mud Parade in previous years, we wore old clothes. Nonetheless, they were clean – all the better to offer a target for the revelers.

Each "mas" group, the troupe that follows the bands, is provided with mud of a different color. Just a few minutes after arriving, ochre-colored handprints were slapped on our backs, initiating us into the world of mud. Soon we were smeared in an artist's palette of tinted dirts. Red mud appeared on our cheeks. Gray mud streaked our legs.

Until sunrise, we shuffled through the streets, part of a mass of humanity that, for a few days, was determined to forget about reality and to experience the joy of **Carnival.** It is the largest such Carnival in the Caribbean, and second only to Rio's blowout.

Following Christmas, preparations begin for Carnival. For weeks, residents celebrate with steel band practices, parties, and special events. January marks the **Chutney Soca Monarch Competition,** featuring the unique chutney music that combines calypso and soca, played using East Indian instruments such as the dholak and the dhantal.

The action really heats up in February when nearly daily events include **National Pan and Junior Calypso contests** and competitions for Carnival King and Queen. The events come to a climax in the days before **Ash Wednesday,** starting with **Dimanche Gras** on Sunday night, featuring the most lavish costumes of Carnival, and followed by **J'Ouvert.** On

The Islands

Monday and Tuesday, bands process through the streets and past judges in Carnival activities throughout both islands, the largest which is held in Port of Spain and culminates at **Queen's Park Savannah.**

Carnival is certainly the largest event in Trinidad, but it's just one of the many festivals that give couples the chance to take part in the "real Caribbean." Few places on earth offer as many types of festivals as do Trinidad and Tobago. With a diverse population that traces its roots back to India, Africa, China, and the Middle East, these islands present a myriad of opportunities to celebrate. In Trinidad and Tobago, Christian churches, Hindu temples, and Muslim mosques stand side by side, each contributing to the joyous festivals found throughout the year.

On Tobago, the **Tobago Heritage Festival** in late July, celebrates the island's culture. One of the top events is the Old Time Wedding, a re-enactment of an 1800s wedding, complete with top hats and morning coats, at a historic church. Actually a play that changes every year, the vows are interrupted by dramatic events and locals roar with laughter when the ceremony is overshadowed by the groom's pregnant ex-girlfriend. Following the vows, the wedding party and the onlookers head down to the festival grounds. If you missed Carnival, here's your chance to learn chipping (a slow bump and grind) and shuffle along as the whole parade gyrates down the street.

Sweet Dreams

Price Chart

Rates reflect high winter season (expect prices to be as much as 40% lower during the off season) for a standard room for two adults for one night; prices are in US dollars.

$ . . . . under $150
$$ . . . . between $150 and $300
$$$ . . . . between $300 and $450
$$$$ . . . . over $450

Trinidad

Trinidad Hilton

PO Box 442, Lady Young Road, Port of Spain
Reservations: ☎ *800-445-8667*
☎ *868-624-3211, ext. 6040; fax 868-624-4485*
www.hilton.com
$$

Conrad Hilton's personal project still exudes an air of comfort and elegance amid the bustling city. This hotel is known as the "upside-down Hilton" because the lobby and ground level make up the top floor and the guest rooms are located downhill.

Visitors are met by walkways of smooth teak, grown on the island and used in furniture and railings throughout the hotel. Rooms are similar to those found in other traditional business-oriented hotels, but all include a private balcony overlooking Queen's Park Savannah. Carnival is held directly across the street from the hotel, so during that time come prepared to party.

Special Features/Activities: downtown, fine and casual dining, shopping arcade, freshwater pool, tennis.

The Normandie Hotel

10 Nook Ave., PO Box 851, Port of Spain
Reservations: ☎ *800-223-6510*
☎ *868-624-1181-4; fax 868-624-0108*
www.normandiett.com
$

The Normandie Hotel is a small (53 rooms) and intimate place in which to enjoy the downtown region in a setting much like a country inn. The property may be small in size, but has a large number of amenities to offer its guests: an excellent shopping arcade, an outdoor rum shop, La Fantasie fine dining restaurant, a gallery featuring local artists, and cultural events scheduled every month. Rooms here are simple and, for the most part, adequate.

Special Features/Activities: downtown, fine and casual dining, shopping arcade, freshwater pool, nightclub.

The Islands

Tradewinds Hotel

38 London Street, San Fernando
☎ *868-652-9463; fax 868-652-9463*
www.tradewindshotel.net
$

Tradewinds is located in the residential area of San Fernando and offers easy access to Trinidad's tourist attractions. This hotel offers its guests several room choices. For couples who plan on seeing the sights of the island, Caribbean-style superior and executive rooms are available, but for lovers who want to stay in more and enjoy each other's company, Tradewinds offers studio and one-bedroom apartments with full kitchens.

Special Features/Activities: computer room with Internet access, complimentary breakfast, restaurant.

Tobago

Blue Waters Inn

Batteaux Bay, Speyside
☎ *868-660-4341; fax 868-660-5195*
Reservations: ☎ *800-742-4276*
www.bluewatersinn.com
$

Located in Speyside on Batteaux Bay, this casual resort is perfect for lovers who plan to spend time enjoying nature, either on the resort's 46 acres of tropical foliage, or in the clear waters best known as the home of giant manta rays. Activity is the name of the game here, and it comes in forms such as scuba diving, snorkeling, windsurfing, glass-bottom boat tours of the reef, deep-sea fishing, tennis, and more.

Special Features/Activities: beachfront, casual dining, dive shop.

♥ Coco Reef Resort

PO Box 434, Coconut Bay, Scarborough
Reservations: ☎ *800-221-1294*
☎ *868-639-8571; fax 868-639-8574*
www.cocoreef.com
$$

This luxurious hotel hugs the Caribbean coastline, combining tropical elegance with island casualness for a wonderfully romantic atmosphere. This new property is located just a mile from the Crown Point International Airport. Lacking its own natural beach, the resort constructed a sand beach protected by an offshore breaker, so the calm waters are ideal for lazy afternoon floats. Next door lies Store Bay, a very popular beach, and Pigeon Point, another well-known Tobago stretch of sand.

> *The most romantic room at Coco Reef is, without a doubt, the Sunset Villa. Set apart from the rest of the hotel, this charming villa is constructed in true Caribbean fashion with a red tin roof, gingerbread trim, and its own private lawn overlooking the sea. Decks lead down from the villa's porch to overlook the water; indoors, the villa reveals its true luxury, with two baths sporting gold-tone fixtures and marble floors, a full size living room with wet bar, and a sprawling bedroom with its own patio as well. Romance couldn't ask for a better setting.*

Special Features/Activities: beachside, fine and casual dining, freshwater pool, dive operator, shopping arcade, spa, watersports.

Grafton Beach Resort

PO Box 25, Black Rock, Scarborough
☎ *868-639-0191; fax 868-639-0030*
Reservations: ☎ *800-223-6510*
www.grafton-resort.com
$$

From its beach bar to its restaurant to its swim-up pool bar, Grafton Beach Resort exudes fun. The 114-room property includes some rooms with king-size beds (which are saved for honeymooners, so be sure to let reservations know!). Every unit at the resort comes with television, mini-bar, and air conditioning.

Special Features/Activities: beachfront, casual and fine dining, freshwater pool, squash, watersports.

The Islands

♥ Le Grand Courlan Resort and Spa

PO Box 25, Black Rock, Scarborough
☎ *868-639-9667; fax 868-639-9292*
Reservations: ☎ *800-INSIGNIA*
www.legrandcourlan-resort.com
$$

Tobago's most elegant resort features a new spa with a teak floor for aerobics, massage rooms, juice bar, and hot and cold whirlpools. Le Grand Courlan also boasts some romantic rooms with hot tubs that are filled upon check-in.

> *Two wedding packages are available and include legal fees, marriage license, cake, champagne, and flowers, as well as options such as steel band music, traditional fruit cake, and photos.*

Special Features/Activities: beachfront, pool, fine and casual dining, spa.

Manta Lodge

PO Box 433, Winward Road, Speyside
☎ *868-660-5268; fax 868-660-5030*
www.mantalodge.com
$

If you love diving, check out the Manta Lodge, one of Tobago's best known properties for scuba enthusiasts. This 22-room property attracts bird lovers too. All come to enjoy peace and quiet, reflected by the lack of telephones and televisions in the guest rooms. This end of the island is home of Tobago's manta population, located in the deep waters just offshore from the resort. Nearby, undeveloped areas are filled with colorful birdlife.

Special Features/Activities: dive shop, swimming pool, casual restaurant.

♥ Plantation Villas

PO Box 435, Stonehaven Bay, Scarborough
☎ *868-639-9377; fax 868-639-0455*
Reservations: ☎ *800-74-CHARMS*
www.plantationbeachvillas.com
$$$

For villa lovers, these two-story homes are a dream come true. They lie just steps from the sea and from both the Le Grand Courlan and Grafton Beach Resorts. The villas, each with a full kitchen, living and dining room, and three bedrooms, are filled with locally crafted furniture. Each tempt residents with wide porches across the back of the homes, overlooking a tropical garden. Housekeeping services are provided daily, and cooking and babysitting are also available.

Special Features/Activities: beachfront, freshwater pool, bar.

Rex Turtle Beach

PO Box 201, Great Courland Bay, Scarborough
☎ *868-639-2851; fax 868-639-1495*
Reservations: ☎ *800-255-5859*
www.rexcaribbean.com
$

Like its name suggests, this hotel is located right on a beach favored by turtles as a nesting site. The atmosphere is casual and fun, enjoyed by an international array of visitors who come to soak up Tobago's sun. The hotel offers 125 rooms, each with ocean view.

Honeymooners are treated to sparkling wine and a fruit basket, and those who'd like to get married on their honeymoon will find the services of a wedding coordinator on-site to help simplify arrangements.

Special Features/Activities: beachfront, casual dining, watersports, tennis, golf.

Tables for Two

Dining is a true pleasure in either Trinidad or Tobago. On both islands you'll find tasty treats like the **roti,** a burrito-like fast food that traces its roots to India. Look for **"buss up shot"** at most diners; this is a roti that's torn up like a "busted up shirt" and is eaten with a fork rather than by hand. **Curried dishes** are the star of just about every menu. You'll also find an excellent selection of Chinese food, especially in Port of Spain.

$\mathcal{P}$rice $\mathcal{C}$hart

Restaurant prices are for dinner per person, including a drink, appetizer or salad, and entrée.

$........................ under $15
$$ .... $15 to $30
$$$ .... $30 to $45
$$$$ .... over $45

$\mathcal{T}$rinidad

♥ $\mathcal{R}$afters

6 Warner St., Newton, Port of Spain
☎ *868-628-9258*
Dress code: casually elegant
Reservations: recommended
$$-$$$

This elegant eatery is the perfect spot for a quiet evening in bustling Port of Spain. Attentive service, white table linens, and a décor that highlights the brick walls of this former warehouse, make a special night out. Start with Caribbean crab back, chicken scallopini, or smoked seafood pâté and then move on to the house specialties: chicken teriyaki, flame-broiled tenderloin served with jumbo shrimp, seafood au gratin, and garlic shrimp. For beef lovers, there's porterhouse steak and rib-eye, and seafood fans can select Tobago lobster tail, curried shrimp, or crab and lobster on a bed of spinch and mushrooms.

$\mathcal{M}$onsoon

Port of Spain
☎ *868-638-2268*
Dress code: casual
Reservations: not needed
$

When you dine at Monsoon, the two of you may well be the only vacationers in the restaurant. Have a look around, though, and you'll see faces from around the globe. This purple and green decorated diner is a lunchtime favorite with downtown businesspeople, many of whom have relocated to this island from other lands.

Rotis are the favorite dish here, and you can take your pick from many fillings: chicken, duck, beef, goat, pork, lamb, shrimp, conch, fish, and vegetable. Rotis are served with vegetables including potato, pumpkin, and bodi, a curried vegetable much like green beans.

Tiki Village
Kapok Hotel
☎ *868-622-6441*
Dress code: casual
Reservations: not needed
$-$$

This restaurant, located at the Kapok Hotel, has a good Polynesian and Chinese food menu. We recommend the Chinese buffet for a lunchtime treat.

Davises
100 Oxford Street
☎ *868-625-0144*
Dress code: casual
Reservations: not needed
$-$$

This local eatery offers new island cuisine, using local ingredients with a classic gourmet style.

Tobago

Blue Crab
5 Robenson Street, Scarborough
☎ *868-639-2737*
Dress code: casual
Reservations: required
$

This charming outdoor eatery offers local cuisine such as king-fish with pumpkin, pigeon peas, breadfruit salad, and oildown, a breadfruit dish that tastes somewhat like potato salad made

The Islands

with callaloo, coconut milk, and herbs. Blue Crab is a favorite with locals for lunch and dinner, and a delightful place to sit out the heat of the day and enjoy a refreshing lime punch.

Kariwak Village
Crown Point, Scarborough
☎ *868-639-8442*
Dress code: casual
Reservations: optional
$$

This small inn is a favorite with diners looking for all natural ingredients. The Dalai Lama recently dined here and conducted a seminar in the open-air restaurant perched beneath thatched palapa roofs. On Friday and Saturday nights, stop by for the all-you-can-eat buffet with favorites such as lamb chops, grilled fish, curried plantains, rice, and eggplant casserole, all followed up, if you're lucky, by Guinness ice cream.

Lalls Roti Shop
Scarborough
☎ *868-639-8748*
Dress code: casual
Reservations: no
$

There's nothing fancy about this roti shop. Wild chickens run for their lives just outside the door. There's no air conditioning and orders are taken at the counter. Drinks are kept in a self-serve refrigerator that also serves as a TV stand.

But the product here is the real thing: rotis and buss-up shot made by islanders for islanders.

▌ *For a taste of Tobago off the tourist trail, go to Lalls.*

♥ Jemma's
Speyside
☎ *868-660-4066*
Dress code: casual
Reservations: not needed
$

Located on the island's north tip, this restaurant is perched up in the trees, a full story above ground. It offers a bird's-eye view of the sea, although for many diners it's tough to tear your eyes away from the restaurant's offerings, including a top-notch callaloo soup. Jemma's is the perfect place for lovebirds to nest for a lingering beachside lunch.

Cocrico Inn
North Street, Plymouth
☎ *868-639-2961*
Dress code: casual
Reservations: not needed
$

This simple diner, located in front of a charming guesthouse, serves some of the island's best dishes: creole stew, Indian-style curried chicken, saucy shrimp, and marinated flying fish. Every dish is as fresh as can be, prepared with breadfruit, okra, callaloo, and lettuce from the owner's garden. Lobster is caught by fishermen at the water's edge. The mood here is friendly and unassuming and as delightful as going to enjoy Sunday dinner at your favorite grandmother's house.

Black Rock Café
Main Road, Black Rock
☎ *868-639-7625*
Dress code: casual
Reservations: not needed
$$-$$$

Open for breakfast, lunch and dinner, this open-air restaurant is casual and fun. Breakfast consists of exotic dishes such as grilled flying fish or black pudding with buljol or smoked herring, as well as traditional American eggs and toast. Lunch entrées include grilled flying fish and cheeseburgers; for dinner there is crab back, lobster creole, Tobago river lobster (crayfish), and shrimp kebab, all served with creole rice, roasted potatoes, or French fries. Don't miss the Englishman's Bay Sunset, a potent cocktail made of pineapple juice, rum, triple sec, lime juice, and grenadine syrup that's as colorful as a sunset itself.

♥ *Rouselles*
Bacolet Street
☎ *868-639-4738*
Dress code: casually elegant
Reservations: optional
$$-$$$

Island cuisine with a chef's touch is the mark of Rouselles, an elegant restaurant that specializes in lobster, seafood in creole sauce, pork chops, and grouper.

> *Dining by candlelight on Rouselles open-air porch is a romantic treat for any couple.*

Romantic Activities

Island Sights

Nature tours are top attractions on Trinidad. The **Asa Wright Nature Centre,** ☎ 868-667-4655, is the top spot for naturalists and birders, who can enjoy guided walks on nature trails, or go off on their own in search of multicolored hummingbirds and other tropical species. Near Port of Spain, the **Caroni Swamp,** ☎ 868-638-6360, is a sanctuary that's home to the scarlet ibis, and in the sunset hours the sky turns truly scarlet as these birds come in to roost in the mangroves. Boat tours are available for a closer look at these beautiful birds; for information, call **KPE Nature Tours,** ☎ 868-637-9664, or fax 625-6980.

In Port of Spain, the **Queen's Park Savannah** is a top stop. This central park, encircled by what's termed the world's longest roundabout, is home to cricket fields, botanical gardens, and tall trucks selling coconut water. Walk around the Savannah, which is lined with grand historic homes.

Although Trinidad is not known for its beaches, **Maracas Bay,** located on the north shore, is a popular spot with both tourists and residents. About an hour from Port of Spain, the drive to this area is a treat in itself, winding through the **Northern Range** with views of forests, where species such as howler and capuchin monkeys, ocelot, Amazon parrots, and wild pigs can be found.

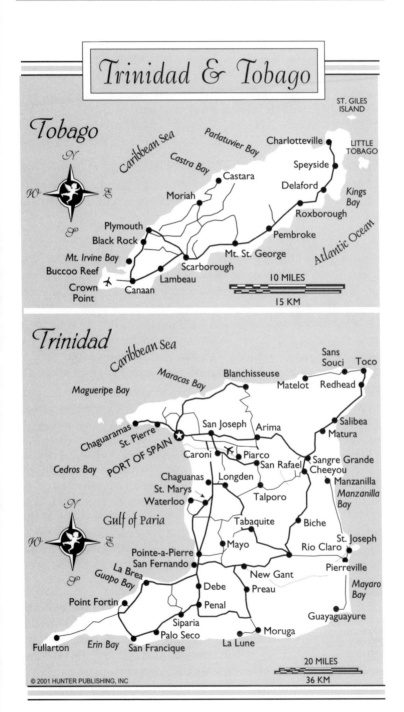

Trinidad & Tobago

Tobago

Caribbean Sea

ST. GILES ISLAND

Parlatuvier Bay

Castra Bay

Charlotteville

LITTLE TOBAGO

Speyside

Castara

Delaford

Kings Bay

Moriah

Roxborough

Plymouth

Pembroke

Black Rock

Mt. Irvine Bay

Mt. St. George

Buccoo Reef

Scarborough

Lambeau

Crown Point

Canaan

Atlantic Ocean

10 MILES

15 KM

Trinidad

Caribbean Sea

Sans Souci

Toco

Blanchisseuse

Matelot

Redhead

Magueripe Bay

Maracas Bay

Chaguaramas

San Joseph

Arima

Salibea

St. Pierre

Matura

Cedros Bay

PORT OF SPAIN

Caroni

Piarco

San Rafael

Sangre Grande

Cheeyou

Chaguanas

Longden

Manzanilla

St. Marys

Manzanilla Bay

Waterloo

Talporo

Gulf of Paria

Tabaquite

Biche

Mayo

St. Joseph

Pointe-a-Pierre

Rio Claro

San Fernando

Pierreville

La Brea

New Gant

Mayaro Bay

Guapo Bay

Debe

Preau

Point Fortin

Penal

Guayaguayure

Siparia

Palo Seco

Moruga

Fullarton

Erin Bay

San Francique

La Lune

20 MILES

36 KM

The Islands

> *Make a stop at the **Hot Bamboo Hut** for a taste of spicy mango slices in pepper and a beautiful view of the coastline.*

Maracas Bay offers a full day of fun, with complete changing facilities, chair rentals, watersports, and local food such as "shark and bake," a fast food snack made with fresh shark encased in a pancake sandwich.

Cultural events are scheduled every month at **The Normandie Hotel,** with entertainment ranging from poetry readings to small plays to opera performances held beneath the trees. ☎ 868-624-1181.

Nature attractions are also a big draw on Tobago. Of special interest are the **leatherback turtles** who come to nest on the leeward side of the island between March and August. Come out after sunset between 7 pm and 5 am, for the best chance of viewing these large marine turtles when they come ashore to lay between 80 and 125 eggs in the sand. The tiny offspring make their run for the sea about two months later. For tours of Tobago's natural wonders, call **Hew's Tours** in Scarborough (☎ 868-639-9058), or **David Rooks Nature Tours** (☎ 868-639-4276).

Water Delights

Cruising Tobago's calm waters is a fun a way to look at the island's beautiful coast. ***The Loafer*** (☎ 868-639-7312), a 50-foot catamaran, departs from **Buccoo Reef,** the most popular beach on the island, for all-day cruises as well as sunset sails and full moon dinners. The all-day-trip includes a swim at the **Nylon Pool,** a calm, shallow area in the sea formed by a sandbar close to the surface, where swimmers of all skills can take a dip.

Divers often head straight to **Speyside,** located on the northern tip of the island. Here, they might have the opportunity to swim with giant manta rays; dolphins, turtles, whale sharks and porpoises are sometimes spotted. This area is especially rich, with a profusion of coral growth and marine life, because of Venezuela's **Orinoco River.** The river's nutrients flow through the Guyana current that brushes Tobago and provides the island with some of the Caribbean's best diving.

To schedule a dive, contact one of these operators: **Aqua-marine Dive at Blue Waters Inn** (☎ 868-660-5445); **Adventure Eco-Divers** at Grafton Beach Resort (☎ 868-639-8729); **Man Friday Diving at Man-O-War Bay** (☎ 868-660-4676) or **Manta Dive Center** at Pigeon Point (☎ 868-639-9209/9969). Day-trips to other islands are a popular activity for travelers who stay on Tobago for a week or longer. Trips to the **Grenadines** and Venezuela's **Angel Falls** are two choices; call **AJM Tours,** ☎ 868-639-0610.

Trinidad & Tobago Shopping

Some of the best shopping on Trinidad is actually found at **Piarco International Airport.** These duty-free shops tempt those departing with local liquor, electronics, watches, jewelry, and more. There's also a good selection of locally made items, ranging from hot sauces to copper jewelry to tiny steel pans. **Port of Spain** is also home to several sprawling malls.

Non-shoppers will love Tobago: it's tough to spend money on this island. The most colorful shopping is found in **Scarborough's open-air market,** where tropical fruits and vegetables explode in an artist's palette of colors. Sample a few items (watch out for the fiery Scotch bonnet peppers!), and buy a bottle of homemade hot sauce and packaged curry, some of the island's top buys.

Foodies will find plenty of gifts to bring home on either island. Coffee lovers can take home **Pong Wing Coffee;** rum drinkers can check out **Royal Oak.** Curry, saffron, and other spices are excellent buys at the markets.

Nightlife

Nowhere do the differences between Trinidad and Tobago reveal themselves more than in the amount of nighttime activity. **Trinidad** pulsates with nightlife, especially in the **pan yards,** where steel bands practice and local residents come to enjoy the sounds. Finding a pan yard involves a little work on your part; no publication lists the yards that are open that night. Have no fear, though, because you'll find that the hotel personnel of Trinidad can tell you where to go for music on any given night.

The Islands

Tobago's nightlife is much more sedate – except when it comes to Sunday evenings. That's the time for **"Sunday School,"** held every Sunday in the community of **Buccoo Village.** This open-air street party doesn't get cranked up until near midnight, so come prepared to stay up late and enjoy the pulsating sounds of calypso and soca.

 *Just the Facts*

Entry Requirements: Visitors from the US, Canada, and the UK must show a valid passport.

No vaccinations are required for admission from the US; however, the Centers for Disease Control recommends a yellow fever vaccine for travelers venturing to the remote areas of Tobago, such as the rain forest. For more information, contact the CDC fax document service at ☎ 404-332-4565. Request document 220150 for Disease Risk and Prevention in the Caribbean and document 221040 for yellow fever.

Getting Around: Taxis are a common means of transportation on both islands. Driving in Port of Spain is a little like participating in a stock car race, so most vacationers opt for a cab. Inexpensive options are the Maxi taxis, vans that cover different areas of the island (locations are designated by the color of the stripe on the side of the vans). Maxi taxis stop anywhere along their routes.

In Tobago, taxis also frequent Scarborough's streets, but visitors on the north end of the island may find rental cars a better option. Thrifty Car Rental and several local companies offer rentals from Crown Point airport.

Language: English

Currency: Trinidad & Tobago dollar: US $1 = TT $6.24.

Electricity: 115 volts and 220 volts, depending on the hotel.

Information: In the US, contact the Trinidad and Tobago Tourist Office at 733 Third Avenue, Suite 1716, New York 10017-3204; ☎ 800-595-1TNT. In Canada, 2005 Sheppard Avenue East, Suite 303, Willowdale, Ontario M2J 5B4; ☎ 416-495-

9442. In the UK, 42 Belgravec Square, London, SWIX 8NT;
☎ 800-960057. Website: www.visittnt.com.

Turks & Caicos

Ever wonder what it's like to discover a Caribbean hideaway? An island bathed in tropical pastels, where the sound of lapping surf fills the warm air with the promise of a walk on a chalk-white beach or a dive in turquoise waters?

You'll feel like the two of you have made a lucky discovery in the Turks and Caicos (pronounced kay-cos), an archipelago of nearly 40 islands. Here, you'll find over 200 miles of pristine beaches, a coral reef system spanning over 65 miles, and a group of islands offering everything from late-night roulette in an elegant casino to Robinson Crusoe-type solitude on uninhabited islands.

The Turks and Caicos islands are located 1½ hours from Miami, tucked halfway between the tip of Florida and Puerto Rico. This British crown colony, ruled by a governor appointed by the Queen, is better known in the world of banking than by travelers. With its tax-free status and the stability of the British government backing the islands, the Turks and Caicos has offered off-shore banking for American corporations for many years.

The same attributes that make these islands so attractive to businesses also make them appealing to travelers. Daily jet service speeds travel. Once there, transport around the islands is easy, although conducted on the left side of the road.

Geography

This chain is composed of nearly 40 limestone islands, only eight are considered destinations. **Providenciales,** or Provo, is home to about 6,000 residents and to most of the tourist industry. No hotels though are over three-stories-tall by law.

The capital of the Turks and Caicos is the island of **Grand Turk,** a short hop from Provo. This seven-square-mile island

The Islands

has some historic buildings and the national museum, a must-see for history buffs.

Other inhabited islands include **North Caicos,** the most verdant island in the chain; **South Caicos,** a fishing center; **Middle Caicos,** home of several sea caves; and **Salt Cay,** a tiny island of only 300 residents that was once the world's largest producer of salt.

The Turks and Caicos are home to an extensive national park and nature reserve system. Over 31 national parks dot the islands, including Provo's **Princess Alexandra National Park,** with 13 miles of protected beaches; the **NW Point Marine,** with spectacular wall diving; and **Chalk Sound,** with small boat sailing on the west end of the island. National park rules make it illegal to hunt or fish, remove any animal or coral, moor vessels over 60 feet except on fixed buoys, or drive boats within 100 yards of shore.

If you take a boat trip to one of the cays, you might be lucky enough to see the unofficial mascot of the islands: **JoJo.** This wild dolphin has been sighted for over a dozen years along Provo's north shore, the only case ever documented of prolonged interaction between an individual wild dolphin and humans. Often seen swimming near boats, JoJo is protected by his governmental status as an official national treasure.

Although it is rare to spot JoJo, vacationers are certain to view wildlife on daytrips to nearby **Water Cay,** located northeast of Provo. Here numerous iguanas greet boat passengers and hope for handouts of a tasty grape or mango.

Festivals

The Turks and Caicos are home to several festivals, although most take place on one island only. In late May, South Caicos holds a sailing regatta (call the tourist board for entry details, ☎ 800-241-0824 or 305-891-4117), with plenty of local food.

In early June, Grand Turk celebrates the **Queen's Official Birthday,** with a uniformed parade (and we mean uniforms – everyone from the police force to the Girl Scouts and Boy Scouts takes to the streets) and medals from Her Majesty the Queen are presented by the governor.

Late June brings **Fun in the Sun** on tiny Salt Cay. The event is a beauty pageant for the youngest residents of Salt Cay, along with dances and local food. This celebration is a good way to meet the handful of local residents who make this island home; the festival has a real small-town feel.

In mid-August, dance to the sounds of the **Rake and Scrape Music Festival** on Grand Turk. Like the name says, this event features plenty of "rake and scape," music produced using drums and handsaws.

Sweet Dreams

Price Chart

Rates reflect high winter season (expect prices to be as much as 40% lower during the off season) for a standard room for two adults for one night; prices are in US dollars.

$ . . . . under $150
$$ . . . . between $150 and $300
$$$ . . . . between $300 and $450
$$$$ . . . . over $450

Providenciales

Ocean Club
PO Box 240, Grace Bay Road
☎ *649-946-5880; fax 649-946-5845*
Reservations: ☎ *800-457-8787*
www.oceanclubresorts.com
$$

The Ocean Club is casual elegance at its best: rooms with cool tile floors, ceiling fans, fully equipped kitchens, and large screened balconies where the two of you can sit and discuss the underwater beauty you beheld that day.

Special Features/Activities: beachfront, casual dining and bar, freshwater pool, shopping arcade, tennis, walking distance to golf course and club, watersports, dive shop.

♥ Grace Bay Club
PO Box 128, Grace Bay Road
☎ *649-946-5757; fax 649-946-5758*
Reservations: ☎ *800-946-5757*
www.gracebay.com
$$$$

Provo's most exclusive property, this Swiss-owned hotel has 22 suites and a regard for privacy. We have seen few accommodations in the Caribbean with this level of style. Furnished with items from Mexico and India, the rooms are decorated in subdued beige tones to put the emphasis on the brilliant color of the sea just beyond the balcony.

Guests can choose from a list of complimentary activities, or pamper themselves with a facial, body wrap, or even a massage on the beach.

> *The hotel can arrange to drop the two of you off on an uninhabited island with a picnic lunch.*

At the end of the day, enjoy a cocktail in the palapa bar, dinner at Anacaona, the finest restaurant on the island, and some dancing to live music under the stars. This resort isn't for the budget conscious, but for those who can afford it, this is luxury itself.

Special Features/Activities: beachfront, tennis, fine dining, complimentary watersports, sailing, golf at nearby course.

Allegro Resort Turks and Caicos
PO Box 205, Grace Bay Road
☎ *649-946-5555; fax 649-946-5629*
Reservations: ☎ *800-992-2015*
www.jacktar.com or www.allegroresorts.com
$$

The only casino in the country is found here. The full-service hotel has comfortable rooms, an excellent beach, and a relaxed atmosphere that we enjoyed.

Late afternoon sun makes the pool shimmer.
Courtesy of Allegro Resort Turks and Caicos.

Special Features/Activities: beachfront, freshwater pool, dive shop, tennis, watersports, casual and fine dining, casino.

Le Deck

PO Box 144, Grace Bay Road
☎ 649-946-5547; fax 649-946-5770
Reservations: ☎ 800-528-1905
www.ledeck.com
$$

Though not fancy, Le Deck has comfortable rooms, a great restaurant, and a central location on Grace Bay.

Special Features/Activities: beachfront, freshwater swimming pool, casual restaurant and bar.

Erebus Inn

PO Box 238, Turtle Cove Marina
☎ 649-946-4240; fax 649-946-4704
Reservations: ☎ 800-645-1179
www.erebus.tc
$

Overlooking Turtle Cove Marina, this modest inn is a charming spot for those on a budget – plus it offers a great view.

The Islands

Special Features/Activities: mountainside, freshwater pool, gym, restaurant.

Turtle Cove Inn
PO Box 131, Turtle Cove Marina
☎ *649-946-4203; fax 649-946-4141*
Reservations: ☎ *800-887-0477*
www.turtlecoveinn.com
$

When divers come up for air, many head here, where they find an on-site dive center and packages including two-tank morning dives. A honeymoon package, featuring champagne, dinner, a dune buggy rental or day sail, picnic lunch for two, and more is available. Located directly off the marina, rooms here are simple but include telephone, cable TV, and a private balcony.

Special Features/Activities: freshwater pool, casual restaurant and bar, dive shop.

Beaches Turquoise Resort and Spa
PO Box 186, Lower Bight Road
☎ *649-946-8000; fax 649-946-8001*
Reservations: ☎ *800-BEACHES*
www.beaches.com
$$-$$$

This Sandals is open to couples, singles and families. Here you can expect all-inclusive fun while taking advantage of the Grace Bay location. Includes full European Spa, kid's program, and five restaurants. Rooms have cable TV, mini-bar, safes, coffee makers, hairdryers, dataports, and balconies.

Special Features/Activities: beachfront, all-inclusive, fine and casual dining, watersports, spa.

Grand Turk

Sitting Pretty Hotel
PO Box 42, Duke Street
☎ *649-946-2135; fax 649-946-1460*
Reservations: ☎ *800-548-8462*
$

This 43-room hotel is simple and rather spartan. All rooms include TVs and air conditioning, as well as private patios. The hotel is primarily a rest stop for dedicated divers, who will find three wrecks just offshore and many other dive sites just 10 minutes away.

Special Features/Activities: some beachfront rooms, freshwater pool, restaurant and bar, dive shop.

Salt Cay

Mount Pleasant Guest House
☎ 649-946-6927
Reservations: ☎ 800-821-6670
www.turksandcaicos.tc/mtpleasant
$

This inn, with seven guest rooms (and a dorm room with multiple beds), is a favorite with scuba divers. All rooms are furnished with antiques.

Although divers may comprise the biggest part of their guest list, the owners of this inn haven't forgotten romantics as well.

> *At Mount Pleasant you'll find one of the most romantic offerings in the Caribbean – and at no extra cost. You can arrange to spend a night on a private, uninhabited island. The inn will take you out by boat and provide a tent, bedding, a gas grill, and a bottle of wine. The rest is up to you. As the owner says, "You can reinvent the wheel as a couple" in this truly Robinson Crusoe-type setting.*

Special Features/Activities: casual dining, horseback riding.

Windmills Plantation
North Beach Road
☎ 649-946-6962; fax 649-946-6930
Reservations: ☎ 800-822-7715
$$$$

It's somewhat surprising to find this exclusive eight-room hotel tucked away on tiny Salt Cay. Perhaps that's what makes this

The Islands

inn so special. Add furniture imported from Costa Rica, a library with over a thousand volumes, a restaurant featuring Caribbean food, including Salt Cay lobster, horseback and nature trails, and you've got a romantic getaway for those looking for the ultimate in privacy. You can even splurge and book a suite with its own plunge pool.

Special Features/Activities: fine dining, pool.

Tables for Two

With the high number of both American visitors and expatriates, you'll find many cuisines represented on the islands. For a real taste of island food, sample the **conch,** served as fritters, salad, and sandwiches, as well as **grouper, hogfish, soft-shell crab,** and **spiny lobster.**

Price Chart

Restaurant prices are for dinner per person, including a drink, appetizer or salad, and entrée.

$.	under $15
$$	$15 to $30
$$$	$30 to $45
$$$$	over $45

♥ *Anacaona*
Grace Bay Club, Grace Bay Road, Providenciales
☎ *649-946-5050*
Dress Code: dressy
Reservations: suggested
$$$

Save one night for a special dinner at Anacaona, an Indian word that translates into "feather of gold." This open-air restaurant is true gold, a gem of a property that combines European elegance with Caribbean tranquillity. The two of you can enjoy an elegant meal beneath a thatched palapa that rests on Roman columns. The menu is complemented with an extensive wine list and Cuban cigars. Reservations recommended.

After dinner at Acacoana one night, we walked back along the beach to our room at Turquoise Reef, carrying our shoes. With the sound of the surf and the light of the moon, we remember this as one of our most romantic walks in the Caribbean, a treat that we could fully enjoy thanks to the low crime rate on this peaceful island.

Gecko Grill
Ocean Club, Providenciales
☎ *649-946-5880*
Dress code: casually elegant
Reservations: suggested
$$-$$$

Start with a drink at the bar, then choose an indoor or outdoor table. We always dine outside beneath the ficus trees, lit with small, white Christmas lights. The Gecko Grille is one of our favorite dining spots in these islands, thanks to the creations of Chef John A. Brubaker.

Brubaker's menu puts a gourmet spin on Caribbean favorites. We started with ocean escargot, tender young conch served in a garlic herb butter. Especially impressive at the Gecko Grille is its extensive wine and champagne list.

Gilley's Café at Leeward
Leeward Marina, Providenciales
☎ *649-946-5094*
Dress code: casual
Reservations: optional
$$

This delightful eatery, located just steps from the marina at Leeward, serves up breakfast, lunch and dinner. We dined on cracked conch, fried to tender perfection; other options include lobster salad, sirloin, seafood and broccoli quiche, and more. The restaurant is simple with long tables that encircle a central bar.

The Islands

Tiki Hut

Turtle Cove Inn, Providenciales
☎ *649-941-5341*
Dress code: casual
Reservations: optional
$

Start the day with a breakfast of Grand Marnier croissant French toast, Belgian waffles, or tropical pancakes. We enjoyed an excellent lunch here and sampled the conch fritters, made from the Conch Farm's own product, fish and chips and jerk chicken sandwich. Friday through Monday you can also enjoy dinner at this excellent restaurant.

Romantic Activities

With the number of tourists relatively low, you'll find that the number of attractions are equally sparse. Don't expect the shopping of St. Thomas or the reggae clubs of Jamaica. For most couples, the real attraction is being able to do nothing at all. Days are spent on the beach or in the water that's so clear it's often cited as the world's top scuba destination.

Island Sights & Museums

One unique attraction is the **Conch Farm,** ☎ 649-945-5942, the only farm in the world that raises Queen conch, the shellfish that's become a favorite meal throughout much of the Caribbean. On a guided tour, you'll see conch in various stages, from the larvae in the hatchery, to juveniles about four millimeters in length, to full grown. In Provo, the product of this unique farm is served at the Anacaona Restaurant and the Tiki Hut.

History buffs will find reason enough to take a day-trip to Grand Turk to visit the **Turks and Caicos National Museum,** ☎ 649-946-2160, one of the most fascinating museums in the entire Caribbean. The main exhibit features the Molasses Reef shipwreck, which occurred in the Turks and Caicos nearly 500 years ago. The Spanish caravel hit the reef and quickly sank in only 20 feet of water, where it remained until the 1970s.

Once excavated, it was recognized as the oldest European ship-wreck in the New World.

The museum, located in a 150-year-old house on the island's main street, features artifacts from the wreck, with interactive displays, video presentations, and scientific exhibits.

The name of this ship was never learned because, like drug-running planes of today, this was a ship with an illegal booty. Kept off the official records of Spain, it was carrying slaves probably bound for the plantations of nearby Hispaniola.

Underwater Delights

Scuba diving and snorkeling are the top attractions of these islands. Visibility ranges from 80 to 100 feet, or better, and water temperatures hover at about 82° in the summer, and 75 or so in the winter months. Beneath the calm waves swim colorful marine animals as exotic as hawksbill turtles, nurse sharks, and octopus. With a one-mile vertical coral wall located offshore, Provo is a diver's paradise. Scuba diving and snorkeling are the top attractions of these islands.

Some good shallow sites are found off Grace Bay; wreck divers are also challenged at sites such as the 1985 wreck of the freighter *Southwind*.

You'll find top operators here as well. In Provo, call **Dive Provo,** ☎ 800-234-7768, or **Turtle Inn Divers,** ☎ 800-359-DIVE. In Grand Turk, check with **Blue Water Divers,** ☎ 649-946-2432; **Sea Eye Diving,** ☎ 649-946-1407; or **Aquanaut,** ☎ 649-946-2160; in Salt Cay, call **Porpoise Divers;** ☎ 649-946-6927.

Other Activities

Save a day to cruise over to **Water Cay,** an island inhabited by friendly iguanas and tropical birds.

Provo Golf Club, ☎ 649-946-5991, has a nice clubhouse with restaurant, a good place to stop for a drink after playing a round.

The Islands

Shopping

You will find limited shopping on Provo, most in a complex called **Ports of Call,** designed to resemble an old Caribbean seaside town. Look for restaurants, crafts and art in this new development near Grace Bay.

Conch shells (pronounced Konk) make a wonderful souvenir from these islands. Stop by the Conch Farm on Provo to purchase a beautiful shell; you'll also find some large piles next to several island bars where you can stop and make an inexpensive purchase.

For Caribbean art, check out the **Bamboo Gallery** on Provo, an excellent gallery that's been featured in many newspaper and magazine articles. Here you'll find Haitian, Jamaican, and even some Turks and Caicos artwork. Near Ports of Call, **Maison Creole** also has magnificent artwork with crafts from Haiti and other Caribbean islands.

Nightlife

Nightlife is somewhat limited in the Turks and Caicos because of the islands' secluded atmosphere and because scuba divers, after a day in the sun and sea, are ready to hit the sack early and prepare for another day underwater. The two of you will find a few good options, though.

Try your luck at the **Port Royale Casino, ☎** 649-946-5508, at the Allegro Resort in Provo. The nation's only casino has plenty of action, including over 100 slot machines, Caribbean stud poker, roulette, blackjack, craps, and more.

The hottest dance spot on the island, **Erebus Inn, ☎** 649-946-4240, is popular with both locals and vacationers. The outdoor club blasts live music under the stars late into the night.

Every night of the week you can find live music at one location. Look to these nightspots for live music on some nights:

♥ **Club Med-Turkoise, ☎** 649-946-5500. We recently bought a night pass at this all-inclusive; you buy tickets for drinks. They have dancing and an evening show.

- ♥ **Le Jardin Restaurant** at Le Deck Hotel and Beach Club, ☎ 649-946-5547. Live music entertains diners and a late-night crowd on Thursdays and Sundays.

- ♥ **Lone Star Bar and Grill** at Ports of Call, ☎ 649-946-5832. Live music on Friday nights brings in a crowd.

- ♥ **Beaches Resort and Spa,** ☎ 649-946-8000. You can buy a night pass at this all-inclusive resort to enjoy their evening show.

Just the Facts

Entry Requirements: US, Canadian, and UK visitors are required to have proof of citizenship, such as an official birth certificate or voter registration card and photo identification, or a passport. Visitors must also show a return ticket.

Getting Around: Rental cars are available, but limited numbers make them tough to obtain and expensive. Once you have a rental car, you'll find that gasoline prices are equally expensive: about $2.50 a gallon. Taxi service is easier.

Language: English

Currency: US dollar

Electricity: 110 volts

Information: In the US, contact the Turks and Caicos Tourist Office, 11645 Biscayne Boulevard, Suite 302, North Miami, Florida 33181, or call ☎ 800-241-0824 or ☎ 305-891-4117; fax 305-891-7096. In the UK, c/o Mitre House, 66 Abbey Road, Bush Hill Park, Enfield, Middlesex EN1 2QE; ☎ 44-208-350-1017. Website: www.turksandcaicostourism.com.

The Islands

US Virgin Islands

A trip to the US Virgin Islands is truly "no problem" because you never leave American soil. No need to change money or buy foreign postage stamps. You're still at home, but, oh, what a beautiful and unique home it is.

While still part of the US, the US Virgin Islands are a special mix of American and Caribbean. English is spoken, but with a distinct Caribbean lilt called calypso. Driving is on the left side of the road. And restaurant menus feature a few items that you may not recognize (but you should try).

License plates proudly proclaim that this is "America's Paradise." It's America's own vacation land, a place for lovers to enjoy some of the greatest duty-free shopping, dance to a Caribbean beat, swim in some of the region's clearest waters, or do some "limin'," the Virgin Islanders' word for just kicking back and enjoying a taste of paradise.

Geography

The US Virgin Islands offer three distinct vacations for couples. Shoppers and high-energy types will love **St. Thomas,** where poinciana-covered hills overlook streets filled with some of the Caribbean's finest duty-free shopping, one of the region's busiest cruise ship ports, and some of the most luxurious resorts in the isles.

Next door, tiny **St. John** is custom-made for nature lovers, who can camp and hike in the national park that covers two-thirds of this unspoiled island. And, last and largest, **St. Croix** enchants travelers with its small-town charm, picturesque Danish architecture, and one of the Caribbean's finest snorkeling trails.

Island hopping is part of life here. St. Thomas and St. John are just a 20-minute ferry ride apart, and it's just another short hop over the British Virgin Islands, a very popular day-trip.

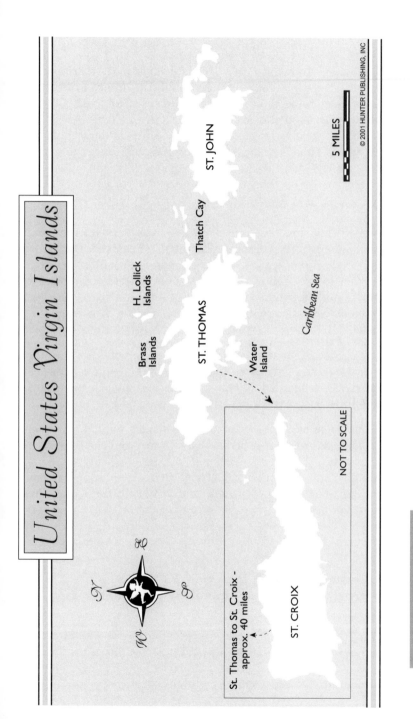

United States Virgin Islands

Brass
Islands

H. Lollick
Islands

Thatch Cay

ST. THOMAS

ST. JOHN

Water
Island

Caribbean Sea

5 MILES

© 2001 HUNTER PUBLISHING, INC

NOT TO SCALE

St. Thomas to St. Croix -
approx. 40 miles

ST. CROIX

The Islands

Forty miles to the south, St. Croix is connected to its sister islands by 25-minute flights or by high-speed catamaran.

You'll enjoy the largest duty-free allowance in the Caribbean in the US Virgin Islands, double that found on other Caribbean islands. Each member of your party can spend up to $1,200 without duty, and you may mail up to $100 in gifts daily. All visitors over 21 years old can return with five fifths of liquor duty free (six fifths if one is a Virgin Islands product). Tourist items also have no sales tax.

Festivals

The USVI parties year-round. On St. Croix, partying reaching a crescendo with the **Crucian Christmas Festival.** The month-long festival comes alive with costumes as colorful as the tropical fish just offshore; the two of you can stroll the historic streets and sample local dishes at the food fair, dance to local tunes at the music competition, or join in the Three Kings Day Parade, following the steel pan bands through the streets.

Any visit to St. John is celebration enough, but several times a year the island parties with a purpose. The biggest blowout is **Carnival,** scheduled for the July 4th weekend. Carnival rocks the entire island with pulsating parades and live music.

On St. Thomas, Carnival is also the biggest annual event. The St. Thomas carnival is scheduled in April and the celebration brings the island alive with colorful parades, calypso, mocko jumbies, and dancing in the streets. It's a time when vacationers can party with islanders and celebrate during a whole month of activity.

St. Croix

With the smell of molasses hanging in the humid air, we toured the **Cruzan Rum distillery.** Along with us, a group of Danish tourists peered into the giant vats where sugar is transformed into St. Croix's most popular export.

But the Danes were not just here for the frothy piña coladas that awaited us at the end of the tour. "We are here," one sun-burned blonde explained, "to see what a mistake our country made."

From 1733 to 1917, Denmark owned St. Croix. It then sold all of the USVI to the United States for $25 million in gold. Concerned for the security of Panama Canal, the US made the islands a territory, giving its residents right of American citizenship, except for a vote in the presidential election. While the stars and stripes may wave there, the island still boasts its own unique spirit.

What results is a mélange of American and Caribbean, with a peppering of other cultures as well. The island is rich in history and has flown seven flags throughout the years: Spanish, Dutch, British, French, Knights of Malta, Danish, and American.

That combination of cultures, mixed with a rich history and natural beauty, brings visitors to St. Croix, an island that offers a sampling of the other Virgin Islands. "St. Croix is a combination of St. Thomas and St. John," explains Elizabeth Armstrong of the Buccaneer Hotel. "St. Croix has such a good mixture: the rolling hills, the beaches, and the small towns."

St. Croix is the largest Virgin Island, an 82-square-mile land-mass dotted with pastel-tinted brick and mortar architecture, found in the towns of **Frederiksted** and **Christiansted,** named for Danish kings.

To view the structures the Danes designed at a time when Americans were still English citizens, we headed off on an island tour, a feat accomplished in five or six hours. We started on the north shore in the town of Christiansted, just minutes from where Columbus landed over 500 years ago and named this island Santa Cruz. Today residents born on St. Croix are known as Crucians.

As appealing as Christiansted's charms are, the real beauty of the island lies beyond the city limits. Here, on rolling hills littered with historic sugar mills, the island takes on a country charm. Bucolic cattle dot open fields, small homes cling to the hillsides along winding roads, and the occasional shy mon-

The Islands

goose, imported to kill snakes, scampers like a large squirrel across the road to take cover.

Sweet Dreams

Price Chart

Rates reflect high winter season (expect prices to be as much as 40% lower during the off season) for a standard room for two adults for one night; prices are in US dollars.

$ . . . . under $150
$$ . . . . between $150 and $300
$$$ . . . . between $300 and $450
$$$$ . . . . over $450

♥ The Buccaneer

PO Box 25200, Gallows Bay
☎ 340-773-2100; fax 340-778-8215
Reservations: ☎ 800-255-3881
www.thebuccaneer.com
$$$

No other hotel in St. Croix, and few in the Caribbean, can boast the impressive history of The Buccaneer, located east of Christiansted. Once owned by Charles Martel, one of the Knights of Malta, the estate was built with walls three feet thick, tucked just behind a hill to hide it from view of pirates. Later, the stately manor was the residence of the young Alexander Hamilton.

Today, the original estate is supplemented with modern rooms to complete the 146-room resort, but the rich historic atmosphere remains. Every week, guests and staff come together at the manager's cocktail party, hosted in a stone sugar mill that stands as a reminder of the island's early plantation past.

History at the Buccaneer doesn't just end with the facilities – it extends to the resort owners as well. The ninth generation of the Armstrong family to reside on St. Croix operates the expansive resort.

The Buccaneer is also well known for its sports facilities, especially tennis and golf. Eight tennis courts are located halfway down the hill from the main house. Golfers can take their best swing at an 18-hole course with views of the sea. Packages with unlimited golf are available.

Special Features/Activities: beachfront, tennis, freshwater pools, dive shop, watersports, fitness center and spa, shopping arcade, fine and casual dining, golf, hosted nature walks.

Carambola Beach Resort
PO Box 3031, Davis Bay, Kingshill
☎ *800-924-4399, 340-778-3800; fax 340-778-1682*
$$$

We loved this hotel from the moment our transport began descending the steep hill on the island's western side and we caught sight of the hotel's trademark red roofs. The guest rooms, scattered throughout the lush grounds, are housed in two-story villas, each with louvered windows and private screened porch. During our stay here, we began every morning with a room service breakfast on the screened porch, listening to the sea. Most of our evenings ended there as well, watching the palms sway in the moonlight.

> *This ranks as one of the most romantic places to stay in the Caribbean. Second-floor rooms are the top choice. Ceilings soar to a West Indian peak, and porches are above the view of pedestrian beachcombers.*

No matter where you stay, you're only steps away from the beach along walkways that wind through grounds filled with hibiscus, bougainvillea, oleander, elephant's ear, philodendrons, banana trees, and towering palms.

Carambola was once part of the Rockresort chain, a handful of exclusive resorts developed by Laurance Rockefeller in the 1960s and 70s. Rockefeller himself had a vacation home at Carambola, the 200-year-old Davis Bay Suite, which once was a sugar mill. Damaged in Hurricane Marilyn, the suite has been restored to its original splendor, and is now one of many popular wedding sites on this lavish property. The suite features two bedrooms and two bathrooms, as well as a living room and veranda. A wedding planner at the Westin Carambola can help lovers select plenty of other beautiful sites, from seaside to quiet shaded areas tucked beneath towering banana trees.

Special Features/Activities: beachfront, casual and fine dining, freshwater pool, golf, tennis, watersports, dive shop.

♥ **Divi Carina Bay Resort and Casino**
25 Estate Turner Hole, Christiansted
☎ *340-773-9700; fax 340-773-6802*
Reservations: ☎ *800-823-9352*
www.divicarina.com
$$$

This resort offers both oceanfront rooms as well as villas. Rooms include private patios, mini-refrigerators, microwaves, and a sitting area; villas have a full kitchen. Rooms are decorated in tropical colors.

Special Features/Activities: beach, casino, two restaurants, three bars, watersports center, two freshwater pools, tennis, fitness and massage rooms.

Hibiscus Beach Hotel
4131 La Grande Princesse
☎ *340-773-4042; fax 340-773-4668.*
Reservations: ☎ *800-442-0121*
www.1hibiscus.com
$$

The 37 guest rooms (each with an ocean view) are stark, almost in the style of a chain motel. It does have a pretty stretch of beach, though, and is an economical choice for those on a budget. Plus, this property is very convenient, just 15 minutes from the airport and about 10 minutes from Christiansted. The best feature, however, is its Friday night dance show (see *Nightlife*, page 356).

> *The Hibiscus offers a package called "Weddings Cruzan Style," which includes an officiating minister, a bridal bouquet and boutonniere; a wedding cake; a photographer for three hours, including a roll of 36 prints, proofs, and negatives; a bottle of champagne; and dinner for two at the hotel with wine or champagne.*

Special Features/Activities: freshwater pool, casual restaurant and bar.

Hotel Caravelle

44A Queen Cross Street, Christiansted
☎ *340-773-0687; fax 340-778-7004*
Reservations: ☎ *800-524-0410*
www.hotelcaravelle.com
$

This modest European-style hotel is especially convenient for those who want to immerse themselves in the shopping of Christiansted. Located downtown on the waterfront, the 43-room inn is within walking distance of just about everything in Christiansted, from art galleries to the historic fort to fine dining. It's an excellent choice for anyone on a budget, and you can splurge with the penthouse suite, with a living room, full kitchen, large bedroom, and two baths, for less than the cost of a standard room at many other island properties.

> *Get married on the high seas with a special wedding package offered at Hotel Caravelle.*

The Caravelle offers a "St. Croix Married at Sea" package aboard the *Renegade,* a 42-foot catamaran that's large enough for 38 guests. Vows are conducted by Captain "Big Beard," who has performed over 300 weddings. The package includes a sunset wedding ceremony on the sea; a bottle of champagne; wedding cake; dinner for two at the hotel restaurant; an Island Safari tour; a room with king-size bed and more. The staff of Hotel Caravelle can coordinate all the arrangements (with a 10-day notice). For landlubbers, they can also arrange for a wedding on the harbor or at the hotel pool.

Special Features/Activities: downtown location, swimming pool.

Hotel on the Cay
PO Box 4020, Christiansted
☎ *800-524-2035, 340-773-2035; fax 340-773-7046*
$$

Known to its fans as "Hot C," this charming property is located on a tiny cay with an unbeatable view of Christiansted. Protestant Cay rises from the turquoise waters of the harbor just a one minute ferry ride (free for guests) from downtown.

Along with 55 guest rooms (each with a kitchenette), Hotel on the Cay also offers the only beach in downtown Christiansted. It's also enjoyed by guests from many nearby hotels.

Special Features/Activities: beachfront, casual restaurant, watersports center.

Tamarind Reef Hotel
5001 Tamarind Reef, Christiansted
☎ *800-619-0014, 340-773-4455; fax 340-773-3989*
www.usvi.net-hotel-tamarind
$$

This is one of our favorite budget-priced accommodations in the Caribbean, thanks to sparkling clean rooms, an excellent snorkel trail, and the hotel's friendly on-site owners, Dick and Marcy Pelton. St. Croix's newest hotel, the 46-room property is located east of Christiansted just off the reef. All of the rooms include a refrigerator, coffee maker, air conditioning, phones, and many also include kitchenettes. The atmosphere here is laid-back and comfortable, perfect for couples (and families) to enjoy the tranquil east end of St. Croix and the snorkel trail in the inlet just in front of the hotel.

Just a few steps from the hotel, the Green Cay Marina is home to boats that offer daily tours to Buck Island as well as deep-sea fishing excursions and scuba diving trips.

Special Features/Activities: beachside, freshwater pool, watersports, nearby marina, casual restaurant and bar.

Tables for Two

St. Croix has a wide variety of dining options, from gourmet restaurants to fast food chains. You'll find many cuisines represented here as well, including Caribbean, Italian, French, and, yes, Danish.

Don't miss the **conch** here, it's an island specialty. The shellfish is often served with a side dish called **fungi** (pronounced foon-GEE), a tasty accompaniment that's somewhat like cornbread dressing. The most popular beer here is Heineken.

Price Chart

Restaurant prices are for dinner per person, including a drink, appetizer or salad, and entrée.

$	under $15
$$	$15 to $30
$$$	$30 to $45
$$$$	over $45

Christiansted

Brass Parrot
Buccaneer Hotel, Gallows Bay
☎ *340-777-6750*
Dress code: casually elegant
Reservations: suggested
$$$

This is one of our favorite restaurants, both for its unsurpassed cuisine and for its unbeatable night-time view of the lights of Christiansted twinkling in the distance. The glass-walled restaurant features a Northern Italian menu with lots of regional classics.

The Islands

♥   *Tutto Bene*
2 Company St.
☎ *340-773-5229*
Dress code: casually elegant
Reservations: suggested
$$$

This Italian restaurant is popular with locals and visitors alike. Lunch is served weekdays, and dinner daily, in this café that's been praised by both *Gourmet* and *Bon Appétit* magazines. Favorites include beef or cheese ravioli, spinach lasagna, spaghetti carbonara, and veal marsala.

♥   *Top Hat*
52 Company St.
☎ *340-773-2346*
Dress code: casually elegant
Reservations: suggested
$$$

This elegant restaurant features continental cuisines as well as Danish dishes. Reservations are recommended.

Comanche Club
Strand St.
☎ *340-773-2665*
Dress code: casual
Reservations: suggested
$$

Located on the second floor in what's known as the Comanche Restaurant Bridge, this open-air restaurant is a romantic yet casual spot for a seafood dinner by candlelight. Start with an appetizer of conch in mushroom caps, escargot, or conch fritters, then move on to prawns stuffed with shellfish, fried scallops, lobster or, our favorite, tender conch creole with fungi.

♥   *Le St. Tropez*
67 King Street, Frederiksted
☎ *340-772-3000*
Dress code: casually elegant
Reservations: suggested
$$

Just a block from the cruise pier, this French bistro offers plenty of Gallic delights: s*oupe de poissons, escargots Provençal, coq au vin Bourguignon,* and more. Open for lunch on weekdays, and romantic candlelight dinners daily, except Sunday.

Romantic Activities

Island Sights & Museums

The best way to see what St. Croix has to offer you and your mate is to get an overview aboard a guided island tour. **St. Croix Safari Tours,** ☎ 340-773-6700 (or 773-9561, evenings) offer excellent tours in open-air safari vehicles with bench seats. Tours last about 5½ hours and include visits to both island cities, as well as all the major attractions.

In **Christiansted,** save time to admire the Danish architecture such as the **Old Scalehouse.** This seaside building was constructed in 1856 to weigh sugar, the product of over 100 stone mills scattered across the island in the late 19th century. Near the Old Scalehouse, **Fort Christianvaern** is now operated by the US Park Department. Sneak a kiss as you view the city from the yellow fortress, open for self-guided tours.

Traveling west from Christiansted, the island becomes progressively more lush. This natural abundance is best seen at the **St. George Botanical Gardens**, ☎ 340-692-2874, a 16-acre park where 800 species of Caribbean plants thrive among the ruins of a sugar plantation. Bougainvillea as colorful as crepe paper lines the walkways that lead visitors on a self-guided tour of an orchid house, a rain forest, and even a cactus garden. With a year-round backdrop of tropical splendor, this is one of the most popular wedding sites on the island.

The lavish lifestyle enjoyed by plantation owners during the 19th century is preserved at the **Whim Greathouse,** ☎ 340-673-6201. Here, we toured an elegant home that combines English gentility with Caribbean practicality, filled with fine imported furniture as well as floor-to-ceiling shuttered windows and cool plank floors. If you're lucky, you'll be able to sample some freshly-made johnnycakes, baked in the plantation's de-

The Islands

tached cookhouse. And don't miss the gift shop filled with Caribbean cookbooks, perfumes, and crafts.

St. Croix's southern city, **Frederiksted,** lies just a few miles from the former plantation house. A stop for many cruise ships (a new dock was constructed here in 1994 to replace damage done by Hurricane Hugo), the town is a smaller version of Christiansted with a red, rather than yellow, fortress guarding the waterfront. Shopping includes duty-free boutiques featuring china and crystal, and a vendor's market for inexpensive T-shirts and jewelry.

St. Croix's best treasures, however, are not the man-made ones but the natural areas found at opposite ends of the island. From Frederiksted, take **Rt. 76** (also called **Mahogany Road**), north for a trip to the rain forest. The small rain forest has thick vegetation where the sunlight is filtered through mahogany, yellow cedar, and Tibet trees. This forest is also home of LEAP, the **Life and Environmental Arts Project,** where skilled artisans craft everything from sculptures to spoons from the hardwoods found in the rain forest. Another romantic way to enjoy the rain forest is on horseback. **Paul and Jill's Equestrian Stables,** ☎ 340-772-2880 or 772-2627, offers rides through this lush area.

Just off the coast of the far northeast side of the island lies St. Croix's other natural treasure: **Buck Island.** Several outfitters take snorkelers on half- and full-day-trips to this island to swim along the **Buck Island Reef National Monument.** Here, in about 12 feet of water, snorkelers follow a marked trail for a self-guided tour of this undersea world. Several companies offer tours to this site, including **Big Beard's Adventure Tours,** ☎ 340-773-4482. **Mile Mark Watersports,** ☎ 340-773-2628, is a very friendly group of operators who have a store in downtown Christiansted near the Old Scalehouse.

Shopping

Shopping in St. Croix means a trip to **Christiansted** or **Frederiksted.** Until recently, most shopping took place in Christiansted, the larger of the two communities, but as the cruise ship business has grown, Frederiksted is offering more duty-free shops aimed at those who have only a few hours to shop.

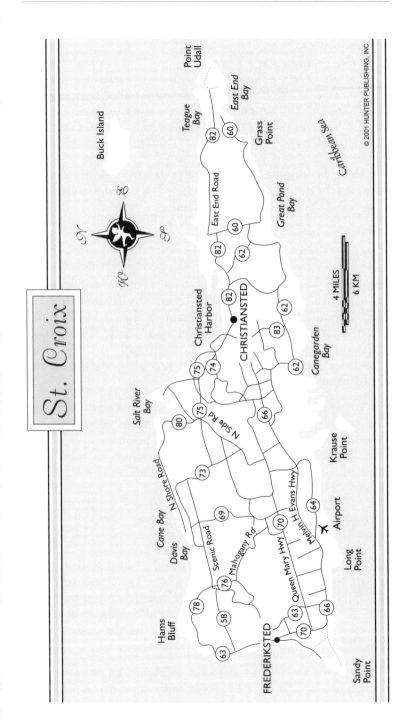

St. Croix

© 2001 HUNTER PUBLISHING, INC

The Islands

> *A unique item is the **"St. Croix Hook,"** developed by Sonya's Ltd. (No. 1 Company Street). While we were selecting a bracelet, the clerk at Sonya's told us that "the Hook" is very popular among divers of both sexes. The bracelet features a simple hook clasp that gives a clue to the wearer's romantic status: if the hook is pointed down, it signifies the wearer is single, pointed up and turned toward the heart, it symbolizes attachment.*

For those looking to bring back a taste of St. Croix, **Cruzan Rum** is sold throughout the island, as is **Chococo,** a chocolate and coconut liqueur made in St. Croix.

Nightlife

Nightlife is pretty quiet in St. Croix, but there are some new additions on the scene. The **Divi Carina Bay Resort and Casino** is home to the USVI's first casino, ☎ 340-773-9700, www.carinabay.com, a fun way to court Lady Luck. The 10,000-square-foot casino has 300 slot machines and 13 gaming tables. **The Buccaneer** has a steel band; call for weekly schedule, ☎ 340-773-2100.

The **Hibiscus Beach Hotel** offers an unbeatable weekly show that pulses with the fervor of island dancing and music. Authentic local steps are performed by the Caribbean Dance Company. The show is available with dinner, or as show only. Reservations are required for this popular presentation; call ☎ 340-773-4042 for times and days.

Just the Facts

Entry Requirements: US citizens need proof of identity upon airport check-in, but incoming travelers do not need to pass through immigration. It's a good idea to bring along your passport, however, in case you decide to take a day-trip to the nearby British Virgin Islands. Canadian and UK citizens need passports and photo ID.

Getting Around: Taxis are easy to obtain on St. Croix. In Christiansted, stop by the taxi stand on King Street near the Little Switzerland shop; in Frederiksted, the taxi stand is located at Fort Frederik. Licensed taxi services bear a license plate number that begins with the letters "TP."

Rental cars are readily available; all you'll need is a valid US driver's license. Remember, though, that driving is on the left side of the road.

Traveling among the USVI is as easy as moving from city to city. You can hop a ferry or seaplane (between St. Croix and St. Thomas), and there's no need to show documents on arrival.

Language: English

Currency: US dollar

Electricity: 110 volts

Information: For brochures on St. Croix and the other United States Virgin Islands, call ☎ 800-372-USVI. Website: www.usvi.net.

St. John

*N*ature lovers, set your sights for tiny St. John. This is the eco-tourism capital of the Caribbean, an island where the two of you, from the luxury of a beautiful resort, posh villa or the inexpensive accommodations of a tent or cabin, can hike, snorkel, and tour an island where two-thirds of the land is preserved as a national park.

The stewardship of the island's natural beauty began with Laurance Rockefeller. Developer of Caneel Bay Resort, the multimillionaire donated much of the island to the National Park Service in the 1950s. Today, preservation of this island's resources lies in the hands of the park service and a developer named Stanley Selengut, a leader in the world of eco-tourism, who operates several eco-friendly properties on the island. St. John leads the world in sustainable tourism resorts where guests make a minimal impact on nature.

Most travelers arrive in St. John by ferry from St. Thomas. The ferry docks in the town of **Cruz Bay,** a funky community filled with artisans, boaters, and campers looking for provisions. Like the rest of the island, Cruz Bay has a laid-back casual atmosphere where shorts and T-shirts are the uniform of both day and night. This is the most relaxed area of the US Virgin Islands and a far cry from the bustling atmosphere of St. Thomas.

Sweet Dreams

Price Chart

Rates reflect high winter season (expect prices to be as much as 40% lower during the off season) for a standard room for two adults for one night. All prices are in US dollars.

$ . . . . under $150
$$ . . . . between $150 and $300
$$$ . . . . between $300 and $450
$$$$ . . . . over $450

Caneel Bay

PO Box 720, Virgin Islands National Park
Reservations: 888-767-3966
☎ *340-776-6111; fax 340-693-8280*
www.caneelbay.com
$$$

Caneel has the air of old-world Caribbean elegance. Tucked within the Virgin Islands National Park, it boasts seven beaches and a natural beauty that is surpassed only by the resort's high-quality service. Spread out across the lush property, 171 cottages combine "casual elegance" with "St. John camping," to come up with a property where you can feel like you are camping while enjoying plenty of pampering. Cooled by trade winds and a ceiling fan, each cottage has furnishings from the Philippines, screened walls that are open to a pristine view, and cool terrazzo floors, as well as an ice chest for daily ice delivery.

Guests check in when they arrive at the airport in St. Thomas and board private ferry service to the resort. (The ferry service is available several times daily, so guests can hop to St. Thomas for a little shopping.) Private ferry service is also available three times a week to the resort's sister property, Little Dix Bay, on Virgin Gorda. (Bring along your passport or proof of citizenship to take this jaunt to the British Virgin Islands.)

Along with plenty of complimentary diversions (including the Peter Burwash International tennis program), introductory scuba diving clinic, windsurfing, Sunfish and kayaks, and movie presentations, other activities are available at additional charge: half- and full-day sails, beach barbecue, sunset cocktail cruise, guided snorkel trips, fishing charters, massages, and boat charters.

But the focal point of Caneel Bay is its beaches: seven pristine stretches of sand. Guests can hop aboard the resort shuttle for quick drop off at any of these beaches. Don't forget to request a picnic lunch to take along!

Turtle Bay Point is especially popular for weddings and vow renewals. Other couples opt for private Honeymoon Beach or Paradise Beach. An on-site wedding planner makes arrangements simple.

Special Features/Activities: beachfront, watersports, scuba diving, freshwater pool, tennis, fine and casual dining.

Cinnamon Bay Campgrounds
PO Box 720, Cruz Bay
Reservations: ☎ *800-539-9998*
☎ *340-776-6330 or 693-5654; fax 340-776-6458*
www.cinnamonbay.com
$

You might not think of camping as romantic – but that just means you haven't seen St. John's campsites. The bare sites, tents, and screened shelters of this popular campground are full year-round. Managed by Caneel Bay, the camp is located on the grounds of the national park and features accommodations near beautiful Cinnamon Bay Beach, St. John's longest stretch of sand.

Tents (which measure 10x14 feet) are outfitted with four cots with bedding, a solid floor, an ice chest, water container, and

The Islands

cooking and eating utensils. Outdoors, a propane stove and lantern, charcoal grill, and picnic table are available.

Cottages (15x15 feet) are actually screened shelters with the same features as the tents, as well as electricity. All accommodations share bathhouses with cool water showers.

The atmosphere is very relaxed, as campers enjoy the Caribbean at their campsite, on the beach, and on daily ranger-led tours of the national park. Don't be surprised to see a family of wild burros roaming the grounds.

> *The most romantic cottages are units 10 A through D, a seashell's throw from the water. Tent site 21 is the closest to the water, and bare site 24 is best for beach buffs. We hear that you practically have to inherit a reservation to secure these most popular sites, but give it a try anyway.*

Special Features/Activities: beachfront, campsites, tents, cabins, general store, snack bar, restaurant, watersports center.

Estate Concordia

Cruz Bay
☎ 340-693-5855; fax 340-643-5960
Reservations: ☎ 800-392-9004
www.maho.org
$

"Eco-tents" are the latest creation in eco-tourism done by the same developer as Maho, Harmony, and Estate Concordia properties. These canvas tent cottages are specifically designed to be light on the land and rely on high-tech advancements such as ultra-light reflective materials and compost toilets. The resident managers of this natural complex, a husband-wife team, came to St. John as honeymooners themselves at Maho Bay. Today they recognize how romantic camping can be for couples looking to experience the Caribbean in a slightly nontraditional way.

Special Features/Activities: mountainside.

Harmony

PO Box 310, Cruz Bay
☎ *340-776-6226; fax 340-776-6540*
Reservations: ☎ *800-392-9004*
www.maho.org/harmony.html
$$

As its name suggests, this resort is in tune with nature. It has solar power, recycled materials, low flush toilets, and a complete awareness of the environment, but with a higher number of creature comforts than are found at its sister property, Maho. Units include energy-efficient refrigerators, comfortable furnishings (either two twin beds in the bedroom studio units or two queen beds in the living room studios), private baths, a deck with furniture, and kitchen.

Special Features/Activities: mountainside, casual restaurant.

Maho Bay Camps

PO Box 310, Cruz Bay
☎ *340-776-6240; fax 340-776-6504*
Reservations: ☎ *800-392-9004*
www.maho.org/maho.html
$

This is no ordinary campground. From the help-yourself center where guests leave unused food, toiletries, books, and items for others to use, to the network of raised boardwalks that connect the tent cabins and protect hillside vegetation, this resort's focus is on environmental camping. Every 16x16-foot unit has screened sides with roll-down privacy shades, a sleeping area with beds and bedding, a futon sofa that pulls down into a sleeper, a cooking and dining area with cooler, propane stove, fan, and an outdoor balcony. Barbecue grills and bathhouses are scattered throughout the property.

The campgrounds enjoy a beautiful open-air restaurant perched high above the sea. Breakfast offerings include (in addition to the obligatory granola) items such as bacon and cheese omelets and amaretto French toast. (Breakfast prices are under $5.) Dinner entrées are also inexpensive and range from jerk chicken to BBQ spare ribs to vegetarian walnut loaf.

Special Features/Activities: mountainside, casual restaurant.

The Islands

♥ *Westin St. John*
PO Box 8310, Great Cruz Bay
Reservations: ☎ *340-693-8000, 888-625-5144, 800-WESTIN-1*
www.westin.com
$$$

The Westin St. John is one of the most beautiful properties in the region, thanks to its location on gently rolling slopes that overlook a stretch of beach and an aqua sea.

The hotel offers several wedding packages. The "Westin Ceremony" includes ceremony arrangements; exclusive use of the Beach Garden Gazebo; a minister or justice of the peace (a rabbi is available for an additional fee); consulting by a Westin catering manager; a nosegay wedding bouquet for the bride; and a boutonniere for the groom. The "Emerald Ceremony" includes all those features, as well as a wedding cake; a photographer to take 60 wedding photos; a bottle of champagne in your room; and keepsake crystal flutes. The grandest package is the "St. John Ceremony," and it includes all of the previously mentioned features, as well as a videographer; one hour of steel pan music; tropical flowers decorating the gazebo; and a wedding bouquet.

Special Features/Activities: beachfront, casual and fine dining, freshwater pool, watersports, dive shop, tennis.

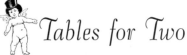 *Tables for Two*

Dining on St. John is often a casual affair, with restaurants featuring a continental mix to satisfy mainlander appetites.

Price Chart

Restaurant prices are for dinner per person, including a drink, appetizer or salad, and entrée.

$. . . . . under $15
$$ . . . . $15 to $30
$$$ . . . . $30 to $45
$$$$. . . . . over $45

♥ *Ellington's*
Gallows Point
☎ *340-693-8490*
Dress code: casually elegant
Reservations: requested
$$

This sunset favorite features lobster, fresh fish, steaks and pasta, accompanied by a fine selection of wine. Caribbean music is featured nightly.

The Fishtrap
Raintree Inn, Cruz Bay
☎ *340-693-9949*
Dress code: casual
Reservations: optional
$$

This casual, open-air restaurant specializes in, you guessed it, fish. Start with shrimp cocktail, conch fritters, or FishTrap chowder, then get serious with rock lobster tail, sea scallops, shrimp scampi, or surf and turf. Burgers and pasta dishes including fettucine alfredo with shrimp or scallops round out the menu.

Mongoose Restaurant
Mongoose Junction, Cruz Bay
☎ *340-693-8677*
Dress code: casual
Reservations: optional
$$

Take a break from your shopping at this casual restaurant that features pork loin, chicken parmesan, and Cajun grilled mahi mahi.

Paradiso
Mongoose Junction
☎ *340-693-8899*
Dress code: casual
Reservations: optional
$$

The Islands

It seems that Italian food remains universally in demand, so if it's pasta that you're craving, head up to the second level of Mongoose Junction for *linguine al pesto e broccoli* or *linguine con fruitti di mare*.

Romantic Activities

The biggest attraction of St. John is the national park. Start with a visit to the **Virgin Islands National Park Visitors Center,** ☎ 340-776-6201, located on the waterfront in Cruz Bay. Here you'll find information on hiking, camping, snorkeling, and guided programs.

After you have your bearings, head out to the park by taxi or rental jeep. Hike on one of the many marked trails, snorkel the guided underwater trail at **Trunk Bay,** stroll along the self-guided **Cinnamon Bay Nature Trail,** or visit ruins of **Annaberg Sugar Plantation.**

St. John is among the few places in the Caribbean that offers **snuba,** a unique blend of scuba and snorkeling that allows would-be divers to descend to 20 feet below the surface. **Snuba St. John,** ☎ 340-693-8063, hooks guests up to a floating air tank, so "C" cards are not required.

Nightlife

As you might expect on an island that emphasizes camping and enjoying nature, nightlife can be a little quiet on St. John. One popular exception is **Fred's,** ☎ 340-776-6363, a hip-hopping joint in Cruz Bay that's a favorite with locals and visitors alike. Located just across from the Lemon Tree Mall, this nightspot charges cover on Wednesday and Friday, but has music nightly, usually until midnight.

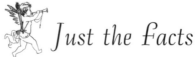

Just the Facts

Entry Requirements: You'll need proof of identity upon airport check-in, but incoming travelers do not need to pass through immigration when they reach St. Thomas. It's a good

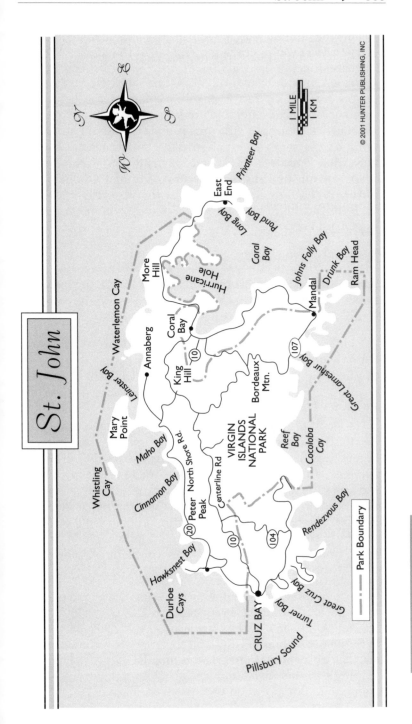

St. John

The Islands

© 2001 HUNTER PUBLISHING, INC

idea to bring along your passport, however, in case you decide to take a day-trip to the nearby British Virgin Islands.

Getting Around: There is plentiful taxi service in St. John, especially from Cruz Bay. Typically, visitors at the hotels and north shore campgrounds don't rent cars but rely on taxi service and shuttles. However, villa guests and visitors to Estate Concordia on the south shore often rent cars because of the distance. Most rentals on the island are small jeeps. Note to young lovers: you must be at least 25 years old to rent a vehicle.

Language: English

Currency: US dollar

Electricity: 110 volts

Information: For questions on the US Virgin Islands, call ☎ 800-372-USVI. Website: www.usvi.net.

St. Thomas

St. Thomas is one island that vacationers seem to either love or hate. Those strong feelings emanate from the island's omnipresent bustling atmosphere. With cruise ships that discharge hundreds of frenzied shoppers on its streets every day, this island is not the place for peace and quiet. It is, however, the spot to go if the two of you enjoy shopping, fine dining, or lavish resorts. St. Thomas' **Charlotte Amalie** (pronounced a-mal-yah) has a busy cosmopolitan atmosphere where the laid-back West Indian ambiance is juxtaposed with traffic jams, congestion, and a hectic pace.

But beyond Charlotte Amalie's boundaries, the island enjoys a slower pace. Here, on overlooks high above the city's lights, couples can share some of the Caribbean's most glorious sunsets. On the island's fringe of powdered sugar beaches, the two of you can catch up on your limin' – just lazing the days away beneath towering palms.

Sweet Dreams

Price Chart

Rates reflect high winter season (expect prices to be as much as 40% lower during the off season) for a standard room for two adults for one night. All prices are in US dollars.

$	under $150
$$	between $150 and $300
$$$	between $300 and $450
$$$$	over $450

Blackbeard's Castle

PO Box 6041, Charlotte Amalie
☎ *800-344-5771, 340-776-1234; fax 340-776-4321*
$

High above Charlotte Amalie, perched on Government Hill, Blackbeard's Castle has stood as a symbol of St. Thomas since 1679. Built to protect Fort Christian, the structure was said to have been used from 1716 to 1718 by the pirate Blackbeard, famed for his long, black beard braided and strung with colored ribbons.

Whether Blackbeard ever eyed the harbor from this tower is uncertain, but one thing is well known: the site is now a romantic hotel. The small property, which formerly was used as a plantation and as a private residence, now has 24 quiet rooms. Couples will enjoy lovely views of the waterfront.

Special Features/Activities: fine dining, freshwater pool.

Elysian Beach Resort

6800 Estate Nazareth
☎ *800-524-6599, 340-775-1000; fax 340-776-0910*
$$

Everything about Elysian spells comfort and casual elegance. You'll ascend a spiral staircase to a king-size sleigh bed in your

The Islands

two-story suite. The private balconies with a view of pools and palms give way to a turquoise sea. The open-air dining areas allow the two of you to enjoy Caribbean specialties over a glass of wine or a tropical drink.

> *Elysian has a wedding consultant on-site to help plan ceremonies. For wedding information, call the consultant at ☎ 800-753-2554.*

Special Features/Activities: beachfront, fine and casual dining, freshwater pool, tennis, watersports.

Marriott's Frenchman's Reef Beach Resort
PO Box 7100, 5 Estate Bakkeroe
☎ 340-776-8500; fax 340-715-6191
Reservations: ☎ 800-524-2000
www.marriott.vi
$$

Each with a bright West Indian décor, the 408 guest rooms include air conditioning, cable television with pay-per-view movies, voice mail, data lines, hair dryer, coffee/tea maker, iron, clock radio, in-room safe, and ice maker. Rooms also include a mini-refrigerator that guests can stock from the on-site deli and grocery located at lobby level. Accessible rooms for the physically challenged are available.

A recent addition to the property is 21 two-story suites. These "Top of the Reef" rooms are on the hotel's top floor, where access will soon be limited by key card. Here 17 Royal Suites offer luxury with a loft bedroom and oversized bathroom reached by spiral staircase. Rooms include a hot tub for two, private balcony, and cathedral ceilings. Each of these Top of the Reef suites can be connected with a deluxe room, a popular option for families.

A renovated pool complex highlighted by waterfalls and a swim-up bar greets guests. Tennis players can take advantage of two lighted seaside courts; a program managed by Peter Burwash International includes professional tennis lessons and clinics. A watersports center can arrange scuba diving, snorkeling, sailing, sunset cruises, boat rentals, sports fishing, and parasailing. Additional sports, such as windsurfing, kayaking, and Jet Skiing can be enjoyed at adjacent Morning Star Beach, accessible by shuttle or via a new beach elevator and seaside walkways. Fitness-conscious guests can maintain a regimen at the health and fitness center.

Five restaurants at Frenchman's Reef and adjoining Morning Star offer a variety of concepts for diners. Windows on the Harbour, an indoor restaurant featuring steaks and a Sunday brunch, is their premier restaurant with a spectacular day and night view of Charlotte Amalie.

Special Features/Activities: beachfront, pool, restaurants, spa, fitness facility, watersports.

Renaissance Grand Beach Resort

Smith Bay Road
☎ *340-775-1510; fax 340-775-2185*
Reservations: 800-HOTELS1
$$$

The Renaissance is proof that you can't keep a good resort down. Struck by 1995's Hurricane Marilyn, the resort rose like an eternal phoenix to reopen even grander than before. From the moment you step in the open-air lobby and look through to powdery beach and Caribbean sea beyond, you'll enjoy a resort that features an airy tropical décor.

Romantic activity here centers on the sea. Step out on the beach, pull up a chaise lounge, and enjoy a lazy day in the sun, or, look for fun on the water in the form of snorkeling, sailing, kayaking, or windsurfing. Dining opportunities include two specialty restaurants as well as poolside lunches (don't miss seeing the resident iguana begging for French fries!).

Special Features/Activities: beachfront, restaurants, pools, watersports.

Wyndham Sugar Bay Beach Club and Resort

6500 Estate Smith Bay
☎ *340-777-7100; fax 340-777-7200*
Reservations: ☎ 800-wyndham
www.wyndham.com
$$$

This 300-room resort is a real rarity in the US Virgin Islands: an all-inclusive property. Here, families can stay, play, and eat

The Islands

for one easy price. "We believe that parents deserve a holiday from high vacation costs," said Bob Marshall, general manager. "Our all-inclusive offerings allow the entire family to enjoy a full breakfast, lunch, and dinner daily, including spectacular theme dinners and all day snacks." The all-inclusive package also includes drinks, an ice cream bar, day and night tennis, all non-motorized watersports, use of snorkel equipment, fitness center and hot tub, daily activity programs, nightly entertainment, and beach volleyball.

Perched high atop a seaside hill, the resort offers spectacular views of St. John and the British Virgin Islands. Much of the activity centers around the spectacular pool area. Three interconnecting pools are alive with the sounds of laughter as well as the roar of a man-made waterfall. Visitors reach the pool area across a suspended bridge (look in the hibiscus for a resident iguana on the way down!) and a casual dining area lies just steps away. Beyond the pool area, the beach offers plenty of watersports, and there's some good snorkeling just yards from the shore, a site where we spotted about 40 small squid one afternoon.

Special Features/Activities: beachfront, all-inclusive, pool complex, restaurants, watersports.

♥ *The Ritz-Carlton St. Thomas*
6900 Great Bay
Reservations: ☎ 800-330–8272
☎ 340-775-3333; fax 340-775-4444
www.ritzcarlton.com
$$$$

Formerly the Grand Palazzo, this is one of the most elegant hotels in the Caribbean, an ultra-luxurious resort designed to make its visitors feel like royalty. From the moment you enter the marble entry of this resort styled to replicate a Venetian palace, you'll know that this is a step above even the luxurious resorts for which the island is known.

> *The Ritz-Carlton maintains a one-to-one guest-to-staff ratio, perfect for those vacationers ready for privacy and pampering.*

The hotel's hibiscus-colored roofs dot the shoreline of Great Bay. Stark white buildings are punctuated with bougainvillea and other tropical splendors. Rooms have marble baths, seer-sucker robes, and French doors leading out to private balconies. Amenities include sailing, snorkeling, and a private yacht. Dining is an elegant affair at The Ritz. The hotel's Dining Room restaurant, filled with palm trees, overlooks Great Bay. Long trousers and collared shirts are requested in the evenings.

Special Features/Activities: beachfront, casual and fine dining, freshwater pool, watersports, tennis.

Sapphire Beach Resort and Marina
PO Box 6577, Route 6, Smith Bay
☎ *800-524-2090, 340-775-6100; fax 340-775-2403*
$$$

This resort sits on a beautiful stretch of sand and offers excel-lent snorkeling in calm, shallow waters just offshore. Located about half an hour from the airport, this resort includes beach-front and yacht harbor view suites and villas, each with fully equipped kitchens, television, and daily maid service.

> *Sapphire Beach has a special package for lovers, which includes a sunset sail for two, champagne, air-port transfers, T-shirts, and more.*

Weddings are popular at Sapphire. During our stay, we watched a beautiful beach wedding. The bride and groom were in traditional formal dress against the backdrop of the sea, which could genuinely be described as sapphire.

Special Features/Activities: beachfront, casual dining, water-sports, dive shop, shuttle to Charlotte Amalie and Red Hook.

Secret Harbour Beach Resort
6280 Estate Nazareth, Charlotte Amalie
Reservations: ☎ *800-524-2250*
☎ *340-775-6550; fax 340-775-1501*
www.st-thomas.com/shb.vi
$$$

They call themselves "the most romantic little beach resort in the Caribbean." Judge for yourself. The resort offers beachfront studios or one- and two-bedroom suites, each with fully equipped kitchens, cable TV, air conditioning, ceiling fans, and beachfront balconies or patios, all looking right out to sea and, in the evenings, to the setting sun.

Special Features/Activities: beachfront, casual restaurant, freshwater pool, hot tub, tennis, watersports, dive shop.

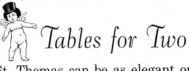 *Tables for Two*

Dining on St. Thomas can be as elegant or as casual as you wish. Just as its shops offer merchandise from around the globe, look for cuisine from many cultures represented here as well. Don't miss the local offerings, though: **fungi** (foon-GEE), a side dish much like a cornbread stuffing, and **conch** (konk), a shellfish that's prepared as an entrée or appetizer.

Price Chart

Restaurant prices are for dinner per person, including a drink, appetizer or salad, and entrée.

$............................	under $15
$$	$15 to $30
$$$	$30 to $45
$$$$........................	over $45

Gladys' Café
Royal Dane Mall West, Charlotte Amalie
☎ *340-774-6604*
Dress code: casual
Reservations: not needed
$$

Popular with locals and visitors, this restaurant specializes in local fare. If you like conch, here's the place. Conch fritters, conch chowder, conch salad platter, conch in lemon butter sauce, you name it, they have it. Also look for sautéed shrimp in lemon and garlic sauce. Don't miss the fungi!

Caesar's
Marriott's Morningstar Hotel
☎ *340-776-8500*
Dress code: casual
Reservations: not needed
$

This open-air eatery is a good stop for lunch. Start with Caesar or pesto bread and follow up with grilled chicken or clams chioggia linguine with baby clams.

Banana Tree Grille
Bluebeard's Castle Resort
☎ *340-776-4050*
Dress code: casually elegant
Reservations: recommended
$$-$$$

Guests can enjoy delicious dishes and enjoy one of the island's best views at Banana Tree Grille. Dine on coconut shrimp, lobster tail and other tasty dishes while gazing over the Charlotte Amalie Harbor. Check in with the restaurant for their live entertainment schedule or place an order for take-out and enjoy your meal in your hotel room or at a beach-side picnic.

Herve's
Government Hill, Charlotte Amalie
☎ *340-777-9709*
Dress code: elegant
Reservations: recommended
$$$

Couples can make a dinner at Herve's the evening's entertainment. Start with a glass of fine French wine, then select from a menu of French dishes, all served with a spectacular view of Charlotte Amalie below.

The Islands

Romantic Activities

Beaches

St. Thomas' most romantic attractions are undoubtedly its beaches. The number one stretch of sand is **Magens Bay,** a picture postcard-perfect beach where you'll find everything you need, from beach chairs to a beach bar, to allow you to luxuriate all day. Another top beach is **Coki Beach,** a favorite with both locals and tourists. Located near the Renaissance, this beach has good snorkeling. **Sapphire Beach** is also popular with snorkelers as well as windsurfers; lovers like this white sand beach for its spectacular view of St. John and the British Virgin Islands.

Underwater Delights

To have a look at the undersea life, take a 50-minute cruise aboard the *Atlantis* submarine, ☎ 800-253-0493 or 340-776-5650. The dives depart from **Havensight Mall** and carry up to 46 passengers to a depth of 90 feet below the surface. Here's a chance for non-divers to enjoy a look at sponges, coral, and an array of colorful tropical fish. The trip is safe and comfortable. Bring along your camera, but because of the portholes, you won't be able to use the flash. (Buy some fast film – 400 ASA or faster – to capture these memories.)

Island Sights

For the best view of St. Thomas from above, ride the **Paradise Point Tramway,** which also departs near Havensight Mall. Aboard ski-lift gondolas, you'll rise to one point that never sees snow: the top of **Flag Hill.** From here you'll see the Charlotte Amalie harbor dotted with cruise ships. Gondolas ascend to the point from 9 am to 4:30 pm every day, or you can take a taxi (on a very crooked and bumpy road) to the point. Once on top, enjoy a frozen Bushwacker or a mango margarita at **The Bar.** Stick around for the best sunset in the islands and watch the lights of Charlotte Amalie come out.

St. Thomas

Atlantic Ocean

Leeward Passage

Grass Cay

Cabrita Point

Water Point

Fish Cay

Redhook Bay

Cabes Point

Deck Point

Smith Bay

Coki Bay

Smith Bay Rd

322

38

32

Thatch Cay

Mandal Bay

Tutu Bay

386

42

Redhook Rd

Turpentine Run

38

Inner Brass Island

Picara Point

Magens Bay

Mahogany Run Rd

Donoe Bypass

394

42

Skyline Drive

40

Weymouth Rhymer

38

Frenchman Bay Rd

Cas Cay

Patricia Cay

Long Point

30

Tropaco Point

Magens Rd

35

Hull Bay Road

St. Peter Mtn Rd

Solberg Road

40

308

CHARLOTTE AMALIE

315

Muhlenfels Point

Hassel Island

Crown Mtn Rd

37

Crown Mtn Rd

33

33

Hardwood

Moravian Hwy

302

304

Mosquito Point

WATER ISLAND

404

333

30

Airport

Brewers Bay

30

Vluck Point

Stumpy Point

West End Rd

Perseverance Bay

Flat Cays

Saba Island

Turtledove Cay

Caribbean Sea

Botany Bay

David Point

Fortuna Rd

30

Fortuna Bay

The Islands

N W E S

2 MILES

2 KM

© 2001 HUNTER PUBLISHING, INC

Another excellent view of Charlotte Amalie is from the lookout on **Skyline Drive.** Here all the guided tours stop for a quick photo and the chance to buy a T-shirt from a conveniently located vendor. Your jitney tour will undoubtedly stop at **Mountain Top,** the peak of **St. Peter Mountain.** A more touristy version of Paradise Point, this look-out is home to a mega-gift shopping complex, mucho tourists, banana daiquiris (they claim to be the home of the original banana daiquiri) and, we must admit, a beautiful view. From the lookout, you'll have a great view of Tortola, Jost Van Dyke, and Magens Bay. Check with **Godfrey Tours** (☎ 340-775-7243; www.godfreytoursvi. com) for guided tours.

Shopping

Ah, a travel writer could do an entire book on the shopping in St. Thomas. This is where serious duty-free shoppers come to seek out bargains from around the globe on jewelry, perfumes, leather goods, and gemstones.

The **Waterfront Highway** (Kyst Vejen), **Main Street** (Dronningens Gade) and **Back Street** (Vimmelskaft Gade) run parallel to the waterfront of **Charlotte Amalie.** These streets, and the alleys that connect Waterfront Highway and Main Street, are filled with shops. Start near the **Vendor's Plaza** (good for craft purchases and inexpensive T-shirts), then begin your walk down crowded Main Street, where the sidewalks are always packed with shoppers and the street is continuously lined with taxis and jitneys.

Our favorite shops are tucked in the alleys, refuges from the crowds where you can shop, dine or drink in a little peace. Here the walls are brick, recalling the area's history. In the 19th century, this was the Danish warehouse district.

These picturesque alleys are also home to several excellent malls. The **A.H. Riise Gift and Liquor Mall**, located between Post Office Alley and Hibiscus Alley off Main Street, includes shops such as **Colombian Emeralds, Calypso Boutique,** and **Gucci.**

Charlotte Amalie is very much a pedestrian city, and you'll be able to shop and dine all day without need of a taxi. After dark, however, use common sense precautions when setting out. Like other cities its size, Charlotte Amalie has had its share of crime.

Nightlife

Much of the nightlife on the island centers around the resort hotels. **Wyndham Sugar Bay** (☎ 340-777-7100), **Bluebeard's Beach Club & Villa** (☎ 340-776-4770), and **Sapphire Beach** (☎ 340-775-6100) each feature popular local bands on a regular basis. **Gladys' Café** (☎ 340-774-6604) in Charlotte Amalie has a jazz band every Friday night.

Just the Facts

Entry Requirements: You'll need proof of identity upon airport check-in, but incoming travelers do not need to pass through immigration when they reach St. Thomas. You can also travel to nearby St. John and St. Croix from St. Thomas without proof of citizenship. It's a good idea to bring along your passport, however, in case you decide to take a day-trip to the nearby British Virgin Islands.

Getting Around: You'll never have to look far for a taxi; in fact, they'll often come looking for you. However, if the two of you need a ride from Charlotte Amalie between about 3 pm and 5 pm, you may have to check with several taxi drivers. During this time, they start picking up cruise passengers to return to the ship and won't take less than a full car or van load. Check for licensed taxi services by looking for license plates that begin with the letters "TP."

The two major towns – Charlotte Amalie and Red Hook – are connected both by road and ferry.

Currency: US dollar

Language: English

Electricity: 110 volts

The Islands

Information: Call the US Virgin Island Tourist office at ☎ 800-372-USVI. Website: www.usvi.net.

Chartered Yachts

If love means nights being rocked to sleep by gentle waves and days spent exploring various anchorages, then consider a vacation aboard a chartered yacht. These luxurious vessels boast the niceties of a fine hotel, including private bath, gourmet meals, television and VCR. They come crewed with a captain and cook. Call **Regency Yacht Vacations,** ☎ 800-524-7676, for information on these unique excursions, where the itinerary is selected based on your desires. A few vessels are small enough for two-person charters, but most accommodate between four and 12 persons. Prices are all-inclusive.

Appendix

Caribbean Tourist Boards

Anguilla

Anguilla Tourist Board
c/o The Wescott Group
39 Monaton Drive
Huntington Station, NY 11746
☎ 800-553-4939
www.net.ai

Antigua & Barbuda

Antigua & Barbuda Tourist Office
610 Fifth Ave., Suite 311
New York, NY 10020
☎ 212-541-4117; fax 212-541-4789
www.antigua-barbuda.org

Aruba

Aruba Tourism Authority
1000 Harbor Blvd.
Weehawken, NJ 07087
☎ 800-TO-ARUBA; fax 201-330-8757
www.aruba.com

Bahamas

Bahamas Tourism Centre
150 East 52nd Street, 28th Floor North
New York, NY 10022
☎ 800-4-BAHAMAS; fax212-753-6531
www.bahamas.com

Barbados

Barbados Tourism Authority
800 2nd Ave., 2nd Floor
New York, NY 10017
☎ 800-221-9831; fax 212-573-9850
www.barbados.org

Bermuda

Bermuda Department of Tourism
310 Madison Avenue, Suite 201
New York, NY 10017
☎ 800-223-6106
www.bermudatourism.com

British Virgin Islands

British Virgin Islands Tourist Board
370 Lexington Ave., Suite 1605
New York, NY 10017
☎ 800-835-8530; fax 212-949-8254
www.bviwelcome.com

Cayman Islands

Cayman Islands Department of Tourism
420 Lexington Ave., Suite 2733
New York, NY 10170
☎ 212-682-5582; fax 212-986-5123
www.caymanislands.ky

Curaçao

Curaçao Tourist Board
475 Park Avenue South, Suite 2000
New York, NY 10016
☎ 800-3CURACAO; fax 212-683-9337
www.curacao-tourism.com

Jamaica

Jamaica Tourist Board
801 2nd Ave., 20th Floor
New York, NY 10017

☎ 800-233-4JTB; fax 212-856-1212
www.jamaicatravel.com

Puerto Rico

Puerto Rico Tourism Company
575 5th Ave., 23rd Floor
New York, NY 10017
☎ 800-223-6530; fax 212-586-1212
www.prtourism.com

St. Barts

St. Barts Tourism Office
French West Indies Tourist Board
444 Madison Ave.
New York, NY 10022
☎ 877-956-1234; fax 212-838-3486
www.stbarths.com

St. Kitts & Nevis

St. Kitts and Nevis Tourism Office
414 East 75th St.
New York, NY 10021
☎ 800-582-6208; fax 212-734-6511
www.stkitts-nevis.com

St. Lucia

St. Lucia Tourist Board
820 Second Ave., 9th Floor
New York, NY 10017
☎ 800-456-3984; fax 212-867-2795
www.st-lucia.com

St. Martin

St. Martin
French West Indies Tourist Board
444 Madison Ave.
New York, NY 10022
☎ 877-956-1234; fax 212-838-3486
www.st-martin.org

St. Maarten

St. Maarten Tourist Office
675 Third Ave., Suite 1806
New York, NY 10017
☎ 800-786-2278; fax 212-953-2145
www.st-maarten.com

Trinidad & Tobago

Trinidad & Tobago
Sales, Marketing, and Reservations Tourism Services
7000 Boulevard East
Guttenberg, NJ 07093
☎ 201-869-0060
www.visittnt.com

Turks & Caicos

Turks & Caicos Tourist Board
PO Box 128, Pond St.
Grand Turk
Turks and Caicos Islands
☎ 800-241-0824; fax 649-946-2733
www.turksandcaicostourism.com

US Virgin Islands

US Virgin Islands Division of Tourism
1270 Avenue of the Americas, Room 2108
New York, NY 10020
☎ 800-372-USVI; fax 212-332-2223
www.usvi.net

US Passport Offices

Boston Passport Agency
Thomas P. O'Neill Federal Building
10 Causeway Street, Room 247
Boston, MA 02222-1094
☎ 617-878-0900
Region: Maine, Massachusetts, New Hampshire, Rhode Island, Up-
state New York, and Vermont.

Chicago Passport Agency
Kluczynski Federal Building
230 S. Dearborn Street, Suite 380
Chicago, IL 60604-1564
☎ 312-341-6020
Region: Illinois, Indiana, Michigan, and Wisconsin.

Honolulu Passport Agency
First Hawaiian Tower, 1132 Bishop Street, Suite 500
Honolulu, HI 96813-2809
☎ 808-522-8283 or 522-8286
Region: American Samoa, Federated States of Micronesia,
Guam, Hawaii, & Northern Mariana Islands.

Houston Passport Agency
Mickey Leland Federal Building, 1919 Smith Street, Suite 1100
Houston, TX 77002-8049
☎ 713-751-0294
Region: Kansas, Oklahoma, New Mexico, and Texas.

Los Angeles Passport Agency
Federal Building, 11000 Wilshire Boulevard, Suite 1000
Los Angeles, CA 90024-3615
☎ 310-575-5700
Region: California (all counties south of and including San Luis
Obispo, Kern and San Bernardino), and Nevada (Clark County
only).

Miami Passport Agency
Claude Pepper Federal Office Building
51 SW First Avenue, 3rd Floor
Miami, FL 33130-1680
☎ 305-539-3600
Region: Florida, Georgia, Puerto Rico, South Carolina,
and US Virgin Islands.

New Orleans Passport Agency
Postal Services Building, 701 Loyola Avenue, Suite T-12005
New Orleans, LA 70113-1931
☎ 504-412-2600
Region: Alabama, Arkansas, Iowa, Kentucky, Louisiana, Missis-
sippi, Missouri, North Carolina, Ohio, Tennessee, and Virginia (except DC suburbs).

New York Passport Agency
376 Hudson Street
New York, NY 10014
☎ 212-206-3500
Region: New York City and Long Island
Note: New York Passport Agency accepts only emergency applications from those leaving within two weeks.

Philadelphia Passport Agency
US Custom House, 200 Chestnut Street, Room 103
Philadelphia, PA 19106-2970
☎ 215-418-5937
Region: Delaware, New Jersey, Pennsylvania, and West Virginia

San Francisco Passport Agency
95 Hawthorne Street, 5th Floor
San Francisco, CA 94105-3901
☎ 415-538-2700
Region: Arizona, California (all counties north of and including Monterey, Kings, Oulare, and Inyo), Nevada (except Clark Co.), and Utah.

Seattle Passport Agency
Henry Jackson Federal Building, 915 Second Avenue, Suite 992
Seattle, WA 98174-1091
☎ 206-220-7788
Region: Alaska, Colorado, Idaho, Minnesota, Montana, Nebraska, North Dakota, Oregon, South Dakota, Washington, and Wyoming.

Stamford Passport Agency
One Landmark Square, Broad and Atlantic Streets
Stamford, CT 06901-2667
☎ 203-969-9000
Region: Connecticut and Westchester County (New York).

Washington Passport Agency
1111 19th Street, NW
Washington, D.C. 20524
☎ 202-647-0518
Region: Maryland, Northern Virginia (including Alexandria, Arlington, and Fairfax Counties), and the District of Columbia.

National Passport Center
31 Rochester Avenue
Portsmouth, NH 03801-2900
Handles applications for Passport by Mail (Form DSP-82) and workload transfers from regional passport agencies.

Embassies & Consulates

Antigua & Barbuda

American Consular Agent
Hospital Hill, Nelson's Dockyard PO
English Harbour, Antigua
☎ 268-460-1569
Assists Americans in Antigua & Barbuda, St. Kitts & Nevis, and the British West Indies.

Bahamas

American Embassy
Queen Street
Nassau, Bahamas
☎ 242-322-1181 or 328-2206

Barbados

American Embassy
Canadian Imperial Bank of Commerce Bldg., Broadstreet
Bridgetown, Barbados
☎ 246-436-4950

American Consulate
ALICO Building, Cheapside
Bridgetown, Barbados
☎ 246-431-0225

Cayman Islands

American Consular Agent
George Town, Grand Cayman
☎ 246-949-7955

Appendix

Dominican Republic

American Embassy
Calle Cesar Nicolas Penson and Calle Leopoldo Navarro
Santo Domingo, Dominican Republic
☎ 809-221-2171

American Consular Agent
Calle Beller 51, Second Floor, Office 6
Puerto Plata, Dominican Republic
☎ 809-586-4204

Jamaica

American Embassy
Jamaica Mutual Life Center, 2 Oxford Road
Kingston, Jamaica
☎ 876-929-4850/4859

American Consular Agent
St. James Place, 2nd Floor, Gloucester Avenue
Montego Bay, Jamaica
☎ 876-949-7955

Netherlands Antilles

American Consulate General
J.B. Gorsiraweg No. 1
Willemstad, Curaçao
☎ 599-9-461-3066

Trinidad & Tobago

American Embassy
15 Queen's Park West, Port of Spain, Trinidad
☎ 868-622-6371

French Government Tourist Offices

444 Madison Ave.
New York, NY 10022

9454 Wilshire Blvd., Suite 715
Beverly Hills, CA 90212
☎ 310-271-6665
676 N. Michigan Ave., Suite 3360
Chicago, IL 60611
☎ 312-751-7800

1981 Ave. McGill College (490)
Montreal, Québec H3A 2W9
☎ 514-288-4264

30 St. Patrick St., Suite 700
Toronto, Ontario M5T 3A3
☎ 416-593-6427

Index

A

Romantic Weekends Guides Available from Hunter Publishing

America's Southwest
Don & Marjorie Young
Romantic getaways in Arizona, Colorado, Nevada, New Mexico and Utah.
288 pages, $15.95, 1-55650-823-9

Central & Northern Florida
Janet Groene & Gordon Groene
From the Panhandle to Sanibel Island to Jacksonville to Vero Beach,
here's a variety of places to rekindle your relationship.
352 pages, $15.95, 1-55650-855-7

The Carolinas & The Georgia Coast
Norman & Kathy Renouf
A collection of sexy Southern getaways to spice up your love life.
556 pages, $17.95, 1-55650-854-9

New England
Patricia & Robert Foulke
Special places in New Hampshire, Vermont, Coastal Maine,
Massachusetts, Newport, Block Island, Martha's Vineyard and Nantucket.
408 pages, $16.95, 1-55650-813-1

Southern California
Louann W. Murray
52 Southern California locales. Historic places to stay, whale-watching,
beachcombing, murder-mystery weekends.
275 pages, $15.95, 1-55650-774-7

Texas
Mary Lu Abbott
Locations in and around Houston, San Antonio, Austin and El Paso, with
everything from hidden ranches in the desert to luxurious city hotels.
304 pages, $15.95, 1-55650-834-4

Virginia, Maryland & Washington D.C., 2nd Edition

Norman & Kathy Renouf

From tavern-hopping in Annapolis to lighthouse retreats overlooking the
Chesapeake, you'll find romance abundant here.

420 pages, $16.95, 1-55650-835-2

Available at bookstores nationwide or from the publisher. Secure **credit card** orders may be placed at our Web site, www.hunterpublishing.com, which also has in-depth descriptions of the hundreds of travel guides we offer.

- -

ORDER FORM

Yes! Send the following *Romantic Weekends* guides:

TITLE	ISBN #	PRICE	QTY	TOTAL
	SUBTOTAL			
	SHIPPING & HANDLING (United States only)			
	(1-2 books, $4; 3-5 books, $5; 6-10 books, $8)			
	ENCLOSED IS MY CHECK FOR			

NAME:	
ADDRESS:	
CITY: STATE: ZIP:	
PHONE:	

Make checks payable to Hunter Publishing, Inc.,
and mail with order form to:
HUNTER PUBLISHING, INC.
239 SOUTH BEACH RD
HOBE SOUND FL 33455
561 546 7986 / FAX 561 546 8040